PRINCIPLES OF FOREIGN EXCHANGE TRADING

PRINCIPLES OF FOREIGN EXCHANGE TRADING

LALIT LILOTHIA

CYBER TECH PUBLICATIONS
4264/3, Ansari Road, Daryaganj, New Delhi-110002 (India)
Ph.: 011-23244078, 011-43559448 Fax: 011-23280028
E-Mail: cyberpublicationsdelhi@yahoo.com
Website: www.cybertechpublications.com

PRINCIPLES OF FOREIGN EXCHANGE TRADING

Lalit Lilothia

First Edition 2011

Published by :

G.S. Rawat for **Cyber Tech Publications**
4264/3, Ansari Road, Daryaganj, New Delhi-110002 (India)
Ph.: 011-23244078, 011-43559448 Fax: 011-23280028
E-Mail: cyberpublicationsdelhi@yahoo.com
Website: www.cybertechpublications.com

CONTENTS

Preface

1. Introduction 1
2. Foreign Exchange Management Act, 1999 10
3. Overview of Money Market Instruments 109
4. Foreign Exchange 145
5. Forward Outrights and Swaps 156
6. Hedging Swaps with Deposits, FRAs and Futures, Covered Interest Arbitrage and Creating Synthetic FRAs 183
7. Analysing Currency Movements 200

Glossary 232

Bibliography 255

Index 256

1

Introduction

SOME BASIC CONCEPTS

Throughout the book, we have generally used ISO codes (also used by the SWIFT system) to abbreviate currency names – for example, GBP for sterling, USD for US dollars and EUR for euros. You can find a list of codes in Appendix C.

Hedging, speculation and arbitrage

Some activity in the financial markets is driven by underlying commercial needs. Companies, banks and individuals borrow money because they need to finance their activities. Conversely, investors with surplus funds need to keep their money somewhere and wish to earn a return on it because otherwise it will dwindle in real value because of inflation. Through the mechanisms of the financial markets, the investors effectively lend, directly or indirectly to the borrowers. Also, organizations involved internationally need at some point to convert cashflows from one currency to another. Other organizations need to buy or sell commodities because that is an essential part of their business.

Beyond these activities, however, there are at least three distinct motivations for dealing: speculation, hedging and arbitrage – al-though deals often contain elements of more than one category:

- Speculation A trader in a bank or elsewhere will often deliber-ately establish a risky position where there was no risk in the first place, because he believes he can make a profit by doing so. This is *speculation*. For example, a trader who believes that the price of gold is going up might buy gold, without any commercial need to do so. If the price of gold does rise as he expects, he will make a profit. If it falls, he will make a loss.

- Hedging In the opposite way to this, to *hedge* (or to *cover*) means to protect against the risks arising from potential market movements in exchange rates, interest rates or other variables. This could be a company protecting against the risk that the value of its future income in a foreign currency is vulnerable because that currency might weaken soon, or a company protecting against the possible future increase of interest rates, which would increase the company's borrowing costs. Alternatively, it might be a bank dealer deciding that a speculative position he has already taken has now become too risky and choosing to insulate the position against any further market movements.
- Arbitrage The third broad category involves packages of more than one deal in different but related markets. If a dealer sees that the prices of two financial instruments which should be in line are in fact not in line, he can deal in both instruments simultaneously in such a way as to lock in a profit but take no, or little, risk. This is *arbitrage.*

Spot, forward, value dates and short dates

In general, each type of financial transaction has a normal time-cycle for settlement. For example, if a dealer does a straightforward foreign exchange deal today to buy US dollars and sells euros then, under normal circumstances, he expects that he will receive the dollars and pay the euros not today, but in two business days' time.

This delay is essentially to allow enough time for the mechanics of the cash trans-fers involved. In foreign exchange, this is referred to as trading for value *spot*. Each market has its own normal convention, sometimes for settlement after a delay like this, and sometimes for settlement on the same day as the transaction. In both the foreign exchange and international money markets, for example, the usual convention is spot, as just described. Money market deals in a domestic market, however – i.e. in the same currency as the market in which they take place (for example, a US dollar deposit in the USA) – are generally settled on the same day as they are transacted.

Preface

STraditionally, trading currencies was reserved for huge corporations, hedge funds, fiscal institutions, and millionaires. In other words, public and corporations with entree to big cash reserves. However, the good get at to the net and the miss of physical location have made forex currency dealing a possibleness for the intermediate human being. Although foreign exchange currency dealing is start to us, on that point are essential matter we require to understand regarding the overseas switch market before we start trading.

The first thing you must realize is why gbp bot are essential. It may seem simple enough, except the fact is that outside currencies play a huge role in nearly each view of our lives. If you utterly need French cheese, the grocery depot where you shop must purchase that cheese in euros. The alike is genuine if were to travel to another state and buy particulars on that point; you will need to switch your currency to buy the needed points. No matter if it is items from the grocery shop or your preferred textile, foreign currency invades each piece of our lives. The need for all nations to switch foreign currency is the major cause that foreign exchange currency dealing is so lucrative.

Because there are so a lot of people involved and so a good deal money engrossed in dealing outside currency, forex dealers act very quickly on information as it's dispersed. When this information is released to sellers, sharp ebbs and flows would occur, making extreme profits and massive releases. Although the market alters in currency are little, the leverage granted to dealers causes the market place to be very isolated. Dealing in the foreign shift market requires a deep figuring of outside currency and its grandness in the market.

Now that you have a basic understanding of forex currency dealing, it is essential to realize the importance of discovering foreign switch values. As a forex dealer, you would deal in outside currency and therefore would be reliable for conscious the outside shift pace of the currencies in which you do business. Do exploration on-line and locate elsewhere outside exchange rates for general currencies you intend to buy and sell. With no this information, you would be dealing blindly.

— *Author*

In many markets, it is also possible to undertake a transaction where the two parties agree that the settlement will be on a later date than normal. This is called a *forward* deal. Similarly, with a transaction such as a foreign exchange spot deal or an international money market deal, it is possible to agree on settlement earlier than normal.

A futures contract is very similar in concept to a forward, but is traded on a recognized exchange, rather than between any two parties. This gives rise to certain important mechanical differences.

Both money market deposits and foreign exchange forwards are normally quoted for certain regular dates - for example, 1, 2, 3, 6 and 12 months forward. These dates are quoted over the spot date. This means that the 1-month forward rates are calculated for one calendar month after the present spot value date. For example, if today is 19 April and the spot value date is 21 April, then the 1-month forward value date will be 21 May. No adjustment in the forward value date is made for any weekends or public holidays between the spot date and the forward delivery date. However, if the forward delivery date falls on a weekend or holiday, the value date becomes the next business day.

One exception to this last rule is when the spot value date is at or close to the end of the month. Suppose that the spot value date is earlier than the last business day of the month, but the forward value date would fall on a non-business day. If moving the forward value date to the next business day would result in it falling in the next month, it is instead brought back to the previous business day in order to stay in the same calendar month. This is called the *modified following* convention.

Another exception arises if the spot value date is exactly the last business day of a month. In this case, the forward value date is the last business day of the corresponding forward month. This is referred to as dealing *end-end.*

Any month that is not a regularly quoted date, for example for 4 or 5 months' maturity, is called an *in-between* month because it is between the regular dates. A forward deal may in fact be arranged for value on any business day (or any day which is a business day in both currencies for foreign exchange). Dates which do not fit in with calendar month dates are called *broken dates* or *odd dates.*

Example

Today is Monday 27 October 2003.

The spot value date is Wednesday 29 October 2003.

The 1-month value date is Friday 28 November 2003 (modified following convention because 29 November is a Saturday and the next business day - Monday 1 December - is in the next month).

The 2-month value date is Monday 29 December.

Example

Today is Wednesday 25 February 2004.

The spot value date is Friday 27 February 2004 (which is the last business day of February because 29 February is a Sunday).

The 1-month value date is Wednesday 31 March 2004 (end-end convention).

The 2-month value date is Friday 30 April 2004 (end-end con-vention).

Short dates

Value dates earlier than 1 month are referred to as *short dates.* There are certain regular dates usually quoted, and the terminology used is the same in the deposit market and the foreign exchange market, as follows:

·*Overnight:* A deposit or foreign exchange swap from today until tomorrow.

·*Tom-next:* A deposit or foreign exchange swap from tomorrow until the next day (spot)

·*Spot-next:* A deposit or foreign exchange swap from spot until the next day.

·*Spot-a-week:* A deposit or foreign exchange swap from spot until a week later.

·*Tomorrow* means the next working day after today and next means the next working day following (i.e. spot).

SOME BASIC TERMINOLOGY

- The cash market *Cash market* is an expression sometimes used for the spot market in something as opposed to the forward market. It is also used, quite separately, for transactions where, on the settlement date, the whole value of something will potentially be settled in the normal way.

This is distinct from *contracts for differences*, where the cash amount to be settled is never intended to be the full principal amount underlying the transaction; instead settlement is made of only the difference between two prices or rates.

- Bid, offer and spread In general, dealers who make a market in anything (i.e. dealers whose business is to quote prices to any creditworthy counterparty who asks) quote a *two-way* price. This means that the dealer quotes two prices simultaneously – one at which he buys something or borrows money, and the other at which he sells something or lends money. The *bid* price or rate is the price at which the dealer quoting the price is prepared to buy or borrow. The *offer* (or *ask*) price is the price at which he is prepared to sell or lend. The difference between them, representing a profit to the dealer, is called the *spread*.
- Long, short and square A *long* position is a surplus of purchases over sales of a given currency or asset, or a situation which naturally gives rise to an organization benefiting from a strengthening of that currency or asset. To a money market dealer, however, a long position is a surplus of borrowings taken in over money lent out (which gives rise to a benefit if that currency weakens rather than strengthens).

  A *short* position is a surplus of sales over purchases of a given currency or asset, or a situation which naturally gives rise to an organization benefiting from a weakening of that currency or asset. To a money market dealer, however, a short position is a surplus of money lent out over borrowings taken in (which gives rise to a benefit if that currency strengthens rather than weakens). A *square* position is one in which sales exactly match purchases, or in which assets exactly match liabilities.
- Eurocurrency Historically, the terms Euro and *Eurocurrency* have been used to describe any instrument which is owned outside the country whose currency is involved. The term does not imply 'European'. For example, a US dollar deposit made by a US resi-dent in New York is in domestic dollars, but a dollar deposit made in Tokyo is in Eurodollars.

Similarly, US dollar commercial paper issued outside the USA is Eurocommercial paper while US dollar commercial paper issued inside the USA is domestic US commer-cial paper. Confusingly, this term has nothing whatever to do with the European Monetary Union currency also called the 'euro'.

ESSENTIAL FINANCIAL ARITHMETIC

PERCENTAGES

When using interest rates, '4.7%', '4.7/100' and '0.047' all mean exactly the same. Throughout the book, when we have used an interest rate in a calculation, we have not multiplied it by 100. For example, if we do a calculation involving an interest rate of 4.7%, we generally write this in the calculation as '0.047' and not '4.7'. Similarly, whenever we speak of 'an interest rate', we always mean a number like 0.047, not a number like 4.7.

When referring to interest rates, a *basis point* always means 0.01% (which is the same as 0.01/100 or 0.0001). Note that this is not necessarily the same as a foreign exchange *point*.

There are some exceptions to the two conventions above. For example, Swedish Treasury bills and some other markets use a convention called *30/360* (also known as 30(E)/360 or 360/360), which is also used in some European bond markets. In this convention, the 'year' has 360 days and the number of days in the period is calculated differently from the calendar.

Each month is assumed to have 30 days, regardless of what the calendar says, so that the 31st day of any month is treated as if it were the 30th day of that month. To calculate the number of days in any period therefore, use the following rules:

- First, change any date which is 31st to 30th.
- Second, multiply the difference between the months by 30.
- Third, add the difference between the days.

Example : Interest is quoted on a EUR 1 million deposit at 5.3% on a 30/360 basis (unusually!). The deposit runs from 31 October 2003 to 5 March 2004. What is the amount of interest paid?

First, change 31 October to 30 October. Second, there are 5 months from October to March and 5 x 30 = 150. Third, there are —25 days from 30th to 5th. There are therefore 125 days from 31 October to 5 March on a 30/360 basis.

The ACT/365 and 30/360 conventions are sometimes referred to as *bond basis* (because bond markets use similar conventions). The ACT/360 convention is sometimes referred to as *money market basis*.

In Appendix A we have given a list of the conventions used in some markets.

Converting between the different conventions

It is possible to convert an interest rate quoted on one basis to what it would be if it were quoted on another basis. For example:

Example : *A* dealer quotes for a EUR 1 million deposit from 5 May to 31 August, at 4.7% on an ACT/360 basis in the usual way. What would the quote be if the customer wanted it converted to an ACT/365 basis or a 30/360 basis?

There are 118 actual calendar days from 5 May to 31 August.

The amount we have calculated is known as the *present value* of USD 1,018,550.00 because it is the value now of that cashflow in the future. Given a choice between receiving USD 1,018,550.00 after 126 days, or USD 1,000,000 now, I would be equally happy with either, because if I start with the USD 1,000,000 now and put it on deposit, I can accumulate USD 1,018,550.00 by the end of 126 days. The present value so calculated depends on the interest rate used and the time until the future cashflow.

In general, this calculation demonstrates the fundamental principle behind market calculations – the *time value of money*. As long as interest rates are not negative, it is better to have any given amount of money sooner rather than later because, if you have it sooner, you can place it on deposit to earn interest on it. The extent to which it is worthwhile having the money sooner depends on the interest rate and the time period involved.

Present values are fundamental to pricing money market instru-ments, because the present value of a future cashflow is its value, or worth, now. It is therefore the amount of money which one is prepared to pay now for any instrument which generates that cashflow in the future.

In the money market and foreign exchange market, prices are gener-ally quoted for standard periods such as 1 month, 2 months etc. If a dealer needs to quote a price for an *odd date* (or *broken date)* between these periods, he needs to *interpolate.* In the money markets, straight-line interpolation is generally used, as follows.

These calculations assume that all interim cashflows can be rein-vested at the same original interest rate. Although this is unrealistic, it is a useful simplifying assumption to make, in order to be able to compare interest rates with different interest payment frequencies. It is possible to use a formula to convert the 5.3% quoted with quarterly interest payments to the semi-annual equivalent rate of 5.335%:

In the example we have been considering, the customer has agreed to pay the 5.3% in quarterly instalments – that is, effectively four times per year (even though the loan only lasts for 6 months). We want to calculate what this is worth to the dealer if interest were paid 6-monthly – that is, effectively twice per year (again, even though the loan only lasts for 6 months).

Note that the calculation method we have given here is almost always satisfactory but is not quite correct mathematically. This is because the 6-month period of 182 days used in our example is not exactly half a year (that would be $182^1{}_2$ days, which is not realistic). Similarly, if interest were paid quarterly, the payment periods would not be exactly equal periods of 91 $^1{}_4$ days but slightly different periods, depending on weekends etc.

Effective rates

The equivalent yield with interest paid only once per year is known as the annual equivalent rate, or the *effective rate.* Consider, for example, a deposit for 3 months. The effective yield is the interest which would be accumulated by the end of the year if the deposit were rolled over three times – i.e. the principal and interest at the end of 3 months were all reinvested at the same rate, and then all again at the end of 6 months and all again at the end of 9 months.

The same idea can be extended to a deposit for an odd period, such as, say, 59 days. If the deposit is rolled over repeatedly, its maturity will never quite coincide with exactly one year, because 365 is not an exact multiple of 59.

Example : *A* dealer is trying to compare two different US dollar investments. The first is for 153 days at a yield of 9.1% and the second is for 87 days at a yield of 9.05%. Assuming that there are no other significant differences between the two investments, which is better? It may be, for example, that the dealer believes that interest rates will be higher after 87 days than now - in which case he would probably prefer the 87-day investment because then he could roll it over at a higher yield when it matures. Ignoring any such expectations, however, it is useful to be able to compare the two investments on a like-for-like basis.

One approach therefore is to compare the effective rate of each investment.

2

Foreign Exchange Management Act, 1999

An Act to consolidate and amend the law relating to foreign exchange with the objective of facilitating external trade and payments and for promoting the orderly development and maintenance of foreign exchange market in India.

BE it enacted by Parliament in the Fiftieth Year of the Republic of India as follows:—

CHAPTER I

PRELIMINARY

Short title, extent, application and commencement.

1. (1) This Act may be called the Foreign Exchange Management Act, 1999.

(2) It extends to the whole of India.

(3) It shall also apply to all branches, offices and agencies outside India owned or controlled by a person resident in India and also to any contravention thereunder committed outside India by any person to whom this Act applies.

(4) It shall come into force on such date as the Central Government may, by notification in the Official Gazette, appoint:

Provided that different dates may be appointed for different provisions of this Act and any reference in any such provision to the commencement of this Act shall be construed as a reference to the coming into force of that provision.

Definitions

2. In this Act, unless the context otherwise requires,—

(a) "Adjudicating Authority" means an officer authorised under sub-section (1) of section 16;

(b) "Appellate Tribunal" means the Appellate Tribunal for Foreign Exchange established under section 18;

(c) "authorised person" means an authorised dealer, money changer, off-shore banking unit or any other person for the time being authorised under sub-section (1) of section 10 to deal in foreign exchange or foreign securities;

(d) "Bench" means a Bench of the Appellate Tribunal;

(e) "capital account transaction" means a transaction which alters the assets or liabilities, including contingent liabilities, outside India of persons resident in India or assets or liabilities in India of persons resident outside India, and includes transactions referred to in sub-section (3) of section 6;

(f) "Chairperson" means the Chairperson of the Appellate Tribunal;

(g) "chartered accountant" shall have the meaning assigned to it in clause (b) of sub-section (1) of section 2 of the Chartered Accountants Act, 1949 (38 of 1949);

(h) "currency" includes all currency notes, postal notes, postal orders, money orders, cheques, drafts, travellers cheques, letters of credit, bills of exchange and promissory notes, credit cards or such other similar instruments, as may be notified by the Reserve Bank;

(i) "currency notes" means and includes cash in the form of coins and bank notes;

(j) "current account transaction" means a transaction other than a capital account transaction and without prejudice to the generality of the foregoing such transaction includes:-

(i) payments due in connection with foreign trade, other current business,services, and short-term banking and credit facilities in the ordinary course of business,

(ii) payments due as interest on loans and as net income from investments,

(iii) remittances for living expenses of parents, spouse and children residing abroad, and

(iv) expenses in connection with foreign travel, education and medical care of parents, spouse and children;

(k) "Director of Enforcement" means the Director of Enforcement appointed under sub-section (1) of section 36;

(l) "export", with its grammatical variations and cognate expressions, means—

(i) the taking out of India to a place outside India any goods,

(ii) provision of services from India to any person outside India;

(m) "foreign currency" means any currency other than Indian currency;

(n) "foreign exchange" means foreign currency and includes,—

(i) deposits, credits and balances payable in any foreign currency,

(ii) drafts, travellers cheques, letters of credit or bills of exchange, expressed or drawn in Indian currency but payable in any foreign currency,

(iii) drafts, travellers cheques, letters of credit or bills of exchange drawn by banks, institutions or persons outside India, but payable in Indian currency;

(o) "foreign security" means any security, in the form of shares, stocks, bonds, debentures or any other instrument denominated or expressed in foreign currency and includes securities expressed in foreign currency, but where redemption or any form of return such as interest or dividends is payable in Indian currency;

(p) "import", with its grammatical variations and cognate expressions, means bringing into India any goods or services;

(q) "Indian currency" means currency which is expressed or drawn in Indian rupees but does not include special bank notes and special one rupee notes issued under section 28A of the Reserve Bank of India Act, 1934 (2 of 1934);

(r) "legal practitioner" shall have the meaning assigned to it in clause (i) of sub-section (1) of section 2 of the Advocates Act, 1961 (25 of 1961);

(s) "Member" means a Member of the Appellate Tribunal and includes the Chairperson thereof;

(t) "notify" means to notify in the Official Gazette and the expression "notification" shall be construed accordingly;

(u) "person" includes—

(i) an individual,

(ii) a Hindu undivided family,

(iii) a company,

(iv) a firm,

(v) an association of persons or a body of individuals, whether incorporated or not,

(vi) every artificial juridical person, not falling within any of the preceding sub-clauses, and

(vii) any agency, office or branch owned or controlled by such person;

(v) "person resident in India" means—

(i) a person residing in India for more than one hundred and eighty-two days during the course of the preceding financial year but does not include—

(A) a person who has gone out of India or who stays outside India, in either case—

(a) for or on taking up employment outside India, or

(b) for carrying on outside India a business or vocation outside India, or

(c) for any other purpose, in such circumstances as would indicate his intention to stay outside India for an uncertain period;

(B) a person who has come to or stays in India, in either case, otherwise than—

(a) for or on taking up employment in India, or

(b) for carrying on in India a business or vocation in India, or

(c) for any other purpose, in such circumstances as would indicate his intention to stay in India for an uncertain period;

(ii) any person or body corporate registered or incorporated in India,

(iii) an office, branch or agency in India owned or controlled by a person resident outside India,

(iv) an office, branch or agency outside India owned or controlled by a person resident in India;

(w) "person resident outside India" means a person who is not resident in India;

(x) "prescribed" means prescribed by rules made under this Act;

(y) "repatriate to India" means bringing into India the realised foreign exchange and—

(i) the selling of such foreign exchange to an authorised person in India in exchange for rupees, or

(ii) the holding of realised amount in an account with an authorised person in India to the extent notified by the Reserve Bank, and includes use of the realised amount for discharge of a debt or liability denominated in foreign exchange and the expression "repatriation" shall be construed accordingly;

(z) "Reserve Bank" means the Reserve Bank of India constituted under sub-section (1) of section 3 of the Reserve Bank of India Act, 1934 (2 of 1934);

(za) "security" means shares, stocks, bonds and debentures, Government securities as defined in the Public Debt Act, 1944 (18 of 1944), savings certificates to which the Government Savings Certificates Act, 1959 (46 of 1959) applies, deposit receipts in respect of deposits of securities and units of the Unit Trust of India established under sub-section (1) of section 3 of the Unit Trust of India Act, 1963 (52 of 1963) or of any mutual fund and includes certificates of title to securities, but does not include bills of exchange or promissory notes other than Government promissory notes or any other instruments which may be notified by the Reserve Bank as security for the purposes of this Act;

(zb) "service" means service of any description which is made available to potential users and includes the provision of facilities in connection with banking, financing, insurance, medical assistance, legal assistance, chit fund, real estate, transport, processing, supply of electrical or other energy, boarding or lodging or both, entertainment, amusement or the purveying of news or other information, but does not include the rendering of any service free of charge or under a contract of personal service;

(zc) "Special Director (Appeals)" means an officer appointed under section 18;

(zd) "specify" means to specify by regulations made under this Act and the expression "specified" shall be construed accordingly;

(ze) "transfer" includes sale, purchase, exchange, mortgage, pledge, gift, loan or any other form of transfer of right, title, possession or lien.

REGULATION AND MANAGEMENT OF FOREIGN EXCHANGE

Dealing in foreign exchange, etc.

3. Save as otherwise provided in this Act, rules or regulations made thereunder, or with the general or special permission of the Reserve Bank, no person shall—

(a) deal in or transfer any foreign exchange or foreign security to any person not being an authorised person;

(b) make any payment to or for the credit of any person resident outside India in any manner;

(c) receive otherwise through an authorised person, any payment by order or on behalf of any person resident outside India in any manner;

Explanation.—For the purpose of this clause, where any person in, or resident in, India receives any payment by order or on behalf of any person resident outside India through any other person (including an authorised person) without a corresponding inward remittance from any place outside India, then, such person shall be deemed to have received such payment otherwise than through an authorised person;

(d) enter into any financial transaction in India as consideration for or in association with acquisition or creation or transfer of a right to acquire, any asset outside India by any person.

Explanation.—For the purpose of this clause, "financial transaction" means making any payment to, or for the credit of any person, or receiving any payment for, by order or on behalf of any person, or drawing, issuing or negotiating any bill of exchange or promissory note, or transferring any security or acknowledging any debt.

Holding of foreign exchange, etc.

4. Save as otherwise provided in this Act, no person resident in India shall acquire, hold, own, possess or transfer any foreign exchange, foreign security or any immovable property situated outside India.

Current account transactions.

5. Any person may sell or draw foreign exchange to or from an authorised person if such sale or drawal is a current account transaction:

Provided that the Central Government may, in public interest and in consultation with the Reserve Bank, impose such reasonable restrictions for current account transactions as may be prescribed.

Capital account transactions.

6. (1) Subject to the provisions of sub-section (2), any person may sell or draw foreign exchange to or from an authorised person for a capital account transaction.

(2) The Reserve Bank may, in consultation with the Central Government, specify—

(a) any class or classes of capital account transactions which are permissible;

(b) the limit up to which foreign exchange shall be admissible for such transactions :

Provided that the Reserve Bank shall not impose any restriction on the drawal of foreign exchange for payments due on account of amortization of loans or for depreciation of direct investments in the ordinary course of business.

(3) Without prejudice to the generality of the provisions of sub-section (2), the Reserve Bank may, by regulations, prohibit, restrict or regulate the following—

(a) transfer or issue of any foreign security by a person resident in India;

(b) transfer or issue of any security by a person resident outside India;

(c) transfer or issue of any security or foreign security by any branch, office or agency in India of a person resident outside India;

(d) any borrowing or lending in foreign exchange in whatever form or by whatever name called;

(e) any borrowing or lending in rupees in whatever form or by whatever name called between a person resident in India and a person resident outside India;

(f) deposits between persons resident in India and persons resident outside India;

(g) export, import or holding of currency or currency notes;

(h) transfer of immovable property outside India, other than a lease not exceeding five years, by a person resident in India;

(i) acquisition or transfer of immovable property in India, other than a lease not exceeding five years, by a person resident outside India;

(j) giving of a guarantee or surety in respect of any debt, obligation or other liability incurred—

(i) by a person resident in India and owed to a person resident outside India; or

(ii) by a person resident outside India.

(4) A person resident in India may hold, own, transfer or invest in foreign currency, foreign security or any immovable property situated outside India if such currency, security or property was acquired, held or owned by such person when he was resident outside India or inherited from a person who was resident outside India.

(5) A person resident outside India may hold, own, transfer or invest in Indian currency, security or any immovable property situated in India if such currency, security or property was acquired, held or owned by such person when he was resident in India or inherited from a person who was resident in India.

(6) Without prejudice to the provisions of this section, the Reserve Bank may, by regulation, prohibit, restrict, or regulate establishment in India of a branch, office or other place of business by a person resident outside India, for carrying on any activity relating to such branch, office or other place of business.

Export of goods and services.

7. (1) Every exporter of goods shall—

(a) furnish to the Reserve Bank or to such other authority a declaration in such form and in such manner as may be specified, containing true and correct material particulars, including the amount representing the full export value or, if the full export value of the goods is not ascertainable at the time of export, the value which the exporter, having regard to the prevailing market conditions, expects to receive on the sale of the goods in a market outside India;

(b) furnish to the Reserve Bank such other information as may be required by the Reserve Bank for the purpose of ensuring the realisation of the export proceeds by such exporter.

(2) The Reserve Bank may, for the purpose of ensuring that the full export value of the goods or such reduced value of the goods as the Reserve Bank determines, having regard to the prevailing market conditions, is received without any delay, direct any exporter to comply with such requirements as it deems fit.

(3) Every exporter of services shall furnish to the Reserve Bank or to such other authorities a declaration in such form and in such manner as may be specified, containing the true and correct material particulars in relation to payment for such services.

Realisation and repatriation of foreign exchange.

8. Save as otherwise provided in this Act, where any amount of foreign exchange is due or has accrued to any person resident in India, such person shall take all reasonable steps to realise and repatriate to India such foreign exchange within such period and in such manner as may be specified by the Reserve Bank.

Exemption from realisation and repatriation in certain cases.

9. The provisions of sections 4 and 8 shall not apply to the following, namely:—

(a) possession of foreign currency or foreign coins by any person up to such limit as the Reserve Bank may specify;

(b) foreign currency account held or operated by such person or class of persons and the limit up to which the Reserve Bank may specify;

(c) foreign exchange acquired or received before the 8th day of July, 1947 or any income arising or accruing thereon which is held outside India by any person in pursuance of a general or special permission granted by the Reserve Bank;

(d) foreign exchange held by a person resident in India up to such limit as the Reserve Bank may specify, if such foreign exchange was acquired by way of gift or inheritance from a person referred to in clause (c), including any income arising therefrom;

(e) foreign exchange acquired from employment, business, trade, vocation, services, honorarium, gifts, inheritance or any other legitimate means up to such limit as the Reserve Bank may specify; and

(f) such other receipts in foreign exchange as the Reserve Bank may specify.

Authorised Person

10. (1) The Reserve Bank may, on an application made to it in this behalf, authorise any person to be known as authorised person to deal in foreign exchange or in foreign securities, as an authorised dealer, money changer or off-shore banking unit or in any other manner as it deems fit.

(2) An authorisation under this section shall be in writing and shall be subject to the conditions laid down therein.

(3) An authorisation granted under sub-section (1) may be revoked by the Reserve Bank at any time if the Reserve Bank is satisfied that—

(a) it is in public interest so to do; or

(b) the authorised person has failed to comply with the condition subject to which the authorisation was granted or has contravened any of the provisions of the Act or any rule, regulation, notification, direction or order made thereunder:

Provided that no such authorisation shall be revoked on any ground referred to in clause (b) unless the authorised person has been given a reasonable opportunity of making a representation in the matter.

(4) An authorised person shall, in all his dealings in foreign exchange or foreign security, comply with such general or special directions or orders as the Reserve Bank may, from time to time, think fit to give, and, except with the previous permission of the Reserve Bank, an authorised person shall not engage in any

transaction involving any foreign exchange or foreign security which is not in conformity with the terms of his authorisation under this section.

(5) An authorised person shall, before undertaking any transaction in foreign exchange on behalf of any person, require that person to make such declaration and to give such information as will reasonably satisfy him that the transaction will not involve, and is not designed for the purpose of any contravention or evasion of the provisions of this Act or of any rule, regulation, notification, direction or order made thereunder, and where the said person refuses to comply with any such requirement or makes only unsatisfactory compliance therewith, the authorised person shall refuse in writing to undertake the transaction and shall, if he has reason to believe that any such contravention or evasion as aforesaid is contemplated by the person, report the matter to the Reserve Bank.

(6) Any person, other than an authorised person, who has acquired or purchased foreign exchange for any purpose mentioned in the declaration made by him to authorised person under sub-section (5) does not use it for such purpose or does not surrender it to authorised person within the specified period or uses the foreign exchange so acquired or purchased for any other purpose for which purchase or acquisition of foreign exchange is not permissible under the provisions of the Act or the rules or regulations or direction or order made thereunder shall be deemed to have committed contravention of the provisions of the Act for the purpose of this section.

Reserve Bank's powers to issue directions to authorised person.

11. (1) The Reserve Bank may, for the purpose of securing compliance with the provisions of this Act and of any rules, regulations, notifications or directions made thereunder, give to the authorised persons any direction in regard to making of payment or the doing or desist from doing any act relating to foreign exchange or foreign security.

(2) The Reserve Bank may, for the purpose of ensuring the compliance with the provisions of this Act or of any rule, regulation, notification, direction or order made thereunder, direct any

authorised person to furnish such information, in such manner, as it deems fit.

(3) Where any authorised person contravenes any direction given by the Reserve Bank under this Act or fails to file any return as directed by the Reserve Bank, the Reserve Bank may, after giving reasonable opportunity of being heard, impose on the authorised person a penalty which may extend to ten thousand rupees and in the case of continuing contravention with an additional penalty which may extend to two thousand rupees for every day during which such contravention continues.

Power of Reserve Bank to inspect authorised person.

12. (1) The Reserve Bank may, at any time, cause an inspection to be made, by any officer of the Reserve Bank specially authorised in writing by the Reserve Bank in this behalf, of the business of any authorised person as may appear to it to be necessary or expedient for the purpose of—

(a) verifying the correctness of any statement, information or particulars furnished to the Reserve Bank;

(b) obtaining any information or particulars which such authorised person has failed to furnish on being called upon to do so;

(c) securing compliance with the provisions of this Act or of any rules, regulations, directions or orders made thereunder.

(2) It shall be the duty of every authorised person, and where such person is a company or a firm, every director, partner or other officer of such company or firm, as the case may be, to produce to any officer making an inspection under sub-section (1), such books, accounts and other documents in his custody or power and to furnish any statement or information relating to the affairs of such person, company or firm as the said officer may require within such time and in such manner as the said officer may direct.

Contravention And Penalties

Penalties

13. (1) If any person contravenes any provision of this Act, or contravenes any rule, regulation, notification, direction or order

issued in exercise of the powers under this Act, or contravenes any condition subject to which an authorisation is issued by the Reserve Bank, he shall, upon adjudication, be liable to a penalty up to thrice the sum involved in such contravention where such amount is quantifiable, or up to two lakh rupees where the amount is not quantifiable, and where such contravention is a continuing one, further penalty which may extend to five thousand rupees for every day after the first day during which the contravention continues.

(2) Any Adjudicating Authority adjudging any contravention under sub-section (1), may, if he thinks fit in addition to any penalty which he may impose for such contravention direct that any currency, security or any other money or property in respect of which the contravention has taken place shall be confiscated to the Central Government and further direct that the foreign exchange holdings, if any of the persons committing the contraventions or any part thereof, shall be brought back into India or shall be retained outside India in accordance with the directions made in this behalf.

Explanation.—For the purposes of this sub-section, "property" in respect of which contravention has taken place, shall include—

(a) deposits in a bank, where the said property is converted into such deposits;

(b) Indian currency, where the said property is converted into that currency; and

(c) any other property which has resulted out of the conversion of that property.

Enforcement of the orders of Adjudicating Authority.

14. (1) Subject to the provisions of sub-section (2) of section 19, if any person fails to make full payment of the penalty imposed on him under section 13 within a period of ninety days from the date on which the notice for payment of such penalty is served on him, he shall be liable to civil imprisonment under this section.

(2) No order for the arrest and detention in civil prison of a defaulter shall be made unless the Adjudicating Authority has issued and served a notice upon the defaulter calling upon him to appear before him on the date specified in the notice and to show cause why he should not be committed to the civil prison,

and unless the Adjudicating Authority, for reasons in writing, is satisfied—

(a) that the defaulter, with the object or effect of obstructing the recovery of penalty, has after the issue of notice by the Adjudicating Authority, dishonestly transferred concealed, or removed any part of his property, or

(b) that the defaulter has, or has had since the issuing of notice by the Adjudicating Authority, the means to pay the arrears or some substantial part thereof and refuses or neglects or has refused or neglected to pay the same.

(3) Notwithstanding anything contained in sub-section (1), a warrant for the arrest of the defaulter may be issued by the Adjudicating Authority if the Adjudicating Authority is satisfied, by affidavit or otherwise, that with the object or effect of delaying the execution of the certificate the defaulter is likely to abscond or leave the local limits of the jurisdiction of the Adjudicating Authority.

(4) Where appearance is not made pursuant to a notice issued and served under sub-section (1), the Adjudicating Authority may issue a warrant for the arrest of the defaulter.

(5) A warrant of arrest issued by the Adjudicating Authority under sub-section (3) or sub-section

(4) may also be executed by any other Adjudicating Authority within whose jurisdiction the defaulter may for the time being be found.

(6) Every person arrested in pursuance of a warrant of arrest under this section shall be brought before the Adjudicating Authority issuing the warrant as soon as practicable and in any event within twenty-four hours of his arrest (exclusive of the time required for the journey):

Provided that, if the defaulter pays the amount entered in the warrant of arrest as due and the costs of the arrest to the officer arresting him, such officer shall at once release him.

Explanation.—For the purposes of this sub-section, where the defaulter is a Hindu undivided family, the karta thereof shall be deemed to be the defaulter.

(7) When a defaulter appears before the Adjudicating Authority pursuant to a notice to show cause or is brought before the

Adjudicating Authority under this section, the Adjudicating Authority shall give the defaulter an opportunity showing cause why he should not be committed to the civil prison.

(8) Pending the conclusion of the inquiry, the Adjudicating Authority may, in his discretion, order the defaulter to be detained in the custody of such officer as the Adjudicating Authority may think fit or release him on his furnishing the security to the satisfaction of the Adjudicating Authority for his appearance as and when required.

(9) Upon the conclusion of the inquiry, the Adjudicating Authority may make an order for the detention of the defaulter in the civil prison and shall in that event cause him to be arrested if he is not already under arrest:

Provided that in order to give a defaulter an opportunity of satisfying the arrears, the Adjudicating Authority may, before making the order of detention, leave the defaulter in the custody of the officer arresting him or of any other officer for a specified period not exceeding fifteen days, or release him on his furnishing security to the satisfaction of the Adjudicating Authority for his appearance at the expiration of the specified period if the arrears are not satisfied.

(10) When the Adjudicating Authority does not make an order of detention under sub-section (9), he shall, if the defaulter is under arrest, direct his release.

(11) Every person detained in the civil prison in execution of the certificate may be so detained,—

(a) where the certificate is for a demand of an amount exceeding rupees one crore, up to three years, and

(b) in any other case, up to six months:

Provided that he shall be released from such detention on the amount mentioned in the warrant for his detention being paid to the officer-in-charge of the civil prison.

(12) A defaulter released from detention under this section shall not, merely by reason of his release, be discharged from his liability for the arrears, but he shall not be liable to be arrested under the certificate in execution of which he was detained in the civil prison.

(13) A detention order may be executed at any place in India

in the manner provided for the execution of warrant of arrest under the Code of Criminal Procedure, 1973 (2 of 1974).

Power to compound contravention.

15. (1) Any contravention under section 13 may, on an application made by theperson committing such contravention, be compounded within one hundred and eighty days from the date of receipt of application by the Director of Enforcement or such other officers of the Directorate of Enforcement and Officers of the Reserve Bank as may be authorised in this behalf by the Central Government in such manner as may be prescribed.

(2) Where a contravention has been compounded under sub-section (1), no proceeding or further proceeding, as the case may be, shall be initiated or continued, as the case may be, against the person committing such contravention under that section, in respect of the contravention so compounded.

Adjudication And Appeal

Appointment of Adjudicating Authority.

16. (1) For the purpose of adjudication under section 13, the Central Government may, by an order published in the Official Gazette, appoint as many officers of the Central Government as it may think fit, as the Adjudicating Authorities for holding an inquiry in the manner prescribed after giving the person alleged to have committed contravention under section 13, against whom a complaint has been made under sub-section

(2) (hereinafter in this section referred to as the said person) a reasonable opportunity of being heard for the purpose of imposing any penalty:

Provided that where the Adjudicating Authority is of opinion that the said person is likely to abscond or is likely to evade in any manner, the payment of penalty, if levied, it may direct the said person to furnish a bond or guarantee for such amount and subject to such conditions as it may deem fit.

(2) The Central Government shall, while appointing the Adjudicating Authorities under sub-section (1), also specify in the order published in the Official Gazette, their respective jurisdictions.

(3) No Adjudicating Authority shall hold an enquiry under sub-section (1) except upon a complaint in writing made by any officer authorised by a general or special order by the Central Government.

(4) The said person may appear either in person or take the assistance of a legal practitioner or a chartered accountant of his choice for presenting his case before the Adjudicating Authority.

(5) Every Adjudicating Authority shall have the same powers of a civil court which are conferred on the Appellate Tribunal under sub-section (2) of section 28 and—

(a) all proceedings before it shall be deemed to be judicial proceedings within the meaning of sections 193 and 228 of the Indian Penal Code (45 of 1860);

(b) shall be deemed to be a civil court for the purposes of sections 345 and 346 of the Code of Criminal Procedure, 1973 (2 of 1974).

(6) Every Adjudicating Authority shall deal with the complaint under sub-section (2) as expeditiously as possible and endeavour shall be made to dispose of the complaint finally within one year from the date of receipt of the complaint :

Provided that where the complaint cannot be disposed off within the said period, the Adjudicating Authority shall record periodically the reasons in writing for not disposing off the complaint within the said period.

Appeal to Special Director (Appeals).

17. (1) The Central Government shall, by notification, appoint one or more Special Directors (Appeals) to hear appeals against the orders of the Adjudicating Authorities under this section and shall also specify in the said notification the matter and places in relation to which the Special Director (Appeals) may exercise jurisdiction.

(2) Any person aggrieved by an order made by the Adjudicating Authority, being an Assistant Director of Enforcement or a Deputy Director of Enforcement, may prefer an appeal to the Special Director (Appeals).

(3) Every appeal under sub-section (1) shall be filed within forty-five days from the date on which the copy of the order made

by the Adjudicating Authority is received by the aggrieved person and it shall be in such form, verified in such manner and be accompanied by such fee as may be prescribed : Provided that the Special Director (Appeals) may entertain an appeal after the expiry of the said period of forty-five days, if he is satisfied that there was sufficient cause for not filing it within that period.

(4) On receipt of an appeal under sub-section (1), the Special Director (Appeals) may after giving the parties to the appeal an opportunity of being heard, pass such order thereon as he thinks fit confirming, modifying or setting aside the order appealed against.

(5) The Special Director (Appeals) shall send a copy of every order made by him to the parties to appeal and to the concerned Adjudicating Authority.

(6) The Special Director (Appeals) shall have the same powers of a civil court which are conferred on the Appellate Tribunal under sub-section (2) of section 28 and—

(a) all proceedings before him shall be deemed to be judicial proceedings within the meaning of sections 193 and 228 of the Indian Penal Code (45 of 1860);

(b) shall be deemed to be a civil court for the purposes of sections 345 and 346 of the Code of Criminal Procedure, 1973 (2 of 1974).

Establishment of Appellate Tribunal.

18. The Central Government shall, by notification, establish an Appellate Tribunal to be known as the Appellate Tribunal for Foreign Exchange to hear appeals against the orders of the Adjudicating Authorities and the Special Director (Appeals) under this Act.

Appeal to Appellate Tribunal.

19. (1) Save as provided in sub-section (2), the Central Government or any person aggrieved by an order made by an Adjudicating Authority, other than those referred to sub-section (1) of section 17, or the Special Director (Appeals), may prefer an appeal to the Appellate Tribunal: Provided that any person appealing against the order of the Adjudicating Authority or the Special Director (Appeals) levying any penalty, shall while filing

the appeal, deposit the amount of such penalty with such authority as may be notified by the Central Government : Provided further that where in any particular case, the Appellate Tribunal is of the opinion that the deposit of such penalty would cause undue hardship to such person, the Appellate Tribunal may dispense with such deposit subject to such conditions as it may deem fit to impose so as to safeguard the realisation of penalty.

(2) Every appeal under sub-section (1) shall be filed within a period of forty-five days from the date on which a copy of the order made by the Adjudicating Authority or the Special Director (Appeals) is received by the aggrieved person or by the Central Government and it shall be in such form, verified in such manner and be accompanied by such fee as may be prescribed : Provided that the Appellate Tribunal may entertain an appeal after the expiry of the said period of forty-five days if it is satisfied that there was sufficient cause for not filing it within that period.

(3) On receipt of an appeal under sub-section (1), the Appellate Tribunal may, after giving the parties to the appeal an opportunity of being heard, pass such orders thereon as it thinks fit, confirming, modifying or setting aside the order appealed against.

(4) The Appellate Tribunal shall send a copy of every order made by it to the parties to the appeal and to the concerned Adjudicating Authority or the Special Director (Appeals), as the case may be.

(5) The appeal filed before the Appellate Tribunal under sub-section (1) shall be dealt with by it as expeditiously as possible and endeavour shall be made by it to dispose of the appeal finally within one hundred and eighty days from the date of receipt of the appeal: Provided that where any appeal could not be disposed of within the said period of one hundred and eighty days, the Appellate Tribunal shall record its reasons in writing for not disposing of the appeal within the said period.

(6) The Appellate Tribunal may, for the purpose of examining the legality, propriety or correctness of any order made by the Adjudicating Authority under section 16 in relation to any proceeding, on its own motion or otherwise, call for the records of such proceedings and make such order in the case as it thinks fit.

Composition of Appellate Tribunal.

20. (1) The Appellate Tribunal shall consist of a Chairperson and such number of Members as the Central Government may deem fit.

(2) Subject to the provisions of this Act,—

(a) the jurisdiction of the Appellate Tribunal may be exercised by Benches thereof;

(b) a Bench may be constituted by the Chairperson with one or more Members as the Chairperson may deem fit;

(c) the Benches of the Appellate Tribunal shall ordinarily sit at New Delhi and at such other places as the Central Government may, in consultation with the Chairperson, notify;

(d) the Central Government shall notify the areas in relation to which each Bench of the Appellate Tribunal may exercise jurisdiction.

(3) Notwithstanding anything contained in sub-section (2), the Chairperson may transfer a Member from one Bench to another Bench.

(4) If at any stage of the hearing of any case or matter it appears to the Chairperson or a Member that the case or matter is of such a nature that it ought to be heard by a Bench consisting of two Members, the case or matter may be transferred by the Chairperson or, as the case may be, referred to him for transfer, to such Bench as the Chairperson may deem fit.

Qualifications for appointment of Chairperson, Member and Special Director (Appeals).

21. (1) A person shall not be qualified for appointment as the Chairperson or a Member unless he—

(a) in the case of Chairperson, is or has been, or is qualified to be, a Judge of a High Court; and

(b) in the case of a Member, is or has been, or is qualified to be, a District Judge.

(2) A person shall not be qualified for appointment as a Special Director (Appeals) unless he—

(a) has been a member of the Indian Legal Service and has held a post in Grade I of that Service; or

(b) has been a member of the Indian Revenue Service and has held a post equivalent to a Joint Secretary to the Government of India.

Term of office.

22. The Chairperson and every other Member shall hold office as such for a term of five years from the date on which he enters upon his office : Provided that no Chairperson or other Member shall hold office as such after he has attained,—

(a) in the case of the Chairperson, the age of sixty-five years;

(b) in the case of any other Member, the age of sixty-two years.

Terms and conditions of service.

23. The salary and allowances payable to and the other terms and conditions of service of the Chairperson, other Members and the Special Director (Appeals) shall be such as may be prescribed: Provided that neither the salary and allowances nor the other terms and conditions of service of the Chairperson or a Member shall be varied to his disadvantage after appointment.

Vacancies.

24. If, for reason other than temporary absence, any vacancy occurs in the office of the Chairperson or a Member, the Central Government shall appoint another person in accordance with the provisions of this Act to fill the vacancy and the proceedings may be continued before the Appellate Tribunal from the stage at which the vacancy is filled.

Resignation and removal.

25. (1) The Chairperson or a Member may, by notice in writing under his hand addressed to the Central Government, resign his office: Provided that the Chairperson or a Member shall, unless he is permitted by the Central Government to relinquish his office sooner, continue to hold office until the expiry of three months from the date of receipt of such notice or until a person duly appointed as his successor enters upon his office or until the expiry of term of office, whichever is the earliest.

(2) The Chairperson or a Member shall not be removed from his office except by an order by the Central Government on the

ground of proved misbehaviour or incapacity after an inquiry made by such person as the President may appoint for this purpose in which the Chairperson or a Member concerned has been informed of the charges against him and given a reasonable opportunity of being heard in respect of such charges.

Member to act as Chairperson in certain circumstances.

26. (1) In the event of the occurrence of any vacancy in the office of the Chairperson by reason of his death, resignation or otherwise, the senior-most Member shall act as the Chairperson until the date on which a new Chairperson, appointed in accordance with the provisions of this Act to fill such vacancy, enters upon his office.

(2) When the Chairperson is unable to discharge his functions owing to absence, illness or any other cause, the seniormost Member shall discharge the functions of the Chairperson until the date on which the Chairperson resumes his duties.

Staff of Appellate Tribunal and Special Director (Appeals).

27. (1) The Central Government shall provide the Appellate Tribunal and the Special Director (Appeals) with such officers and employees as it may deem fit.

(2) The officers and employees of the Appellate Tribunal and office of the Special Director (Appeals) shall discharge their functions under the general superintendence of the Chairperson and the Special Director (Appeals), as the case may be.

(3) The salaries and allowances and other conditions of service of the officers and employees of the Appellate Tribunal and office of the Special Director (Appeals) shall be such as may be prescribed.

Procedure and powers of Appellate Tribunal and Special Director (Appeals)

28. (1) The Appellate Tribunal and the Special Director (Appeals) shall not be bound by the procedure laid down by the Code of Civil Procedure, 1908 (5 of 1908) but shall be guided by the principles of natural justice and, subject to the other provisions of this Act, the Appellate Tribunal and the Special Director (Appeals) shall have powers to regulate its own procedure.

(2) The Appellate Tribunal and the Special Director (Appeals)

shall have, for the purposes of discharging its functions under this Act, the same powers as are vested in a civil court under the Code of Civil Procedure, 1908 (5 of 1908); while trying a suit, in respect of the following matters, namely:—

(a) summoning and enforcing the attendance of any person and examining him on oath;

(b) requiring the discovery and production of documents;

(c) receiving evidence on affidavits;

(d) subject to the provisions of sections 123 and 124 of the Indian Evidence Act, 1872 (1 of 1872) requisitioning any public record or document or copy of such record or document from any office;

(e) issuing commissions for the examination of witnesses or documents;

(f) reviewing its decisions;

(g) dismissing a representation of default or deciding it ex parte;

(h) setting aside any order of dismissal of any representation for default or any order passed by it ex parte; and

(i) any other matter which may be prescribed by the Central Government.

(3) An order made by the Appellate Tribunal or the Special Director (Appeals) under this Act shall be executable by the Appellate Tribunal or the Special Director (Appeals) as a decree of civil court and, for this purpose, the Appellate Tribunal and the Special Director (Appeals) shall have all the powers of a civil court.

(4) Notwithstanding anything contained in sub-section (3), the Appellate Tribunal or the Special Director (Appeals) may transmit any order made by it to a civil court having local jurisdiction and such civil court shall execute the order as if it were a decree made by that court.

(5) All proceedings before the Appellate Tribunal and the Special Director (Appeals) shall be deemed to be judicial proceedings within the meaning of sections 193 and 228 of the Indian Penal Code (45 of 1860) and the Appellate Tribunal shall be deemed to be a civil court for the purposes of sections 345 and 346 of the Code of Criminal Procedure, 1973 (2 of 1974)

Distribution of business amongst Benches.

29. Where Benches are constituted, the Chairperson may, from time to time, by notification, make provisions as to the distribution of the business of the Appellate Tribunal amongst the Benches and also provide for the matters which may be dealt with by each Bench.

Power of Chairperson to transfer cases.

30. On the application of any of the parties and after notice to the parties, and after hearing such of them as he may desire to be heard, or on his own motion without such notice, the Chairperson may transfer any case pending before one Bench, for disposal, to any other Bench.

Decision to be by majority.

31. If the Members of a Bench consisting of two Members differ in opinion on any point, they shall state the point or points on which they differ, and make a reference to the Chairperson who shall either hear the point or points himself or refer the case for hearing on such point or points by one or more of the other Members of the Appellate Tribunal and such point or points shall be decided according to the opinion of the majority of the Members of the Appellate Tribunal who have heard the case, including those who first heard it. Right of appellant to take assistance of legal practitioner or chartered accountant and of Government, to appoint presenting officers.

32. (1) A person preferring an appeal to the Appellate Tribunal or the Special Director (Appeals) under this Act may either appear in person or take the assistance of a legal practitioner or a chartered accountant of his choice to present his case before the Appellate Tribunal or the Special Director (Appeals), as the case may be.

(2) The Central Government may authorise one or more legal practitioners or chartered accountants or any of its officers to act as presenting officers and every person so authorised may present the case with respect to any appeal before the Appellate Tribunal or the Special Director (Appeals), as the case may be.

Members, etc. to be public servants.

33. The Chairperson, Members and other officers and employees of the Appellate Tribunal, the Special Director (Appeals)

and the Adjudicating Authority shall be deemed to be public servants within the meaning of section 21 of the Indian Penal Code (45 of 1860).

Civil court not to have jurisdiction.

34. No civil court shall have jurisdiction to entertain any suit or proceeding in respect of any matter which an Adjudicating Authority or the Appellate Tribunal or the Special Director (Appeals) is empowered by or under this Act to determine and no injunction shall be granted by any court or other authority in respect of any action taken or to be taken in pursuance of any power conferred by or under this Act.

Appeal to High Court.

35. Any person aggrieved by any decision or order of the Appellate Tribunal may file an appeal to the High Court within sixty days from the date of communication of the decision or order of the Appellate Tribunal on any question of law arising out of such order:

Provided that the High Court may, if it is satisfied that the appellant was prevented by sufficient cause from filing the appeal within the said period, allow it to be filed within a further period not exceeding sixty days.

Explanation.—In this section "High Court" means—

(a) the High Court within the jurisdiction of which the aggrieved party ordinarily resides or carries on business or personally works for gain; and

(b) where the Central Government is the aggrieved party, the High Court within the jurisdiction of which the respondent, or in a case where there are more than one respondent, any of the respondents, ordinarily resides or carries on business or personally works for gain.

Directorate of Enforcement

36. (1) The Central Government shall establish a Directorate of Enforcement with a Director and such other officers or class of officers as it thinks fit, who shall be called officers of Enforcement, for the purposes of this Act.

(2) Without prejudice to provisions of sub-section (1), the

Central Government may authorise the Director of Enforcement or an Additional Director of Enforcement or a Special Director of Enforcement or a Deputy Director of Enforcement to appoint officers of Enforcement below the rank of an Assistant Director of Enforcement.

(3) Subject to such conditions and limitations as the Central Government may impose, an officer of Enforcement may exercise the powers and discharge the duties conferred or imposed on him under this Act.

Power of search, seizure, etc.

37. (1) The Director of Enforcement and other officers of Enforcement, not below the rank of an Assistant Director, shall take up for investigation the contravention referred to in section 13.

(2) Without prejudice to the provisions of sub-section (1), the Central Government may also, by notification, authorise any officer or class of officers in the Central Government, State Government or the Reserve Bank, not below the rank of an Under Secretary to the Government of India to investigate any contravention referred to in section 13.

(3) The officers referred to in sub-section (1) shall exercise the like powers which are conferred on income-tax authorities under the Income-tax Act, 1961 (43 of 1961) and shall exercise such powers, subject to such limitations laid down under that Act.

Empowering other officers.

38. (1) The Central Government may, by order and subject to such conditions and limitations as it thinks fit to impose, authorise any officer of customs or any central excise officer or any police officer or any other officer of the Central Government or a State Government to exercise such of the powers and discharge such of the duties of the Director of Enforcement or any other officer of Enforcement under this Act as may be stated in the order.

(2) The officers referred to in sub-section (1) shall exercise the like powers which are conferred on the income-tax authorities under the Income-tax Act, 1961 (43 of 1961), subject to such conditions and limitations as the Central Government may impose.

MISCELLANEOUS

Presumption as to documents in certain cases.

39. Where any document—

(i) is produced or furnished by any person or has been seized from the custody or control of any person, in either case, under this Act or under any other law; or

(ii) has been received from any place outside India (duly authenticated by such authority or person and in such manner as may be prescribed) in the course of investigation of any contravention under this Act alleged to have been committed by any person, and such document is tendered in any proceeding under this Act in evidence against him, or against him and any other person who is proceeded against jointly with him, the court or the Adjudicating Authority, as the case may be, shall—

(a) presume, unless the contrary is proved, that the signature and every other part of such document which purports to be in the handwriting of any particular person or which the court may reasonably assume to have been signed by, or to be in the handwriting of, any particular person, is in that person's handwriting, and in the case of a document executed or attested, that it was executed or attested by the person by whom it purports to have been so executed or attested;

(b) admit the document in evidence notwithstanding that it is not duly stamped, if such document is otherwise admissible in evidence;

(c) in a case falling under clause (i), also presume, unless the contrary is proved, the truth of the contents of such document.

Suspension of operation of this Act.

40. (1) If the Central Government is satisfied that circumstances have arisen rendering it necessary that any permission granted or restriction imposed by this Act should cease to be granted or imposed, or if it considers necessary or expedient so to do in public interest, the Central Government may, by notification, suspend or relax to such extent either indefinitely or for such period as may be notified, the operation of all or any of the provisions of this Act.

(2) Where the operation of any provision of this Act has under

sub-section (1) been suspended or relaxed indefinitely, such suspension or relaxation may, at any time while this Act remains in force, be removed by the Central Government by notification.

(3) Every notification issued under this section shall be laid, as soon as may be after it is issued, before each House of Parliament, while it is in session, for a total period of thirty days which may be comprised in one session or in two or more successive sessions, and if, before the expiry of the session immediately following the session or the successive sessions aforesaid, both Houses agree in making any modification in the notification or both Houses agree that the notification should not be issued, the notification shall thereafter have effect only in such modified form or be of no effect, as the case may be; so, however, that any such modification or annulment shall be without prejudice to the validity of anything previously done under that notification.

Power of Central Government to give directions.

41. For the purposes of this Act, the Central Government may, from time to time, give to the Reserve Bank such general or special directions as it thinks fit, and the Reserve Bank shall, in the discharge of its functions under this Act, comply with any such directions.

Contravention by companies.

42. (1) Where a person committing a contravention of any of the provisions of this Act or of any rule, direction or order made thereunder is a company, every person who, at the time the contravention was committed, was in charge of, and was responsible to, the company for the conduct of the business of the company as well as the company, shall be deemed to be guilty of the contravention and shall be liable to be proceeded against and punished accordingly :

Provided that nothing contained in this sub-section shall render any such person liable to punishment if he proves that the contravention took place without his knowledge or that he exercised due diligence to prevent such contravention.

(2) Notwithstanding anything contained in sub-section (1), where a contravention of any of the provisions of this Act or of any rule, direction or order made thereunder has been committed by a company and it is proved that the contravention has taken

place with the consent or connivance of, or is attributable to any neglect on the part of, any director, manager, secretary or other officer of the company, such director, manager, secretary or other officer shall also be deemed to be guilty of the contravention and shall be liable to be proceeded against and punished accordingly.

Explanation.—For the purposes of this section—

(i) "company" means any body corporate and includes a firm or other association of individuals; and

(ii) "director", in relation to a firm, means a partner in the firm.

Death or insolvency in certain cases.

43. Any right, obligation, liability, proceeding or appeal arising in relation to the provisions of section 13 shall not abate by reason of death or insolvency of the person liable under that section and upon such death or insolvency such rights and obligations shall devolve on the legal representative of such person or the official receiver or the official assignee, as the case may be : Provided that a legal representative of the deceased shall be liable only to the extent of the inheritance or estate of the deceased.

Bar of legal proceedings.

44. No suit, prosecution or other legal proceeding shall lie against the Central Government or the Reserve Bank or any officer of that Government or of the Reserve Bank or any other person exercising any power or discharging any functions or performing any duties under this Act, for anything in good faith done or intended to be done under this Act or any rule, regulation, notification, direction or order made thereunder.

Removal of difficulties.

45. (1) If any difficulty arises in giving effect to the provisions of this Act, the Central Government may, by order, do anything not inconsistent with the provisions of this Act for the purpose of removing the difficulty: Provided that no such order shall be made under this section after the expiry of two years from the commencement of this Act.

(2) Every order made under this section shall be laid, as soon as may be after it is made, before each House of Parliament.

Power to make rules.

46. (1) The Central Government may, by notification, make rules to carry out the provisions of this Act.

(2) Without prejudice to the generality of the foregoing power, such rules may provide for,—

(a) the imposition of reasonable restrictions on current account transactions under section 5;

(b) the manner in which the contravention may be compounded under sub-section (1) of section 15;

(c) the manner of holding an inquiry by the Adjudicating Authority under sub-section (1) of section 16;

(d) the form of appeal and fee for filing such appeal under sections 17 and 19;

(e) the salary and allowances payable to and the other terms and conditions of service of the Chairperson and other Members of the Appellate Tribunal and the Special Director (Appeals) under section 23;

(f) the salaries and allowances and other conditions of service of the officers and employees of the Appellate Tribunal and the office of the Special Director (Appeals) under sub-section (3) of section 27;

(g) the additional matters in respect of which the Appellate Tribunal and the Special Director (Appeals) may exercise the powers of civil court under clause (i) of sub-section (2) of section 28;

(h) the authority or person and the manner in which any document may be authenticated under clause (ii) of section 39; and

(i) any other matter which is required to be, or may be, prescribed.

Power to make regulations.

47. (1) The Reserve Bank may, by notification, make regulations to carry out the provisions of this Act and the rules made thereunder.

(2) Without prejudice to the generality of the foregoing power, such regulations may provide for,—

(a) the permissible classes of capital account transactions, the limits of admissibility of foreign exchange for such transactions, and the prohibition, restriction or regulation of certain capital account transactions under section 6;

(b) the manner and the form in which the declaration is to be furnished under clause (a) of sub-section (1) of section 7;

(c) the period within which and the manner of repatriation of foreign exchange under section 8;

(d) the limit up to which any person may possess foreign currency or foreign coins under clause (a) of section 9;

(e) the class of persons and the limit up to which foreign currency account may be held or operated under clause (b) of section 9;

(f) the limit up to which foreign exchange acquired may be exempted under clause (d) of section 9;

(g) the limit up to which foreign exchange acquired may be retained under clause (e) of section 9;

(h) any other matter which is required to be, or may be, specified.

Rules and regulations to be laid before Parliament.

48. Every rule and regulation made under this Act shall be laid, as soon as may be after it is made, before each House of Parliament, while it is in session for a total period of thirty days which may be comprised in one session or in two or more successive sessions, and if, before the expiry of the session immediately following the session or the successive sessions aforesaid, both Houses agree in making any modification in the rule or regulation, or both Houses agree that the rule or regulation should not be made, the rule or regulation shall thereafter have effect only in such modified form or be of no effect, as the case may be; so, however, that any such modification or annulment shall be without prejudice to the validity of anything previously done under that rule or regulation.

Repeal and saving.

49. (1) The Foreign Exchange Regulation Act, 1973 (46 of 1973) is hereby repealed and the Appellate Board constituted under

sub-section (1) of section 52 of the said Act (hereinafter referred to as the repealed Act) shall stand dissolved.

(2) On the dissolution of the said Appellate Board, the person appointed as Chairman of the Appellate Board and every other person appointed as Member and holding office as such immediately before such date shall vacate their respective offices and no such Chairman or other person shall be entitled to claim any compensation for the premature termination of the term of his office or of any contract of service.

(3) Notwithstanding anything contained in any other law for the time being in force, no court shall take cognizance of an offence under the repealed Act and no adjudicating officer shall take notice of any contravention under section 51 of the repealed Act after the expiry of a period of two years from the date of the commencement of this Act.

(4) Subject to the provisions of sub-section (3) all offences committed under the repealed Act shall continue to be governed by the provisions of the repealed Act as if that Act had not been repealed.

(5) Notwithstanding such repeal,—

(a) anything done or any action taken or purported to have been done or taken including any rule, notification, inspection, order or notice made or issued or any appointment, confirmation or declaration made or any licence, permission, authorization or exemption granted or any document or instrument executed or any direction given under the Act hereby repealed shall, in so far as it is not inconsistent with the provisions of this Act, be deemed to have been done or taken under the corresponding provisions of this Act;

(b) any appeal preferred to the Appellate Board under sub-section (2) of section 52 of the repealed Act but not disposed of before the commencement of this Act shall stand transferred to and shall be disposed of by the Appellate Tribunal constituted under this Act;

(c) every appeal from any decision or order of the Appellate Board under sub-section (3) or sub-section (4) of section 52 of the repealed Act shall, if not filed before the commencement of this Act, be filed before the High Court within a period of sixty days of such commencement :

Provided that the High Court may entertain such appeal after the expiry of the said period of sixty days if it is satisfied that the appellant was prevented by sufficient cause from filing the appeal within the said period.

(6) Save as otherwise provided in sub-section (3), the mention of particular matters in sub-sections (2), (4) and (5) shall not be held to prejudice or affect the general application of section 6 of the General Clauses Act, 1897 (10 of 1897) with regard to the effect of repeal.

THE CONSERVATION OF FOREIGN EXCHANGE AND PREVENTION OF SMUGGLING ACTIVITIES ACT, 1974

1. Short title, extent and commencement --- (1) This Act may be called the Conservation of Foreign Exchange and Prevention of Smuggling Activities Act, 1974.

(2) It extends to the whole of India.

(3) It shall come into force on such date as the Central Government may, by notification in the Official Gazette, appoint.

2. Definitions- In this Act, unless the context otherwise requires,

(a) "appropriate Government" means, as respects a detention order made by the Central Government or by an officer of the Central Government or a person detained under such order, the Central Government, and as respects a detention order made by a State Government or by an officer of a State Government or a person detained under such order, the State Government;

(b) "detention order" means an order made under section 3;

(c) "foreigner" has the same meaning as in the Foreigners Act, 1946 (31 of 1946);

(d) "Indian customs waters" has the same meaning as in clause (28) of the Customs Act, 1962 (52 of 1962);

(e) "smuggling" has the same meanings as in clause (39) of section 2 of the Customs Act, 1962, and all its grammatical variations and cognate expressions shall be construed accordingly;

(f) "State Government", in relation to a Union territory, means the Administrator thereof;

(g) any reference in this Act to a law which is not in force in the State of Jammu and Kashmir shall, in relation to that State, be construed as a reference to the corresponding law, if any, in force in that State.

3. Power to make orders detaining certain persons --- (1) The Central Government or the State Government or any officer of the Central Government, not below the rank of a Joint Secretary to that Government, specially empowered for the purposes of this section by that Government, or any officer of the State Government, not below the rank of a Secretary to that Government, specially empowered for the purposes of this section by that Government, may, it satisfied, with respect to any person (including a foreigner), that, with a view to preventing him from acting in any manner prejudicial to the conservation or augmentation of foreign exchange or with a view to preventing him from -

(i) smuggling goods, or

(ii) abetting the smuggling of goods, or

(iii) engaging in transporting or concealing or keeping smuggled goods, or

(iv) dealing in smuggled goods otherwise than by engaging in transporting or concealing or keeping smuggled goods, or

(v) harbouring persons engaged in smuggling goods or in abetting the smuggling of goods, it is necessary so to do, make an order directing that such person be detained: [Provided that no order of detention shall be made on any of the grounds specified in this sub-section on which an order of detention may be made under section 3 of the Prevention of Illicit Traffic in Narcotic Drugs and Psychotropic Substances Act, 1988 or under section 3 of the Jammu and Kashmir Prevention of Illicit Traffic in Narcotic Drugs and Psychotropic Substances ordinance, 1988.] (J & K Ordinance, 1 of 1988).

(2) When any order of detention is made by a State Government or by an officer empowered by a State Government, the State Government shall, within ten days, forward to the Central Government a report in respect of the order.

(3) For the purposes of clause (5) of article 22 of the Constitution, the communication to a person detained in pursuance of a detention order of the grounds on which the order has been made shall be made as soon as may be after the detention, but ordinarily not later than five days, and in exceptional circumstances and for

reasons to be recorded in writing, not later than fifteen days, from the date of detention.

4. Execution of detention orders - A detention order may be executed at any place in India in the manner provided for the execution of warrants of arrest under the Code of Criminal Procedure, 1973 (2 of 1974).

5. Power to regulate place and conditions of detention - Every person in respect of whom a detention order has been made shall be liable -

(a) to be detained in such place and under such conditions including conditions as to maintenance, interviews or communication with others, discipline and punishment for breaches of discipline, as the appropriate Government may, by general or special order, specify; and

(b) to be removed from one place of detention to another place of detention, whether within the same State or in another State by order of the appropriate Government; Provided that no order shall be made by a State Government under clause (b) for the removal of a person from one State to another State except with the consent of the Government of that other State.

5A. Grounds of detention severable -- Where a person has been detained in pursuance of an order of detention under sub-section(1) which has been made on two or more grounds, such order of detention shall be deemed to have been made separately on each of such grounds and accordingly -

(a) such order shall not be deemed to be invalid or inoperative merely because one or some of the grounds is or are -

(i) vague,

(ii) non-existent,

(iii) not relevant,

(iv) not connected or not proximately connected with such person, or

(v) invalid for any other reason whatsoever, and it is not, therefore, possible to hold that the Government or officer making such order would have been satisfied as provided in sub-section (1) of section 3 with reference to the remaining ground or grounds and made the order of detention;

(b) the Government or officer making the order of detention shall be deemed to have made the order of detention under the said sub-section (1) after being satisfied as provided in that sub-section with reference to the remaining ground or grounds.]

6. Detention order not to be invalid or inoperative on certain grounds - No detention order shall be invalid or inoperative merely by reason -

(a) that the person to be detained thereunder is outside the limited of the territorial jurisdiction of the Government or the officer making the order of detention, or

(b) that the place of detention of such person is outside the said limits.

7. Powers in relation to absconding persons(1) If the appropriate Government has reason to believe that a person in respect of whom a detention order has been made has absconded or is concealing himself so that the order cannot be executed, the Government may

(a) make a report in writing of the fact to a Metropolitan Magistrate or a Magistrate of the first class having jurisdiction in the place where the said person ordinarily resides; and thereupon the provisions of sections 82, 83, 84 and 85 of the Code of Criminal Procedure, 1973 (2 of 1974), shall apply in respect of the said person and his property as if the order directing that he be detained were a warrant issued by the Magistrate;

(b) by order notified in the Official Gazette direct the said person to appear before such officer, at such place and within such period as may be specified in the order; and if the said person fails to comply with such direction, he shall, unless he proves that it was not possible for him to comply therewith and that he had, within the period specified in the order, informed the officer mentioned in the order of the reason which rendered compliance therewith impossible and of his whereabouts, be punishable therewith impossible and of his whereabouts, be punishable with imprisonment for a term which may extend to one year or with fine or with both.

(2) Nothwithstanding anything contained in the Code of Criminal Procedure, 1973 (2 of 1974), every offence under clause(b) of sub-section (1) shall be cognizable.

8. Advisory Board- For the purposes of sub-clause (a) of clause (c) of clause (7) of article 22 of the Constitution,-

(a) the Central Government and each State Government shall, wherever necessary, constitute one or more Advisory Boards each of which shall consist of a Chairman and two other persons possessing the qualifications specified in sub-clause (a) of clause (4) of article 22 of the Constitution;

(b) save as otherwise provided in section 9, the appropriate Government shall, within five weeks from the date of detention of a person under a detention order make a reference in respect thereof to the Advisory Board constituted under clause (a) to enable the Advisory Board to make the report under sub-clause (a) of clause (4) of article 22 of the Constitution;

(c) the Advisory Board to which a reference is made under clause (b) shall after considering the reference and the materials placed before it and after calling for such further information as it may deed necessary from the appropriate Government or from any person called for the purpose through the appropriate Government, from the person concerned, and if, in any particular case, it considers it essential so to do or if the person concerned desires to be heard in person, after hearing him person, prepare its report specifying in a separate paragraph thereof its opinion as to whether or not there is sufficient cause for the detention of the person concerned and submit the same within eleven weeks from the date of detention of the person concerned;

(d) when there is a difference of opinion among the members forming the Advisory Board the opinion of the majority of such members shall be deemed to be the opinion of the Board;

(e) a person against whom an order of detention has been made under this Act shall not be entitled to appear by any legal practitioner in any matter connected with the reference to the Advisory Board, and the proceedings of the Advisory Board and its report, excepting that part of the report in which the opinion of the Advisory Board is specified, shall be confidential;

(f) in every case where the Advisory Board has reported that there is in its opinion sufficient cause for the detention of a person, the appropriate Government may confirm the detention order and continue the detention of the person concerned for such period as it thinks fit and in every case where the Advisory Board has reported that there is in its opinion no sufficient cause for the detention of the person concerned, the appropriate Government shall revoke the detention order and cause the person to be released forthwith.

9. Cases in which and circumstances under which persons may be detained for period longer than three months without obtaining the opinion of Advisory Board- (1)Notwithstanding anything contained in this Act, any person (including a foreigner) in respect of whom an order of detention is made under this Act at any time before the 31st July, 1996, may be detained without obtaining, in accordance with the provisions of sub-clause (a) of clause (4) of article 22 of the Constitution, the opinion of an Advisory Board for a period longer than three months but not exceeding six months from the date of his detention, where the order of detention has been made against such person with a view to preventing him from smuggling goods or abetting the smuggling of goods or engaging in transporting or concealing or keeping smuggled goods and the Central Government or any Officer of the Central Government, not below the rank of an Additional Secretary to that Government, specially empowered for the purpose of this section by that Government, is satisfied that such person,

(a) smuggles or is likely to smuggle goods into, out of or through any area highly vulnerable to smuggling; or

(b) abets or is likely to abet the smuggling of goods into, out of or through any area highly vulnerable to smuggling; or

(c) engages or is likely to engage in transporting or concealing or keeping smuggled goods in any area highly vulnerable to smuggling, and makes a declaration to that effect within five weeks of the detention of such person.

Explanation 1 - In this sub-section, "area highly vulnerable to smuggling" means, -

(i) the Indian customs waters, contiguous to the State of Goa, Gujarat,Karnataka, Kerala, Maharashtra, Tamil Nadu and the Union territories of Daman and Diu and Pondicherry;

(ii) the Inland area fifty kilometres in width from the coast of India falling within the territories of the States of Goa, Gujarat,Karnataka, Kerala, Maharashtra,Tamil Nadu and the Union territories of Daman and Diu and Pondicherry;

(iii) the inland area fifty kilometres in width from the India-Pakistan border in the State of Gujarat,Jammu and Kashmir, Punjab and Rajasthan;

(iv) the customs air port of Delhi; and

(v) such further or other Indian customs waters, or inland area not exceeding one hundred kilometres in width from any other coast or border of India, or such other customs station, as the Central Government may, having regard to the vulnerability of such waters, area or customs station, as the case may be, to smuggling, by notification in the Official Gazette, specify in this behalf.

Explanation 2 - (1) For the purposes of Explanation 1, "customs airport" and "customs station" shall have the same meaning as in clauses (10) and (13) of section 2 of the Customs Act, 1962 (52 of 1962), respectively.

(2) In the case of any person detained under a detention order to which the provisions of sub-section (1) apply, section 8 shall have effect subject to the following modifications, namely:-

(i) in clause (b), for the words "shall, within five weeks", the words "shall, within four months and two weeks" shall be substituted;

(ii) in clause (c), -

(1) for the words "the detention of the person concerned", the words "the continued detention of the person concerned" shall be substituted;

(2) for the words "eleven weeks", the words "five months and three weeks" shall be substituted;

(iii) in clause (f), for the words "for the detention", at both the places where they occur, the words "for the continued detention" shall be substituted.

10. Maximum period of detention - The maximum period for which any person may be detained in pursuance of any detention order to which the provisions of section 9 do not apply and which has been confirmed under clause (f) of section 8 shall be a period of one year from the date of detention or the specified period, whichever period expires late and the maximum period for which any person may be detained in pursuance of any detention order to which the provisions of section 9 apply and which has been

confirmed under clause (f) of section 8 read with sub- section (2) of section 9 shall be a period of two years from the date of detention or the specified period, whichever period expires later; Provided that nothing contained in this section shall affect the power of the appropriate Government in neither case to revoke or modify the detention order at any earlier time.

Explanation In this section and section 10A - "specified period" means the period during which the Proclamation of Emergency issued under clause (1) of article 352 of the Constitution on the 3rd day of December, 1971 and the Proclamation of Emergency issued under that clause on the 25th day of June, 1975, are both in operation.

10A. Extension of period of detention - (1) Notwithstanding anything contained in any other provision of this Act, the detention of every person detained under a detention order which has been confirmed under clause (f) of section 8 before the commencement of the Conservation of Foreign Exchange and Prevention of Smuggling Activities (Amendment) Act, 1976, and which is in force immediately before such commencement shall, unless his detention has been continued by the appropriate Government under the said clause for a period shorter than one year from the date of his detention, continue until the expiry of a period of one year from the date of his detention under such order or until the expiry of the specified period, whichever period expires later: Provided that nothing contained in this sub-section shall affect the power of the appropriate Government to revoke or modify such detention order at any earlier time.

(2) Notwithstanding anything contained in any other provision of this Act, the detention of every person detained under a detention order which has been confirmed under clause (f) of section 8 read with sub-section (2) of section 9 before the commencement of the Conservation of Foreign Exchange and Prevention of Smuggling Activities (Amendment) Act, 1976, and which is in force immediately before such commencement, shall, unless his detention has been continued by the appropriate Government under the said clause (f) read with the said sub-section (2) for a period shorter than two years from the date of his detention, continue until the expiry of a period of two years from the date of his detention under such order or until the expiry of the specified period, whichever period expires later: Provided that nothing

contained in this sub-section shall affect the power of the appropriate Government to revoke or modify such detention order at any earlier time.

11. Revocation of detention orders - (1) Without prejudice to provisions of section 21 of the General Clauses Act, 1897 (10 of 1897), a detention order may, at any time, be revoked or modified

(a) notwithstanding that the order has been made by an officer of a State Government, by that State Government or by the Central Government;

(b) notwithstanding that the order has been made by an officer of the Central Government or by a State Government, by the Central Government.

(2) The revocation of a detention order shall not bar the making of another detention order under section (3) against the same person.

12. Temporary release of persons detained - (1) The Central Government may, at any time, direct that any person detained in pursuance of a detention order made by that Government or an officer subordinate to that Government or by a State Government or by an officer subordinate to a State Government, may be released for any specified period either without conditions or upon such conditions specified in the directions as that person accepts, and may, at any time, cancel his release.

(1A) A State Government may, at any time, direct that any person detained in pursuance of a detention order made by that Government or by an officer subordinate to that Government may be released for any specified period either without conditions or upon such conditions specified in the direction as that person accepts, and may, at any time, cancel his release.

(2) In directing the release of any person under sub-section (1) or sub-section (1A) the Government directing the release may require him to enter into a bond with sureties for the due observance of the conditions specified in the direction.

(3) Any person released under sub-section(1) or sub-section(1A) shall surrender himself at the time and place, and to the authority, specified in the order directing his release or cancelling his release, as the case may be.

(4) If any person fails without sufficient cause to surrender

himself in the manner specified in sub-section(3) he shall be punishable with imprisonment for a term which may extend to two years, or with fine, or with both.

(5) If any person released under sub-section(1) or sub-section(1A) fails to fulfill any of the conditions imposed upon him under the said sub-section or in the bond entered into by him, the bond shall be declared to be forfeited and any person bound thereby shall be liable to pay the penalty thereof.

(6) Notwithstanding anything contained in any other law and save as otherwise provided in this section, no person against whom a detention order made under this Act is in force shall be released whether on bail or bail bond or otherwise.

12A. Special provisions for dealing with emergency - (1) Notwithstanding anything contained in this Act or any rules of natural justice, the provisions of this section shall have effect during the period of operation of the Proclamation of Emergency issued under clause (1) of article 352 of the Constitution on the 3rd day of December, 1971, or the Proclamation of Emergency issued under that clause on the 25th day of June, 1975, or a period of twenty four months from the 25th day of June, 1975, whichever period is the shortest.-

(2) When making an order of detention under this Act against any person after the commencement of the Conservation of Foreign and Prevention of Smuggling Activities (Amendment) Act, 1975, the Central Government or the State Government or, as the case may be, the officer making the order of detention shall consider whether the detention of such person under this Act is necessary for dealing effectively with the emergency in respect of which the Proclamations referred to in sub-section (1) have been issued (hereafter in this section referred to as the emergency) and if, on such consideration, the Central Government or the State Government or, as the case may be, the officer is satisfied that it is necessary to detain such person for effectively dealing with the emergency, that Government or officer may make a declaration to that effect and communicate a copy of the declaration to the person concerned: Provided that where such declaration is made by an officer, it shall be reviewed by the appropriate Government within fifteen days from the date of making of the declaration and such declaration shall cease to have effect unless it is confirmed

by that Government, after such review, within the said period of fifteen days.

(3) The question whether the detention of any person in respect of whom a declaration has been made under sub-section (2) continues to be necessary for effectively dealing with the emergency shall be reconsidered by the appropriate Government within four months from the date of such declaration and thereafter at intervals not exceeding four months, and if, one such reconsideration, it appears to the appropriate Government that the detention of the person is no longer necessary for effectively dealing with the emergency, the Government may revoke the declaration.

(4) In making any consideration, review or reconsideration under sub-section (2) or (3) the appropriate Government or officer may, if such Government or officer considers it to be against the public interest to do otherwise, act on the basis of the information and materials in its or his possession without disclosing the facts or giving an opportunity of making a representation to the person concerned.

(5) It shall not be necessary to disclose to any person detained under a detention order to which the provisions of sub-section (2) apply, the grounds on which the order has been made during the period the declaration made in respect of such person under that sub-section is in force, and, accordingly, such period shall not be taken into account for the purpose of sub-section (3) of section 3

(6) In the case of every person detained under a detention order to which the provisions of sub-section (2) apply, being a person in respect of whom a declaration has been made thereunder, the period during which such declaration is in force shall not be taken into account for the purpose of computing -

(i) the periods specified in clauses (b) and (c) of section 8

(ii) the periods of "one year" and "five weeks" specified in sub-section (1), the period of "one year" specified in sub-section (2)(i), and the period of "six months" specified in sub-section (3), of section 9.

13. Protection of action taken in good faith- No suit or other legal proceeding shall lie against the Central Government or a State Government, and no suit, prosecution or other legal proceedings shall lie against any person, for anything in good faith done or intended to be done in pursuance of this Act.

14. Repeal -The Maintenance of Internal Security (Amendment) Ordinance, 1974 (11 of 1974), shall, on the commencement of this Act, stand repealed and accordingly the amendments made in the Maintenance of Internal Security Act, 1971 (26 of 1971), by the said Ordinance shall, on such commencement, cease to have effect.

Customs Valuation (Determination Of Price Of Imported Goods) Rules, 1988

In exercise of the powers conferred by Section 156 of the Customs Act, 1962 (52 of 1962), read with Section 22 of the General Clauses Act, 1897 (10 of 1897), and in supersession of the Customs Valuation Rules, 1963 except as respect things done or omitted to be done before such supersession, the Central Government hereby makes the following rules, namely: -

1. Short title, commencement and application. – (1) (These rules may be called the Customs Valuation (Determination of Price of Imported Goods) Rules, 1988.

2. They shall come into force on the 16th August, 1988.

3. They shall apply imported goods where a duty of customs is chargeable by reference to their value.

2. Definitions. – (1) In these rules, unless the context otherwise requires,-

1[(a) "computed value" means the value of imported goods determined in accordance with rule 7A of these rules;

(aa) " deductive value" means the value determined in accordance with rule 7 of these rules;]

(b) " goods of the same class or kind", means imported goods that are within a group of range of imported goods produced by a particular industry of industrial sector and includes identical goods of similar goods;

(c) " identical goods" means imported goods -

(i) which are same in all respects, including physical characteristics, quality and reputation as the goods being valued except for minor differences in appearance that do not affect the value of the goods;

(ii) produced in the country in which the goods being valued were produced; and

(iii) produced by the same person who produced the goods,

or where no such goods are available, goods produced by a different person, but shall not include imported goods where engineering, development work, art work, design work, plan or sketch undertaken in India were completed directly or indirectly by the buyer on these imported goods free of charge or at a reduced cost for use in connection with the production and sale for export of these imported goods;

(d) " produced" includes grown, manufactured and mined;

(e) " similar goods" means imported goods –

1. which although not alike in all respects, have like characteristics and like component materials which enable them to perform the same functions and to be commercially interchangeable with the goods being valued having regard to the quality, reputation and the existence of trade mark;

2. produced in the country in which the goods being valued were produced; and

3. produced by the same person who produced the goods being valued, or where no such goods are available, goods produced by a different person, but shall not include imported goods where engineering, development work, art work, design work, plan or sketch undertaken in India were completed directly or indirectly by the buyer on these imported goods free of charge or at a reduced cost for use in connection with production and sale for export of these imported goods;

(f) " transaction value" means the value determined in accordance with Rule 4 of these rules.

(2) For the purpose of these rules, persons shall be deemed to be " related " only if –

1. they are officers or directors of one another's businesses;

2. they are legally recognized partners in business;

3. they are employer and exployee;

4. any person directly or indirectly owns, controls or holds 5 percent or more of the outstanding voting stock or shares of both of them;

5. one of them directly or indirectly controls the other;

6. both of them are directly or indirectly controlled by a third person;

7. together they directly or indirectly control a third person; or

8. they are members of the same family.

Explanation I. – The term " person" also includes legal persons.

Explanation II.- Persons who are associated in the business of one another in that one is the sole agent or sole distributor or sole concessionaire, however described, of the other shall be deemed to be related for the purpose of these rules, if they fall within the criteria of this sub-rule.

3. Determination of the method of valuation.– For the purpose of these rules,-

1. the value of imported goods shall be the transaction value;

2. if the value cannot be determined under the provisions of clause (i) above, the value shall be determined by proceeding sequentially through Rules 5 to 8 of these rules.

1. Transaction value. – (1) The transaction value of imported goods shall be the price actually paid or payable for the goods when sold for export to India, adjusted in accordance with the provisions of Rule 9 of these rules.

(2) The transaction value of imported goods under sub-rule (1) above shall be accepted:

Provided that-

1. there are no restrictions as to the disposition or use of the goods by the buyer other than restrictions which-

1. are imposed or required by law or by the public authorities in India;

or

* limit the geographical area in which the goods may be resold; or

* do not substantially affect the value of the goods;

1. the sale or price is not subject to same condition or consideration for which a value cannot be determined in respect of the goods being valued;

* no part of the proceeds of any subsequent resale,disposal or use of the goods by the buyer will accrue directly or indirectly to the seller unless an appropriate adjustment can be made in accordance with the provisions of Rule 9 of these rules; and

* the buyer and seller are not related,or where the buyer and seller are related, that transaction value is acceptable for customs purposes under the provisions of sub-rule

(3) below.

(3) (a) Where the buyer and seller are related, the transaction value shall be accepted provided that the examination of the circumstances of the sale of the imported goods indicate that the relationship did not influence the price.

(b) In a sale between related persons, the transaction value shall be accepte, whenever the importer demonstrates that the declared value of the goods being valued, closely approximates to one of the following values ascertained at or about the same time-

i. the transaction value of identical goods, or of similar goods, in sales to unrelated buyers in India;

(ii) the deductive value for identical goods or similar goods;

2[(iii) the computed value for identical goods or similar goods.]

Provided that in applying the values used for comparison, due account shall be taken of demonstrated difference in commercial levels, quantity levels, adjustments in accordance with the provisions of Rule 9 of these rules and cost incurred by the seller in sales in which he and the buyer are not related;

(c) substitute values shall not be established under the provisions of clause (b) of this sub-rule.

2. Transaction of value of identical goods. - (1) (a) Subject to the provisions of Rule 3 of these rules, the value of imported goods shall be the transaction value of identical goods sold for export to India and imported at or about the same time as the goods being valued.

(b) In applying this rule, the transaction value of identical goods in a sale at the same commercial level and in substantially the same quantity as the goods being valued shall be used to determine the value of imported goods.

(c) Where no sale referred to in clause (b) of sub-rule (1) of this rule, is found, the transaction value of identical goods sold at a different commercial level or in different quantities or both, adjusted to take account of the difference attributable to commercial level or to the quantity or both, shall be used, provided that such adjustments shall be made on the basis of the demonstrated evidence which clearly establishes the reasonableness and accuracy of the adjustments, whether such adjustment leads to an increase or decrease in the value.

(2) Where the cost and charges referred to in sub-rule (2) of Rule 9 of these rules are included in the transaction value of identical goods, an adjustment shall be made, if there are significant differences in such costs and charges between the goods being valued and the identical goods in question arising from differences in distances and means of transport.

(3) In applying this rule, if more than one transaction value of identical goods is found; the lowest such value shall be used to determine the value of imported goods.

6. Transaction value of similar goods. – (1) Subject to the provisions of Rule 3 of these rules, the value of imported goods shall be the transaction value of similar goods sold for export to India and imported at or about the same time as the goods being valued.

(2) The provisions of clauses (b) and (c) of sub-rule (1), sub-rule (2) and sub-rule(3),of Rule 5 of these rules shall, mutatis mutandis, also apply in respect of similar goods.

3[6a. Determination of value when transaction values is not available. – If the value of imported goods cannot be determined under the provisions of rules 4, 5and 6, the value shall be determined under the provisions of rule 7 or, when the value cannot be determined under that rule, under rule 7A: Provided that at the request of the importer, and with the approval of the proper officer, the order of application of rules 7 and 7A shall be reversed.]

7. Deductive value. – (1) Subject to the provisions of Rule 3 of these rules, if the goods being valued or identical or similar imported goods are sold in India, in the condition as imported at or about the time at which the declaration for determination of value is presented, the value of imported goods shall be based on the unit price at which the imported goods or identical or similar imported goods are sold in the greatest aggregate quantity to persons who are not related to the sellers in India, subject to the following deductions :-

1. either the commission usually paid or agreed to be paid or

the additions usually made for profits and general expenses in connection with sales in India of imported goods of the same class or kind;

2. the usual costs of transport and insurance and associated costs incurred within India;

3. the customs duties and other taxes payable in India by reason of importation or sale of the goods.

(2) If neither the imported goods nor identical nor similar imported goods are sold at or about the same time of importation of the goods being valued, the value of imported goods shall, subject otherwise to the provisions of sub-rule (1) of this rule, be based on the unit price at which the imported goods or identical or similar imported goods are sold in India, at the earliest date after importation but before the expiry of ninety days after such importation.

(3) (a) If neither the imported goods not identical nor similar imported goods are sold in India in the conditions as imported, then, the value shall be based on the unit price at which the imported goods, after further processing, are sold in the greatest aggregate quantity to persons who are not related to the seller in India

(b) In such determination, due allowance shall be made for the value added by processing and the deductions, provided for in items (i) to (iii) of sub-rule (1) of this rule.

4[7A. Computed value.- Subject to the provisions of rule 3, the value of imported goods shall be based on a computed value, which shall consist of the sum of:-

1. the cost of value of materials and fabrication or other processing employed in producing the imported goods;

2. an amount for profit and general expenses equal to that usually reflected in sales of goods of the same class or kind as the goods being valued which are made by producers in the country of exportation for export to India;

3. the cost or value of all other expenses under sub-rule (2) of rule 9 of these rules.]

8. Residual method.- (1) Subject to the provisions of Rule 3 of these rules, where the value of imported goods cannot be determined under the provisions of any of the preceding rules,

the value shall be determined using reasonable means consistent with the principles and general provisions of these rules and sub-section (1) of Section 14 of the Customs Act, 1962 (52 of 1962) and on the basis of data available in India.

(2) No value shall be determined under the provisions of (5) this rule on the basis of-

1. the selling price in India of the goods produced in India;

2. a system which provides for the acceptance for customs purposes \ of the highest of the two alternative values;

4. the price of the goods on the domestic market of country of exportation; 6[(iii a) the cost of production other than computed values which have been determined for identical or similar goods in accordance with the provisions of rule 7A.]

6. the price of the goods for the export to a country other than India;

7. minimum customs values; or

8. arbitrary or fictitious values.

9. Cost and services. – (1) In determining the transaction value, there shall be added to the price actually paid or payable for the imported goods,-

(a) the following cost and services, to the extent they are incurred by the buyer but are not included in the price actually paid or payable for the imported goods, namely:-

(i) commissions and brokerage, except buying commissions;

(ii) the cost of containers which are treated as being one for customs purposes with the goods in question;

(iii) the cost of packing whether for labour or materials;

(b) the value, apportioned as appropriate, of the following goods and services where supplied directly or indirectly by the buyer free of charge or at reduced cost for use in connection with the production and sale for export of imported goods, to the extent that such value has not been included in the price actually paid of payable, namely :-

1. materials, components, parts and similar items incorporated in the imported goods;

2. tools, dies, moulds and similar items used in the production of the imported goods;

3. materials consumed in the production of the imported goods;

4. engineering, development, art work, design work, and and plans and sketches undertaken elsewhere than in India and necessary for the production of the imported goods;

(c) royalties and license fees related to the imported goods that the buyer is required to pay, directly or indirectly, as a condition of the sale of the goods being valued, to the extent that such royalties and fees are not included in the price actually paid or payable.

(d) the value of any part of the proceeds of any subsequent resale, disposal or use of the imported goods that accrues, directly or indirectly, to the seller;

(e) all other payments actually made or to be made as a condition of sale of the imported goods, by the buyer to the seller, or by the buyer to a third party to satisfy an obligation of the seller to the extent that such payments are not included in the price actually paid of payable.

(2) For the purposes of sub-section (1) and sub section (1A) of section14 of the Customs Act, 1962 (52 of 1962) and these rules, the value of the imported goods shall be the value of such goods, for delivery at the time and place of importation and shall include-

1. the cost of transport of the imported goods to the place of importation;

2. loading, unloading and handling charges associated with the delivery of the imported goods at the place of importation; and

3. the cost of insurance:

7[Provided that-

1. Where the coast of transport referred to in clause (a) is not ascertainable, such cost shall be twenty percent of the free on board value of the goods;

2. The charges referred to in clause (b) shall be one per cent of the free on board value of the goods plus the coast of transport referred to in clause (a) plus the coast of insurance referred to in clause (c);

3. Where the coast referred to in clause (c) is not ascertainable, such cost shall be 1.125% of free on board value of the goods;

Provided further that in the case of goods imported by air, where the cost referred to in clause (a) is ascertainable, such cost shall not exceed twenty per cent of free on board value of the goods:

Provided also that where the free on board value of the goods is not ascertainable, the coasts referred to in clause (a) shall be twenty per cent of the free on board value of the goods plus cost of insurance for clause (i) above and the cost referred to in clause (c) shall be 1.125 % of the free on board value of the goods plus cost of transport for clause (iii) above].

(3) Additions to the price actually paid or payable shall be made under this rule on the bases of objective and quantifiable data.

(4) No addition shall be made to the price actually paid or payable in determining the value of the imported goods except as provided for in this rule.

10. Declaration by the importer.- 8[(1) The importer or his agent shall furnish –

1. a declaration disclosing full and accurate details relating to the value of imported goods; and

2. any other statement, information or document including an invoice of the manufacturer or producer of the imported goods where the oops are imorted from or through a person other than the manufacturer or producer, as considered necessary by the proper officer for determination of the value of imported goods under these rule.]

(2) Nothing contained in these rules shall be construed as restricting or calling into question the right of the proper officer of customs to satisfy himself as to the truth or accuracy of any statement, information, document or declaration presented for valuation purposes.

(3) The provisions of the Customs Act, 1962 (52 of 1962) relating to confiscation, penalty and prosecution shall apply to cases where wrong declaration, information, statement or documents are furnished under these rules.

9[10A. Rejection of declared value – (1) When the proper officer has reason to doubt the truth or accuracy of the value declared in relation to any imported goods, he may ask the importer of such goods to furnish further information including documents or other evidence and if, after receiving such further information, or in the absence of a response of such importer, the proper officer still has reasonable doubt about the truth or accuracy of the value so declared, it shall be deemed that the value of such imported goods cannot be determined under the provisions of sub-rule (1) of rule 4.

(2) At the request of and importer, the proper officer, shall intimate the importer in writing the grounds for doubting the truth or accuracy of the value declared in relation to goods imported by such importer and provide a reasonable opportunity of being heard, before taking a final decision under sub-rule (1).]

11. Settlement of dispute. – In case of dispute between the importer and the proper officer of customs valuing the goods, the same shall be resolved consistent with the provisions contained in sub-section (1) of Section 14 of the Customs Act, 1962 (52 of 1962).

12. Interpretative Notes. – The interpretative notes specified in the Schedule to these rules shall apply for the interpretation of these rules.

INTERPRETATIVE NOTES

General Note :

Use of generally accepted accounting principles

1. " Generally accepted accounting principles" refer to the recognized consensus or substantial authoritative support within a country at a particular time as to which economic resources and obligations shall be recorded as assets and liabilities, which changes in assets and liabilities should be recorded, how the assets and liabilities and changes in them should be measured, what information should be disclosed and how it should be disclosed and which financial statements should be prepared. These standards may be broad guidelines of general application as well as detailed practices and procedures.

Notes to rules

Note to Rule 2

In Rule 2(2) (v), for the purposes of these rules, one person shall be deemed to control another when the former is legally or operationally in a position to exercise restraint or direction over the latter.

Note to Rule 4

Price actually paid or payable

The price actually paid or payable is the total payment made or to be made by the buyer to or for the benefit of the seller for the imported goods. The payment need not necessarily take the form of a transfer of money. Payment may be made way of letters of credit or negotiable instruments. Payment may be made directly or indirectly. An example of an indirect payment would be the settlement by the buyer, whether in whole or in part, of a debt owed by the seller.

Activities undertaken by the buyer on his own account, other that those for which an adjustment is provided in Rule 9, are not considered to be and indirect payment to the seller, even though they might be regarded as of benefit to the seller. The costs of such activities shall not, therefore, be added to the price actually paid or payable in determining the value of imported goods.

The value of imported goods shall not include the following charges or costs provided that they are distinguished from the price actually paid or payable for the imported goods :

1. Charges for construction, erection, assembly, maintenance or technical assistance, undertaken after importation on imported goods such as industrial plant, machinery or equipment;

2. The cost of transport after importation;

3. Duties and taxes in India.

The price actually paid or payable refers to the price for the imported goods. Thus the flow of dividends or other payments from the buyer to the seller that do not relate to the imported goods are not part of the customs value.

Among restrictions which would not render a price actually paid or payable unacceptable are restrictions which do not substantially affect the value of the goods. An example of such restrictions would be the case where a seller requires a buyer of automobiles no to sell or exhibit them prior to a fixed date which represents the beginning of a model year.

If the sale or price is subject to some condition or consideration for which a value cannot be determined with respect to the goods being valued, the transaction value shall not be acceptable for customs purposes. Some examples of this include:

1. The seller establishes the price of the imported goods on condition that the buyer will also buy other goods in specified quantities;

2. The price of the imported goods is dependent upon the price or prices at which the buyer of the imported goods sells other goods to the seller of the imported goods;

3. The price is established on the basis of a form of payments extraneous to the imported goods, such as where the imported goods are semi-finished goods which have been provided by the seller on condition that he will receive a specified quantity of the finished goods.

However, conditions or considerations relating to the production or marketing of the imported goods shall to result in rejection of the transaction value. For example, the fact that the buyer furnishes the seller with engineering and plans undertaken in India shall not result in rejection of the transaction value for the purposes of Rule 4. Likewise, if the buyer undertakes on his own account, even though by agreement with the seller, activities relating to the marketing or the imported goods, the value of these activities is not part of the value of imported goods nor shall such activities result in rejection of the transaction value.

Rule 4(3)

1. Rule 4(3) (a) and Rule 4(3) (b) provide different means of establishing the acceptability of a transaction value.

2. Rule 4(3) (a) provides that where the buyer and the seller are related, the circumstances surrounding the sale shall be examined and the transaction value shall be accepted as the value of imported goods provided that the relationship did not influence the price. It is not intended that there should be an examination of the circumstances in all cases where the buyer and the seller are related. Such examination will only be required where there are doubts about the acceptability of the price. Where the proper officer of customs has no doubts about the acceptability of the price, it should be accepted without requesting further information from the importer. For example, the proper officer of customs may have previously examined the relationship, or he may already

have detailed information concerning the buyer and the seller, and may already be satisfied from such examination or information that the relationship did not influence the price.

3. Where the proper officer of customs is unable to accept the transaction value without further inquiry, he should give the importer an opportunity to supply such further detailed information as may be necessary to enable him to examine the circumstances surrounding the sale. In this context, the proper officer of customs should be prepared to examine relevant aspects of the transaction, including the way in which the buyer and seller organize their commercial relations and the way in which the price in question was arrived at, in order to determine whether the relationship influenced the price. Where it can be shown that the buyer and seller, although related under the provisions of Rule 2(2) , buy from and sell to each other as if they were not related, this would demonstrate that the price had not been influenced by the relationship. As example of this, if the price had been settled in a manner consistent with the normal pricing practices of the industry in question or with the way the seller settles prices for sales to buyers who are not related to him, this would demonstrate that the price had not been influenced by the relationship. As a further example, where it is shown that the price is adequate to ensure recovery of all costs plus a profit which is representative of the firm's overall profit realized over a representative period of time (e.g. on an annual basis) in sales of goods of the same class or kind, this would demonstrate that the price had not been influenced.

4. Rule 4(3)(b) provides an opportunity for the importer to demonstrate that the transaction value closely approximates to a "test" value previously accepted by the proper offer of customs and is therefor acceptable under the provisions of rule 4. Where a test under rule 4(3) (b) is met, it is not necessary to examine the question of influence under 1[Rule 4(3)(a)]. If the proper officer of customs has already sufficient information to be satisfied, without further detailed inquiries, that one the tests provided in rule 4(3)(b) has been met, there is no reason for him to require the importer to demonstrate that the test can be met. In rule 4(3)(b) the term " unrelated buyers" means buyers who are not related to the seller in any particular case.

Rule 4(3)(b)

A number of factors must be taken into consideration in determining whether one value " closely approximates" to another value. These factors include the nature of the imported goods, the nature of the industry itself, the season in which the goods are imported, and whether the difference in value is commercially significant. Since these factors may vary from case to case, it would be impossible to apply a uniform standard such as a fixed percentage, in each case. For example, a small difference in value in a case involving one type of goods could be unacceptable while a large difference in a case involving another type of goods might be acceptable in determining whether the transaction value closely approximates to the "test" values set forth in rule 4(3)(b).

Notes to Rule 5

1. In applying rule 5, the proper officer of customs shall, wherever possible, use a sale of identical goods at the same commercial level and in substantially the same quantities as the goods being valued. Where no such sale is found, a sale of identical goods that takes place under any one of the following three conditions may be used:

1. a sale at the same commercial level but in different quantities;

2. a sale at a different commercial level but in substantially the same quantities; or

3. a sale at a different commercial level and in different quantities.

1. Having found a sale under any one of these three conditions adjustments will then be made, as the case may be, for:

1. quantity factors only;

(b) commercial level factors only; or

(c) both commercial level and quantity factors.

3. For the purposes of rule 5, the transaction value of identical imported goods means a value, adjusted as provided for in rule 5(1)(b) and (c) and rule 5(2), which has already been accepted under rule 4.

4. A condition for adjustment because of different commercial levels or different quantities is that such adjustment, whether it leads to an increase or a decrease in the value, be made only on

the basis of demonstrated evidence that clearly establishes the reasonableness and accuracy of the adjustment, e.g. valid price lists containing prices referring to different levels or different quantities. As an example of this, if the imported goods being valued consist of a shipment of 10 units and the only identical imported goods for which a transaction value exists involved a sale of 500 units, and it is recognized that the seller grants quantity discounts, the required adjustment may be accomplished by resorting to the seller's price list and using that price applicable to a sale of 10 units. This does not require that a sale had to have been made in quantities of 10 as long as the price list has been established as being bona fide through sales at other quantities. In the absence of such an objective measure, however, the determination of a value under the provisions of rule 5 is not appropriate.

Note to Rule 6

1. In applying rule 6, the proper officer of customs shall, wherever possible, use a sale of similar goods at the same commercial level and in substantially the same quantities as the goods being valued. For the purpose of rule 6, the transaction value of similar imported goods means the value of imported goods, adjusted as provided for in rule 6(2) which has already been accepted under rule 4.

2. All other provisions contained in note to rule 5 shall mutatis mutandis also apply in respect of similar goods.

Note to Rule 7

1. The term "unit/price at which... Goods are sold in the greatest aggregate quantity" means the price at which the greatest number of units is sold in sales to persons who are not related to the persons from whom they buy such goods at the first commercial level after importation at which such sales take place.

2. As an example of this, goods are sold from a price list which grants favorable unit prices for purchases made in larger quantities.

Sale quantity Unit price Number of sales Total quantity sold at each price

1-10 units 100 10 sales of 5 units, 65.

5 sales of 3 units

11-25 units 95 5 sales of 11 units. 55

over 25 units 90 1 sale of 30 units 80

1 sale of 50 units

The greatest number of units sold at a price is 80, therefore, the unit price in the greatest aggregate quantity is 90.

* As another example of this, two sales occur, in the first sale 500 units are sold at a price of 95 currency units each. In the second sale 400 units are sold at a price of 90 currency units each. In this example, the greatest number of units sold at a particular price is 500, therefore, the unit price n the greatest aggregate quantity is 95.

* A third example would be the following situation where various quantities are sold at various prices.

2. Sales sale quantity Unit price

40 units 100

30 units 90

15 units 100

50 units 95

25 units 105

35 units 90

5 units 100

(b) Totals Total quantity sold Unit price

65 90

50 95

60 100

25 105

In this example, the greatest number of units sold at a particular price is 65, therefore, the unit price in the greatest aggregate quantity is 90.

1. Any sale in India, as described in paragraph 1 above to a person who supplies directly or indirectly free of charge or at reduced cost for use in connection with the production and sale for export of the imported goods any of the elements specified in rule 9(1) (b), should not be taken into account in establishing the unit price for the purposes of rule 7.

2. It should be noted that "profit and general expenses" referred to in rule 7(1) should be taken as a whole. The figure for the

purposes of this deduction should be determined on the basis of information supplied by or on behalf of the importer unless his figures are inconsistent with those obtaining in sales in India, of imported goods of the same class or kind. Where the importers figures are inconsistent with such figures, the amount for profit and general expenses may be based upon relevant information other than that supplied by or on behalf of the importer.

3. The "general expenses" include the direct and indirect costs of marketing the goods in question.

4. Local taxes payable by reason of the sale of the goods for which deduction is not made under the provisions of rule 7(1)(iii) shall be deducted under the provisions of rule 7(1)(i).

5. In determining either the commissions or the usual profits and general expenses under the provisions of rule 7(1), the question whether certain goods are "of the same class or kind" as other goods must be determined on a case-by-case basis by reference to the circumstances involved. Sales in India, of the narrowest group or range of imported goods of the same class or kind, which includes the goods being valued, for which the necessary information can be provided, should be examined. For the purposes of rule 7 "goods of the same class or kind" includes goods imported from the same country as the goods being valued as well as goods imported from other countries.

6. For the purposes of rule 7(2) the "earliest date" shall be the date by which sales of the imported goods or of identical or similar imported, goods are made in sufficient quantity to establish the unit price.

7. Where the method in rule 7(3) is used, deductions made for the value added by further processing shall be based on objective and quantifiable data relating to the cost of such work. Accepted industry formulas, recipes, methods or construction, and other industry practices would form the basis of the calculations.

8. It is recognized that the method of valuation provided for in rule 7(3) would normally not be applicable when, as a result of the further processing, the imported goods lose their identity. However there can be instances where, although the identity of the imported goods is lose their identity. However there can be instances where, although the identity of the imported goods is lost, the value added by the processing can be determined

accurately without unreasonable difficulty. On the other hand, there can also be instances where the imported goods maintain their identity but form such a minor elements in the goods sold in the country of importation that the use of this valuation method would be unjustified. In view of the above, each situation of this type must be considered on a case-by-case basis.

2Note to Rule 7A

1. As a general rule, value of imported goods is determined under these rules on the basis of information readily available in India. In order to determine a computed value, however, it may be necessary to examine the costs of producing the goods being valued and other information which has to be obtained from outside India. Furthermore, in most cases, the producer of the goods will be outside the jurisdiction of the proper officer. The use of the computed value method will generally be limited to those cases where the buyer and seller are related, and the producer is prepared to supply to the proper officer the necessary costing and to provide facilities for any subsequent verification which may be necessary.

2. The "cost or value" referred to in clause (a) of rule 7A is to be determined on the basis of information relating to the production of the goods being valued supplied by or on behalf of the producer. It is to be based upon the commercial accounts of the producer, provided that such accounts are consistent with the generally accepted accounting principles applied in the country where the goods are produced.

3. The "cost or value" shall include the cost of elements specified in clauses (1)(a)(ii) and (1)(a)(iii) of rule 9. It shall also include the value, apportioned as appropriate under the provisions of the relevant note to rule 9, of any element specified in rule 9(1)(b) which has been supplied directly or indirectly by the buyer for use in connection with the production of the imported goods. The value of the elements specified in rule 9(1)(b)(iv) which are undertaken in India shall be included only to the extent that such elements are charged to the producer. It is to be understood that no cost or value of the elements referred to in this paragraph shall be counted twice in determining the computed value.

4. The "amount for profit and general expenses" referred to in clause (b) of rule 7A is to be determined on the basis of

information supplied by or on behalf of the producer unless the producer's figures are inconsistent with those usually reflected in sales of goods of the same class or kind as the goods being valued which are made by producers in the country of exportation for export to India.

5. It should be noted in this context that the "amount for profit and general expenses" has to be taken as a whole. It follows that if, in any particular case, the producer's profit figure is low and his general expenses are high, the producer's profit and general expenses taken together may nevertheless be consistent with that usually reflected in sales of goods of the same class or kind. Such a situation might occur, for example, if a product were being launched in India and the producer accepted a nil or low profit to offset high general expenses associated with the launch. Where the producer can demonstrate a low profit on his sales of the imported goods because of particular commercial circumstances, his actual profit figures should be taken into account provided that he has valid commercial reasons to justify them and his pricing policy reflects usual pricing policies in the branch of industry concerned. Such a situation might occur for example, where producers have been forced to lower prices temporarily because of an unforeseeable drop in demand, or where they sell goods to complement a range of goods being produced in India and accept a low profit to maintain competitivity. Where the producer's own figures for profit and general expenses are not consistent with those usually reflected in sales of goods of the same class or kind as the goods being valued which are made by producers in the country of exportation for export to India, the amount for profit and general expenses may be based upon relevant information other than that supplied by or on behalf of the producer of the goods.

6. The "general expenses" referred to in clause(b) of rule 7A covers the direct and indirect costs of producing and selling the goods for export which are not included under clause (a)of rule 7A.

7. Whether certain goods are "of the same class or kind" as other goods must be determined on a case-by-case basis with reference to the circumstances involved. In determining the usual profits and general expenses under the provisions of rule 7A, sales for export to India of the narrowest group or range of goods,

which includes the goods being valued, for which the necessary information can be provided, should be examined. For the purposes of rule 7A "goods of the same class or kind" must be from the same country as the goods being valued].

Note to Rule 8

1. Value of imported goods determined under the provisions of rule 8 should to the greatest extent possible, be based on previously determined customs values.

2. The methods of valuation to be employed under rule 8 may be those laid down in 3(rules 4 to 7A), inclusive, but a reasonable flexibility in the application of such methods would be in conformity with the aims and provision of rule 8.

3. Some examples of reasonable flexibility are as follows :

a. Identical goods.- The requirement that the identical goods should be imported at or about the same time as the goods being valued could be flexibly interpreted; identical imported goods produced in a country other than the country of exportation of the goods being valued could be the basis for customs valuation; customs values of identical imported goods already determined under the provisions of 4(rules 7 and 7A) could be used.

b. Similar goods.- The requirement that the similar goods should be imported at or about the same time as the goods being valued could be flexibly interpreted; similar imported goods produced in a country other than the country of exportation of the goods being valued could be the basis for customs valuation; customs values of similar imported goods already determined under the provisions of 5(rules 7 and 7A) could be used.

c. Deductive method.- The requirement that the goods shall have been sold in the "condition as imported" in rule 7(1) could be flexibly interpreted; the ninety days requirement could be administered flexibly.

Note to Rule 9

In rule 9(1)(a)(i), the term "buying commissions" means fees paid by an importer to his agent for the service of representing him abroad in the purchase of the goods being valued.

Rule 9(1)(b)(ii)

1. There are two factors involved in the apportionment of the elements specified in rule 9(1)(b)(ii) to the imported goods – the

value of the element itself and the way in which that value is to be apportioned to the imported goods. The apportionment of these elements should be made in a seasonable manner appropriate to the circumstances and in accordance with generally accepted accounting principles.

2. Concerning the value of the element, if the importer acquires the element from a sellei not related to him at a given cost, the value of the element is that cost. If the element was produced by the importer or by a person related to him, its value would be the cost of producing it. If the element had been previously used by the importer, regardless of whether it had been acquired or produced by such importer, the original cost of acquisition or production would have to be adjusted downward to reflect its use in order to arrive at the value of the element.

3. Once a value has been determined for the element it is necessary to apportion that value to the imported goods. Various possibilities exist. For example, the value might be apportioned to the first shipment if the importer wishes to pay duty on the entire value at one time. As another example, the importer may request that the value be apportioned over the number of units produced up to the time of the first shipment. As a further example, he may request that the value be apportioned over the entire anticipated production where contracts or firm commitments exists for that production. The method of apportionment used will depend upon the documentation provided by the importer.

4. As an illustration of the above, an importer provides the producer with a mould to be used in the production of the imported goods and contracts with him to buy 10,000 units. By the time of arrival of the first shipment of 1,000 units the producer has already produced 4,000 units. The importer may request the proper officer of customs to apportion the value of the mould over 1,000 units, 4,000 units or 10,000 units.

Rule 9(1)(b)(iv)

1. Additions for the elements specified in rule 9(1)(b)(iv) should be based on objective and quantifiable data. In order to minimize the burden for both the importer and proper officer of customs in determining the values to be added, data readily available in the buyer's commercial record system should be used in so far as possible.

2. For those elements supplied by the buyer which were purchased or leased by the buyer, the addition would be the cost of the purchase or the lease. No addition shall be made for those elements available in the public domain, other than the cost of obtaining copies of them.

3. The case with which it may be possible to calculate the values to be added will depend on a particular firm's structure and management practice, as well as its accounting methods.

4. For example, it is possible that a firm which imports a variety of products from several countries maintains the records of its design center outside the country of importation in such a way as to show accurately the costs attributable to a given product. In such cases, a direct adjustment may appropriately be made under the provisions of rule 9.

5. In another case, a firm may carry the cost of the design centre outside the country of importation as a general overhead expense without allocation to specific products. In this instance, an appropriate adjustment could be made under the provisions of rule 9 with respect to the imported goods by apportioning total design centre costs over total production benefiting from the design center and adding such apportioned cost on a unit basis to imports.

6. Variations in the above circumstances will, of course, require different factors to be considered in determining the proper method of allocation.

7. In cases where the production of the element in question involves a number of countries and over a period of time, the adjustment should be limited to the value actually added to that element outside the country of importation.

Rule 9(1)(c)

1. The royalties and license fees referred to in rule 9(1) (c) may include among other things, payments in respect to patents, trademarks and copyrights. However, the charges for the right to reproduce the imported goods in the country of importation shall not be added to the price actually paid or payable for the imported goods in determining the customs value.

2. Payments made by the buyer for the right to distribute or resell the imported goods shall not be added to the price actually paid or payable for the imported goods if such payments are not

a condition of the sale for export to the country of importation of the imported goods.

Rule 9(3)

Where objective and quantifiable data do not exist with regard to the additions required to be made under the provisions of rule 9, the transaction value cannot be determined under the provisions of rule 4. As an illustration of this, a royalty is paid on the basis of the price in a sale in the importing country of a litre of particular product that was imported by the kilogram and made up into a solution after importation. If the royalty is based partially on the imported goods and partially on other factors, which have nothing to do with the imported goods (such as when the imported goods are mixed with domestic ingredients and are no longer separately identifiable, or when the royalty cannot be distinguished from special financial arrangements between the buyer and the seller), it would be inappropriate to attempt to make an addition for the royalty. However, if the amount of this royalty is based only on the imported goods and can be readily quantified, an addition to the price actually paid or payable can be made.

Smugglers And Foreign Exchange Manipulators

An Act to provide for the forfeiture of illegally acquired properties of smugglers and foreign exchange manipulators and for matters connected therewith or incidental thereto;

Whereas for the effective prevention of smuggling activities and foreign exchange manipulations which are having a deleterious effect on the national economy it is necessary to deprive persons engaged in such activities and manipulations of their ill-gotten gains;

And whereas such persons have been augmenting such gains by violations of wealth-tax, income-tax or other laws or by other means and have thereby been increasing their resources for operating in a clandestine manner;

And whereas such persons have in many cases been holding the properties acquired by them through such gains in the names of their relatives, associates and confidants.

Be it enacted by Parliament in the Twenty-sixth Year of the Republic of India as follows:

1. Short title, extent and commencement:

(1) This act may be called the Smugglers and Foreign Exchange Manipulators (Forfeiture of Property) Act, 1976.

(2) It extends to the whole of India except the State of Jammu and Kashmir.

(3) It shall be deemed to have come into force on the 5th day of November, 1975.

2. Application:

(1) The provisions of this Act shall apply only to the persons specified in sub-section (2).

(2) The persons referred to in sub-section (1) are the following, namely :-

(a) every person-

(i) who has been convicted under the Sea Customs Act, 1878 (8 of 1878), or the Customs Act, 1962 (52 of 1962), of an offence in relation to goods of a value exceeding one lakh of rupees; or

(ii) who having been convicted under the Sea Customs Act, 1878 (8 of 1878), or the Customs Act, 1962 (52 of 1962), has been convicted subsequently under either of those Acts; or

(iii) who having been convicted under the Foreign Exchange Regulation Act, 1947 (7 of 1947), or the Foreign Exchange Regulation Act, 1973 (46 of 1973), has been convicted subsequently under either or those Act;

(b) every person in respect of whom an order of detention has been made under the Conservation of Foreign Exchange and Prevention of Smuggling Activities Act, 1974 (52 of 1974):Provided that-

(i) such order of detention, being an order which the provisions of section 9 or section 12A of the said Act do not apply, has not been revoked on the report of the Advisory Board under section 8 of the said Act or before the receipt of the report of the Advisory Board or before making a reference to the Advisory Board; or

(ii) such order of detention, being an order to which the provisions of section 9 of the said Act apply, has not been revoked before the expiry of the time for, or on the basis of, the review under sub-section (3) of section 9 or on the report of the Advisory board under section 8, read with sub-section (2) of section 9, of the said Act; or

(iii) such order of detention, being an order to which the provisions of section 12A of the said Act apply, has not been revoked before the expiry of the time for, or on the basis of, the first review under sub-section (3) of that section, or on the basis of the report of the Advisory Board under section 8, read with sub-section (6) of section 12A, of that Act; or

(iv) such order of detention has not been set aside by a Court of competent jurisdiction;

(c) every person who is a relative of person referred to in clause (a) or clause (b);

(d) every associate of a person referred to in clause (a) or clause (b);

(e) any holder (hereafter in this clause referred to as the present holder) of any property which was at any time previously held by a person referred to in clause (a) or clause (b) unless the present holder or, as the case may be, any one who held such property after such person and before the present holder, is or was a transferee in good faith for adequate consideration.

Explanation 1: For the purposes of sub-clause (i) of clause (a), the value of any goods in relation to which a person has been convicted of an offence shall be the wholesale price of the goods in the ordinary cause of trade in India as on the date of the commission of the offence.

Explanation 2: For the purposes of clause (c), "relative", in relation to a person, means -

(i) spouse of the person;

(ii) brother or sister of the person;

(iii) brother or sister of the spouse of the person;

(iv) any lineal ascendant or descendant of the person;

(v) any lineal ascendant or descendant of the spouse of the person;

(vi) spouse of a person referred to in clause (ii), clause (iii), clause (iv) or clause (v);

(vii) any lineal descendant of a person referred to in clause (ii) or clause (iii).

Explanation 3: For the purposes of clause (d), "associate", in relation to a person, means-

(i) any individual who, had been or is residing in the residential premises (including out-houses) of such person;

(ii) any individual who had been or is managing the affairs or keeping the accounts of such person;

(iii) any association of persons, body of individuals, partnership firm, or private company within the meaning of the Companies Act, 1956 (1 of 1956), of which such person had been or is a member, partner or director;

(iv) any individual who had been or is a member, partner or director of an association of persons, body of individuals, partnership firm or private company referred to in clause (iii) at any time when such person had been or is a member, partner or director of such association, body, partnership firm or private company;

(v) any person who had been or is managing the affairs, or keeping the accounts, of any association of persons, body of individuals, partnership firm or private company referred to in clause (iii);

(vi) the trustee of any trust, where,-

(a) the trust has been created by such person; or

(b) the value of the assets contributed by such person (including the value of the assets, if any, contributed by him earlier) to the trust amounts, on the date on which the contribution is made, to not less than twenty per cent of the value of the assets of the trust on that date;

(vii) where the competent authority, for reasons to be recorded in writing, considers that any properties of such person are held on his behalf by any other person, such other person.

Explanation 4: For the avoidance of doubt, it is hereby provided that the question whether any person is a person to whom the provisions of this Act apply may be determined with reference to any facts, circumstances or events (including any conviction or detention) which occurred or took place before the commencement of this Act

2A. Act not to apply to certain persons:

On and from the commencement of the provisions of Chapter VA of the Narcotic Drugs and Psychotropic Substances Act, 1985 (61 of 1985), the provisions of this Act shall not apply to persons in relation to whom any order, or proceeding, may be made or taken under that Chapter.

3. Definitions:

(1) In this Act, unless the context otherwise requires,- "Appellate Tribunal" means the Appellate Tribunal for Forfeited Property constituted under section 12; "competent authority" means an officer of the Central Government authorised by it under sub-section (1) of section 5 to perform the functions of a competent authority under this Act; "illegally acquired property", in relation to any person to whom this Act applies, means-

(i) any property acquired by such person, whether before or after the commencement of this act, wholly or partly out of or by means of any income, earnings or assets derived or obtained from or attributable to any activity prohibited by or under any law for the time being in force relating to any matter in respect of which Parliament has power to make laws; or

(ii) any property acquired by such person, whether before or after the commencement of this Act, wholly or partly out of or by means of any income, earnings or assets in respect of which any such law has been contravened; or

(iii) any property acquired by such person, whether before or after the commencement of this Act, wholly or partly out of or by means of any income, earnings or assets the source of which cannot be proved and which cannot be shown to be attributable to any act or thing done in respect of any matter in relation to which Parliament has no power to make laws; or

(iv) any property acquired by such person, whether before or after the commencement of this Act, for a consideration, or by any means, wholly or partly traceable to any property referred to in sub-clauses (i) to (iii) or the income or earnings from such property; and includes- any property held by such person which would have been, in relation to any previous holder thereof, illegally acquired property under this clause if such previous holder had not ceased to hold it, unless such person or any other person who held the property at any time after such previous holder or, where there are two or more such previous holders, the last of such previous holders is or was a transferee in good faith for adequate consideration; any property acquired by such person, whether before or after the commencement of this Act, for a consideration, or by any means, wholly or partly traceable to any property falling under item (A), or the income or earnings therefrom;

"prescribed" means prescribed by rules made under this Act;

"property" includes any interest in property, movable or immovable;

"trust" includes any other legal obligation.

(2) Any reference in this Act to any law which is not in force in any area shall, in relation to that area, be construed as a reference to the corresponding law, if any, in force in that area.

(3) Any reference in this Act to any officer or authority shall, in relation to any area in which there is no officer or authority with the same designation, be construed as a reference to such officer or authority as may be specified by the central Government by notification in the Official Gazette.

4. Prohibition of holding illegally acquired property:

(1) As from the commencement of this Act, it shall not be lawful for any person to whom this Act applies to hold any illegally acquired property either by himself or through any other person on his behalf.

(2) Where any person holds any illegally acquired property in contravention of the provisions of sub-section (1), such property shall be liable to be forfeited to the Central Government in accordance with the provisions of this Act.

5. Competent authority:

(1) The Central Government may, by order published in the Official Gazette, authorise as many officers of the Central Government (non below the rank of a Joint Secretary to the Government), as it thinks fit, to perform the functions of the competent authority under this Act.

(2) The competent authorities shall perform their functions in respect of such persons or classes or persons as the Central Government may, by order, direct.

6. Notice of forfeiture:

(1) If, having regard to the value of the properties held by any person to whom this Act applies, either by himself or through any other person on his behalf, his known sources, of income, earnings or assets, and any other information or material available to it as

a result of action taken under section 18 or otherwise, the competent authority has reason to believe (the reasons for such belief to be recorded in writing) that all or any of such properties are illegally acquired properties, it may serve a notice upon such person (hereinafter referred to as the person affected) calling upon him within such time as may be specified in the notice, which shall not be ordinarily less than thirty days, to indicate the sources of his income, earnings or assets, out of which or by means of which he has acquired such property, the evidence on which he relies and other relevant information and particulars, and to show cause why all or any of such properties, as the case may be, should not be declared to be illegally acquired properties and forfeited to the Central Government under this Act.

(2) Where a notice under sub-section (1) to any person specifies any property as being held on behalf of such person by any other person, a copy of the notice shall also be served upon such other person.

7. Forfeiture of property in certain cases:

(1) The competent authority may, after considering the explanation, if any, to the show-cause notice issued under section6, and the materials available before it and after giving to the person affected (and in a case where the person affected holds any property specified in the notice through any other person, to such other person also) a reasonable opportunity of being heard, by order, record a finding whether all or any of the properties in question are illegally acquired properties.

(2) Where the competent authority is satisfied that some of the properties referred to in the show-cause notice are illegally acquired properties but is not able to identify specifically such properties, then, it shall be lawful for the competent authority to specify the properties which, to the best of its judgment, are illegally acquired properties and record a finding accordingly under sub-section (1).

(3) Where the competent authority records a finding under this section to the effect that any property is illegally acquired property, it shall declare that such property shall, subject to the provisions of this Act, stand forfeited to the central Government free from all encumbrances.

(4) Where any shares in a company stand forfeited to the

Central Government under this Act, then, the company shall, notwithstanding any thing contained in the Companies Act, 1956 (1 of 1956), or the articles of association of the company, forthwith register the Central Government as the transferee of such shares.

8. Burden of proof: In any proceedings under this Act, the burden of proving that any property specified in the notice served under section 6 in not illegally acquired property shall be on the person affected.

9. Fine in lieu of forfeiture:

(1) Where the competent authority makes declaration that any property stands forfeited to the Central Government under section 7 and it is a case where the source of only a part, being less than one-half, of the income, earnings or assets with which such property was acquired has not been proved to the satisfaction of the competent authority, it shall make an order giving an option to the person affected to pay, in lieu of forfeiture, a fine equal to one and one-fifth times the value of such part.

Explanation: For the purposes of this sub-section, the value of any part of income, earnings or assets, with which any property has been acquired, shall be,-

(a) in the case of any part of income of earnings, the amount of such part of income of earnings;

(b) in the case of any part of assets, the proportionate part of the full value of the consideration for the acquisition of such assets.

(2) Before making an order imposing a fine under sub-section (1), the person affected shall be given a reasonable opportunity of being head.

(3) Where the person affected pays the fine due under sub-section (1), within such time as may allowed in that behalf, the competent authority may, by order, revoke the declaration of forfeiture under section 7 and thereupon such property shall stand released.

10. Procedure in relation to certain trust properties: In the case of any person referred to in clause (vi) of Explanation 3 to sub-section (2) of section 2, if the competent authority, on the basis of the information and materials available to it, has reason to believe (the reasons for such belief to be recorded in writing) that

any property held in trusts in illegally acquired property, it may serve a notice upon the author of the trust or, as the case may be, the contributor of the assets out of or by means of which such property was acquired by the trust and the trustees, calling upon them within such time as may be specified in the notice which shall not ordinarily be less than thirty days, to explain the source of the money or other assets out of or by means of which such property was acquired or, as the case may be, the source of the money or other assets which were contributed to the trust for acquiring such property and thereupon such notice shall be deemed to be a notice served under section 6 and all other provisions of this Act shall apply accordingly.

Explanation: For the purposes of this section "illegally acquired property", in relation to any property held in trust, includes-

(i) any property which if it had continued to be held by the author of the trust of the contributor of such property to the trust would have been illegally acquired property in relation to such author or contributor;

(ii) any property acquired by the trust out of any contributions made by any person which would have been illegally acquired property in relation to such person had such person acquired such property out of such contributions.

11. Certain transfers to be null and void: Where after the issue of a notice under section 6 or under section 10, any property referred to in the said notice is transferred by any mode whatsoever such transfer shall, for the purposes of the proceedings under this Act, be ignored and if such property is subsequently forfeited to the Central Government under section 7, then, the transfer of such property shall be deemed to be null and void.

12. Constitution of Appellate Tribunal:

(1) The Central Government may, be notification in the Official Gazette, constitute an Appellate Tribunal to be called the Appellate Tribunal for Forfeited Property consisting of a Chairman and such number of other members (being officers of the Central Government not below the rank of a Joint secretary to the Government) as the Central Government thinks fit, to be appointed by that Government for hearing appeals against the orders made under section 7, sub-section (1) of section 9 or section 10.

(2) The Chairman of the Appellate Tribunal shall be a person

who is or has been or is qualified to be a judge of the Supreme Court or of a High Court.

(3) The terms and conditions of service of the Chairman and other members shall be such as may be prescribed.

(4) Any person aggrieved by an order of the competent authority made under section 7, sub-section (1) of section 9 or section 10, may, within forty-five days from the date on which the order is served on him, prefer an appeal to the Appellate Tribunal. Provided that the Appellate Tribunal may entertain any appeal after the said period of forty-five days, but not after sixty days, from the date aforesaid if it is satisfied that the appellant was prevented by sufficient cause from filling the appeal in time.

(5) On receipt of an appeal under sub-section (4), the Appellate Tribunal may, after giving an opportunity to the appellant to be heard, if he so desires, and after making such further enquiry as it deems fit, confirm, modify or set aside the order appealed against.

(6) The powers and functions of the Appellate tribunal may be exercised and discharged by Benches consisting of three members and constituted by the Chairman of the Appellate Tribunal.

(6A) Notwithstanding anything contained in sub-section (6), where the Chairman considers it necessary so to do for the expeditious disposal of appeals under this section, he may constitute a Bench of two members and a Bench so constituted may exercise and discharge the powers and functions of the Appellate Tribunal: Provided that if the members of a Bench so constituted differ on any point or points, they shall state the point or points on which they differ and refer the same to a third members (to be specified by the chairman) for hearing on such point or points and such point or points shall be decided according to the opinion of that member.

(7) The Appellate Tribunal may regulate its own procedure.

(8) On application to the Appellate Tribunal and on payment of the prescribed fee, the Tribunal may allow a party to any appeal or any person authorised in this behalf by such party to inspect at any time during office hours, any relevant records and registers of the Tribunal and obtain a certified copy of any part thereof.

13. Notice or order not to be invalid for error in description:

No notice issued or served, no declaration made, and no order passed, under this Act shall be deemed to be invalid by reason of any error in the description of the property or person mentioned therein if such property or person is identifiable from the description so mentioned.

14. Bar of jurisdiction: No order passed or declaration made under this Act shall be appealable except as provided therein and no civil court shall have jurisdiction in respect of any matter which the Appellate Tribunal or any competent authority is empowered by or under the Act to determine, and no injunction shall be granted by any Court or other authority in respect of any action taken or to be taken in pursuance of any power conferred by or under this Act.

15. Competent authority and Appellate Tribunal to have powers of civil court: The competent authority and the Appellate tribunal shall have all the powers of a civil court while trying a suit under the Code of Civil Procedure, 1908 (5 of 1908), in respect of the following maters, namely:

(a) Summoning and enforcing the attendance of any person and examining him on oath;

(b) Requiring the discovery and production of documents;

(c) Receiving evidence on affidavits;

(d) Requisitioning any public record or copy thereof from any court or office;

(e) Issuing commissions for examination of witnesses or documents;

(f) Any other matter which may be prescribed.

16. Information to competent authority:

(1) Notwithstanding anything contained in any other law, the competent authority shall have power to require any officer or authority of the central Government or a State Government of a local authority to furnish information in relation to such persons, points or matters as in the opinion of the competent authority will be useful for, or relevant to, the purposes of this Act.

(2) Any officer of the Income-tax Department, the Customs Department or the Central Excise Department or any officer of Enforcement appointed under the Foreign Exchange Regulation Act, 1973 (46 of 1973), may furnish suo motu any information

available with him to the competent authority if in the opinion of the officer such information will be useful to the competent authority for the purposes of this Act.

17. Certain officers to assist competent authority and Appellate Tribunal: For the purposes of any proceedings under this Act, the following officers are hereby empowered and required to assist the competent authority and the Appellate Tribunal, namely:-

(a) officers of the Customs Department;

(b) officers of the Central Excise Department;

(c) officers of the Income-tax Department;

(d) officers of Enforcement appointed under the Foreign Exchange Regulation Act, 1973 (46 of 1973);

(e) officers of Police;

(f) such other officers of the Central of State Government as are specified by the Central Government in this behalf by notification in the Official Gazette.

18. Power of competent authority to require certain officers to exercise certain powers:

(1) For the purposes of any proceedings under this Act or the initiation of any such proceedings, the competent authority shall have power to cause to be conducted any inquiry, investigation or survey in respect of any person, place, property, assets, documents, books of account or any other relevant matters.

(2) For the purposes referred to in sub-section (1), the competent authority may, having regard to the nature of the inquiry, investigation or survey, require an officer of the Income-tax Department to conduct or cause to be conducted such inquiry, investigation or survey.

(3) Any officer of the Income-tax Department who is conducting or is causing to be conducted any inquiry, investigation or survey required to be conducted under sub-section (2), may, for the purpose of such inquiry, investigation or survey, exercise any power (including the power to authorise the exercise of any power) which may be exercised by him for any purpose under the Income-tax Act, 1961 (43 of 1961), and the provisions of the said Act shall, so far as may be, apply accordingly.

19. Power to take possession:

(1) Where any property has been declared to be forfeited to the Central Government under this Act, or where the person affected has failed to pay the fine due under sub-section (1) of section 9 within the time allowed therefore under sub-section (3) of the section, the competent authority may order the person affected as well as any other person who may be in possession of the property to surrender or deliver possession thereof to the competent authority or to any person duly authorised by it in this behalf within thirty days of the service of the order.

(2) If any person refuses or fails to comply with an order made under sub-section (1), the competent authority may take possession of the property and may for that purpose use such force as may be necessary.

(3) Notwithstanding anything contained in sub-section (2), the competent authority may, for the purpose of taking possession of any property referred to in sub-section (1), requisition the service of any police officer to assist the competent authority and it shall be the duty of such officer to comply with such requisition.

20. Rectification of mistakes: With a view to rectifying any mistakes apparent from the record, the competent authority or the Appellate Tribunal, as the case may be, may amend any order made by it within a period of one year from the date of the order: Provided that if any such amendment is likely to affect any person prejudicially, it shall not be made without giving to such person a reasonable opportunity of being heard.

21. Findings under other laws not conclusive for proceedings under this Act: No finding of any officer of authority under any other law shall be conclusive for the purposes of any proceedings under this act.

22. Service of notices and orders: Any notice or order issued or make under this Act shall be served-

(a) by tendering the notice or order or sending it by registered post to the person for whom it is intended or to his agent;

(b) if the notice or order cannot be served in the manner provided in clause (a), by affixing it on a conspicuous place in the property in relation to which the notice or order is issued or made, or on some conspicuous part of the premises in which the person for whom it is intended is known to have last resided or carried on business or personally worked for gain.

23. Protection of action taken in good faith: No suit, prosecution or other proceeding shall lie against the Central Government or any Officer of the Central or State Government for any thing which is done, or intended to be done, in good faith, in pursuance of this Act or the rules made thereunder.

24. Act to have overriding effect: The provisions of this Act shall have effect notwithstanding any thing inconsistent therewith contained in any other law for the time being in force.

25. Provisions of the Act not to apply to certain properties help in trust: Nothing contained in this Act shall apply in relation to any property held by a trust or an institution created or established wholly for public, religious or charitable purposes if

(i) such property has been so held by such trust or institution from a date prior to the commencement of this Act.

(ii) Such property is wholly traceable to any property held by such trust or institution prior to the commencement of this Act.

26. Power to make rules:

(1) The Central Government may, by notification in the Official Gazette, make rules to carry out the provisions of this Act.

(2) In particular and without prejudice to the generality of the foregoing power, such rules may provide for all or any of the following matters, namely;-

(a) the terms and conditions of service of the chairman and other members of the Appellate Tribunal under sub-section (3) of section 12;

(aa) the fees which shall be paid for the inspection of the records and registers of the Appellate Tribunal or for obtaining a certified copy of any part thereof under sub-section (8) of section 12;

(b) the powers of a civil court that may be exercised by the competent authority and the Appellate Tribunal under clause (f) of section 15;

(c) any other matter which has to be, or may be, prescribed.

(3) Every rule made under this Act shall be laid, as soon as may be after it is made, before each House of parliament, while it is in session or the successive sessions, and if, before the expiry of the session immediately.

THE FOREIGN TRADE (DEVELOPMENT AND REGULATION) ACT, 1992

An Act to provide for the development and regulation of foreign trade by facilitating imports into, and augmenting exports from India and for matters connected therewith or incidental thereto.

Be it enacted by Parliament in the Forty-third Year of the Republic of India as follows:-

Chapter I: Preliminary

1. Short title and commencement:

(1) This Act may be called The Foreign Trade (Development and Regulation) Act, 1992.

(2) Sections 11 to 14 shall come into force at once and the remaining provisions of this Act shall be deemed to have come into force on the 19th day of June, 1992.

2. Definitions: In this Act, unless the context otherwise requires:

(a) "Adjudicating Authority" means the authority specified in, or under, section 13;

(b) "Appellate Authority" means the authority specified in, or under, sub-section (1) of section 15.

(c) "Conveyance" means any vehicle, vessel, aircraft or any other means of transport including any animal;

(d) "Director General" means the Director General of Foreign Trade appointed under section 6;

(e) "import" and "export" means respectively bringing into, or taking out of, India any goods by land, sea or air;

(f) "Importer-Exporter Code Number" means the Code Number granted under section 7

(g) "Licence" means a licence to import or export and includes a customs clearance permit and any other permission issued or granted under this Act;

(h) "Order" means any order made by the Central Government under section 3; and

(i) "Prescribed" means prescribed by rules made under this Act.

Chapter II: Power of Central Government to make Orders and Announce Export and Import Policy

3. Powers to make provisions relating to imports and exports:

(1) The Central Government may by Order published in the Official Gazette, make provision for the development and regulation of foreign trade by facilitating imports and increasing exports.

(2) The Central Government may also, by Order published in the Official Gazette, make provision for prohibiting, restricting or otherwise regulating, in all cases or in specified classes of cases and subject to such exceptions, if any, as may be made by or under the Order the import or export of goods.

(3) All goods to which any Order under sub-section (2) applies shall be deemed to be goods the import or export of which has been prohibited under section 11 of the Customs Act, 1962 (52 of 1962) and all the provisions of that Act shall have effect accordingly.

4. Continuance of existing Orders: All Orders made under the Imports and Exports (Control) Act, 1947 (18 of 1947), and in force immediately before the commencement of this Act shall, so far as they are not inconsistent with the provisions of this Act, continue to be in force and shall be deemed to have been made under this Act.

5. Export and Import Policy: The Central Government may, from time to time, formulate and announce by notification in the Official Gazette, the Export and Import Policy and may also, in like manner, amend that policy.

6. Appointment of Director General and his functions:

(1) The Central Government may appoint any person to be the Director General of Foreign Trade for the purposes of this Act.

(2) The Director General shall advise the Central Government in the formulation of the Export and Import Policy and shall be responsible for carrying out that policy.

(3) The Central Government may, by Order published in the Official Gazette direct that any power exercisable by it under this Act (other than the powers under sections 3, 5, 15, 16 and 19) may also be exercised, in such cases and subject to such conditions, by the Director General or such other officer subordinate to the Director General, as may be specified in the Order.

Chapter III: Importer-Exporter Code Number and Licence

7. Importer-Exporter Code Number: No person shall make any import or export except under an Importer-Exporter Code Number granted by the Director General or the officer authorised by the Director General in this behalf, in accordance with the procedure specified in this behalf by the Director General.

8. Suspension and Cancellation of Importer-Exporter Code Number :

(1) Where:

(a) any person has contravened any law relating to Central Excise or Customs or Foreign Exchange or has committed any other economic offence under any other law for the time being in force as may be specified by the Central Government by notification in the Official Gazette, or

(b) the Director General has reason to believe that any person has made an export or import in a manner gravely prejudicial to the trade relations of India with any foreign country or to the interests of other persons engaged in imports or exports or has brought disrepute to the credit or the goods of the country. The Director General may call for the record or any other information from that person and may, after giving to that person a notice in writing informing him of the grounds on which it is proposed to suspend or cancel the Importer-Exporter Code Number and giving him a reasonable opportunity of making a representation in writing within such reasonable time as may be specified in the notice and, if that person so desires, of being heard, suspend for a period, as may be specified in the order, or cancel the Importer-Exporter Code Number granted to that person.

(2) Where any Importer-Exporter Code Number granted to a person has been suspended or cancelled under sub-section (1), that person shall not be entitled to import or export any goods except under a special licence granted, in such manner and subject to such conditions as may be prescribed, by the Director General to that person.

9. Issue ,suspension and cancellation of Licence :

(1) The Central Government may levy fees, subject to such exceptions, in respect of such person or class of persons making an application for a licence or in respect of any licence granted or renewed in such manner as may be prescribed.

(2) The Director General or an officer authorised by him may, on an application and after making such inquiry as he may think fit, grant or renew or refuse to grant or renew a licence to import or export such class or classes of goods as may be prescribed, after recording in writing his reasons for such refusal.

(3) A licence granted or renewed under this section shall-

(a) be in such form as may be prescribed;

(b) be valid for such period as may be specified therein; and

(c) be subject to such terms, conditions and restrictions as may be prescribed or as specified in the licence with reference to the terms, conditions and restrictions so prescribed.

(4) The Director General or the officer authorised under sub-section (2) may, subject to such conditions as may be prescribed, for good and sufficient reasons, to be recorded in writing suspend or cancel any licence granted under this Act:

Provided that no such suspension or cancellation shall be made except after giving the holder of the licence a reasonable opportunity of being heard.

(5) An appeal against an order refusing to grant, or renew or suspending or cancelling, a licence shall lie in like manner as an appeal against an order would lie under section 15.

Chapter IV: Search, Seizure, Penalty and Confiscation

10. Power relating to search and seizure:

(1) The Central Government may, by notification in the Official Gazette, authorise any person for the purposes of exercising such powers with respect to entering such premises and searching, inspecting and seizing of such goods, documents, things and conveyances, subject to such requirements and conditions, as may be prescribed.

(2) The provisions of the Code of Criminal Procedure, 1973(2 of 1974), relating to searches and seizures shall, so far as may be, apply to every search and seizure made under this section.

11. Contravention of provisions of this Act, Rules, Orders and Export and Import Policy:

(1) No export or import shall be made by any person except in accordance with the provisions of this Act, the rules and orders

made thereunder and the Export and Import Policy for the time being in force.

(2) Where any person makes or abets or attempts to make any export or import in contravention of any provision of this Act or any rules or orders made thereunder or the Export and Import Policy, he shall be liable to a penalty not exceeding one thousand rupees ~~or five times the~~ value of the goods in respect of which any contravention is made or attempted to be made, ~~whichever~~ is more.

(3) Where any person, on a notice to him by the Adjudicating Authority, admits any contravention, the Adjudicating Authority may, in such class or classes of cases and in such manner as may be prescribed, determine, by way of settlement, an amount to be paid by that person.

(4) A penalty imposed under this Act may, if it is not paid, be recovered as an arrear of land revenue and the Importer-Exporter Code Number of the person concerned, may, on failure to pay the penalty by him, be suspended by the Adjudicating Authority till the penalty is paid.

(5) Where any contravention of an provision of this Act or any rules or orders made thereunder or the Export and Import Policy has been, is being, or is attempted to be made, the goods together with any package, covering or receptacle and any conveyances shall, subject to such requirements and conditions as may be prescribed, be liable to confiscation by the Adjudicating Authority.

(6) The goods or the conveyance confiscated under sub-section (5) may be released by the Adjudicating Authority, in such manner and subject to such conditions as may be prescribed, on payment by the person concerned of the redemption charges equivalent to the market value of the goods or conveyance, as the case may be.

12. Penalty or confiscation not to interfere with other punishments :No penalty imposed or confiscation made under this Act shall prevent the imposition of any other punishment to which the person affected thereby is liable under any other law for the time being in force.

13. Adjudicating Authority

Any penalty may be imposed or any confiscation may be adjudged under this Act by the Director General or, subject such limits as may be specified, by such other officer as the Central Government may, by notification in the Official Gazette, authorise in this behalf.

14. Giving of opportunity to the owner of the goods, etc:

No order imposing a penalty or of adjudication or of confiscation shall be made unless the owner of the goods or conveyance or other person concerned, has been given a notice in writing:-

(a) informing him of the grounds on which it is proposed to impose a penalty or to confiscate such goods or conveyance; and

(b) to make a representation in writing within such reasonable time as may be specified in the notice against the imposition of penalty or confiscation mentioned therein, and if he so desires, of being heard in the matter.

Chapter V: Appeal and Revision

15. Appeal:

(1) Any person aggrieved by any decision or order made by the Adjudicating Authority under this Act may prefer an appeal:-

(a) where the decision or order has been made by the Director General, to the Central Government,

(b) where the decision or order has been made by an officer subordinate to the Director General, or the Director General or to any officer superior to the Adjudicating Authority authorised by the Director General to hear the appeal, within a period of forty-five days from the date on which the decision or order is served on such person: Provided that the Appellate Authority may, if it is satisfied that the appellant was prevented by sufficient cause from preferring the appeal within the aforesaid period, allow such appeal to be preferred within a further period of thirty days; Provided further that in the case of an appeal against a decision or order imposing a penalty or redemption charges, no such appeal shall be entertained unless the amount of the penalty or redemption charges has been deposited by the appellant; Provided also that, where the Appellate Authority is of opinion that the deposit to be made will cause undue hardship to the appellant, it may, at its discretion, dispense with such deposit either unconditionally or subject to such conditions as it may impose.

(2) The Appellate Authority may, after giving to the appellant a reasonable opportunity of being heard, if he so desires, and after making such further inquiries, if any, as it may consider necessary, make such orders as it thinks fit, confirming, modifying or reversing the decision or order appealed against, or may send back the case with such directions as it may think fit, for a fresh adjudication or decision, as the case may be, after taking additional evidence, if necessary: Provided that an order enhancing or imposing a penalty or redemption charges or confiscating goods of a greater value shall not be made under this section unless the appellant has been given an opportunity of making a representation, and if he so desires, of being heard in his defence.

(3) The order made in appeal by the Appellate Authority shall be final.

16. Revision: The Central Government, in the case of any decision or order, not being a decision or order made in an appeal, made by the Director General, or the Director General in the case of any decision or order made by any officer subordinate to him, may on its or his own motion or otherwise, call for and examine the records of any proceeding in which a decision or an order imposing a penalty or redemption charges or adjudicating confiscation has been made and against which no appeal has been preferred, for the purposeof satisfying itself or himself, as the case may be, as to the correctness, legality or propriety of such decision or order and make such orders thereon as may be deemed fit Provided that no decision or order shall be varied under this section so as to prejudicially affect any person unless such person-

(a) has, within a period of two years from the date of such decision or order, received a notice to show cause why such decision or order shall not be varied, and

(b) has been given a reasonable opportunity of making representation and, if he so desires, of being heard in his defence.

17. Powers of Adjudicating and other Authorities :

(1) Every authority making any adjudication or hearing any appeal or exercising any powers of revision under this Act shall have all the powers of a civil court under the Code of Civil Procedure, 1908,(V of 1908), while trying a suit, in respect of the following matters, namely:-

(a) summoning and enforcing the attendance of witnesses;

(b) requiring the discovery and production of any document;

(c) requisitioning any public record or copy thereof from any court or office.

(d) receiving evidence on affidavits; and

(e) issuing commissions for the examination of witnesses or documents.

(2) Every authority making any adjudication or hearing any appeal or exercising any powers of revision under this Act shall be deemed to be a civil court for the purposes of sections 345 and 346 of the Code of Criminal Procedure, 1973 (2 0f 1974),

(3) Every authority making any adjudication or hearing any appeal or exercising any powers of revision under this Act, shall have the power to make such orders of an interim nature as it may think fit and may also, for sufficient cause, order the stay of operation of any decision or order.

(4) Clerical or arithmetical mistakes in any decision or order or errors arising therein from any accidental slip or omission may at any time be corrected by the authority by which the decision or order was made, either on its own motion or on the application of any of the parties: Provided that where any correction proposed to be made under this sub-section will have the effect of prejudicially affecting any person, no such correction shall be made except after giving to that person a reasonable opportunity of making a representation in the matter and no such correction shall be made after the expiry of two years from the date on which such decision or order was made.

Chapter VI: Miscellaneous

18. Protection of action taken in good faith: No order made or deemed to have been made under this Act shall be called in question in any court, and no Suit, prosecution or other legal proceeding shall lie against any person for anything in good faith done or intended to be done under this Act or any order made or deemed to have been made thereunder

19. Power to make rules:

(1) The Central Government may, by notification in the Official Gazette, make rules for carrying out the provisions of this Act.

(2) In particular, and without prejudice to the generality of the foregoing power, such rules may provide for all or any of the following matters, namely:-

(a) the manner in which and the conditions subject to which a special licence may be issued under sub-section (2) of section 8.

(b) the exceptions subject to which and the person or class of persons in respect of whom fees may be levied and the manner in which a licence may be granted or renewed under sub-section (1) of section 9.

(c) the class or classes of goods for which a licence may be granted under sub-section (2) of section 9.

(d) the form in which and the terms, conditions and restrictions subject to which licence may be granted under sub-section (3) of section 9.

(e) the conditions subject to which a licence may be suspended or cancelled under sub-section (4) of section 9.

(f) the premises, goods, documents, things and conveyances in respect of which and the requirements and conditions subject to which power of entry, search, inspection and seizure may be exercised under sub-section (1) of section 10.

(g) the class or classes of cases for which and the manner in which an amount, by way of settlement, may be determined under sub-section (3) of section 11.

(h) the requirements and conditions subject to which goods and conveyances shall be liable to confiscation under sub-section (5) of section 11.

(i) the manner in which and the conditions subject to which goods and conveyances may be released on payment of redemption charges under sub-section (6) of section 11; and

(j) any other matter which is to be, or may be, prescribed, or in respect of which provision is to be, or may be, made by rules.

(3) Every rule and every Order made by the Central Government under this Act shall be laid, as soon as may be after it is made, before each House of Parliament, while it is in session, for a total period of thirty days which may be comprised in one session or in two or more successive sessions, and if, before the expiry of the session immediately following the session or the

successive sessions aforesaid, both Houses agree in making any modification in the rule or the Order or both Houses agree that the rule or the Order should not be made, the rule or the Order as the case may be, shall thereafter have effect only in such modified form or be of no effect, as the case may be; so, however, that any such modification or annulment shall be without prejudice to the validity of anything previously done under that rule or the Order.

20. Repeal and savings:

(1) The Imports and Exports (Control) Act, 1947 (18 of 1947) and the Foreign Trade (Development and Regulation) Ordinance 1992 are hereby repealed.

(2) The repeal of the Imports and Exports (Control) Act, 1947 shall, however, not affect, -

(a) the previous operation of the Act so repealed or anything duly done or suffered thereunder; or

(b) any right, privilege, obligation or liability acquired, accrued or incurred under the Act so repealed; or

(c) any penalty, confiscation or punishment incurred in respect of any contravention under the Act so repealed; or

(d) any proceeding or remedy in respect of any such right, privilege, obligation, liability, penalty, confiscation or punishment as aforesaid,

And any such proceeding or remedy may be instituted, continued or enforced, and any such penalty, confiscation or punishment may be imposed or made as if that Act had not been repealed.

(3) Notwithstanding the repeal of the Foreign Trade (Development and Regulation) Ordinance, 1992 (11 of 1992) anything done or any action taken under the said Ordinance shall be deemed to have been done or taken under the corresponding provisions of this Act.

THE FOREIGN TRADE (DEVELOPMENT AND REGULATION) ACT, 1992

An Act to provide for the development and regulation of foreign trade by facilitating imports into, and augmenting exports from India and for matters connected therewith or incidental thereto.

Be it enacted by Parliament in the Forty-third Year of the Republic of India as follows:-

Chapter I: Preliminary

1. Short title and commencement:

(1) This Act may be called The Foreign Trade (Development and Regulation) Act, 1992.

(2) Sections 11 to 14 shall come into force at once and the remaining provisions of this Act shall be deemed to have come into force on the 19th day of June, 1992.

2. Definitions: In this Act, unless the context otherwise requires:

(a) "Adjudicating Authority" means the authority specified in, or under, section 13;

(b) "Appellate Authority" means the authority specified in, or under, sub-section (1) of section 15.

(c) "Conveyance" means any vehicle, vessel, aircraft or any other means of transport including any animal;

(d) "Director General" means the Director General of Foreign Trade appointed under section 6;

(e) "import" and "export" means respectively bringing into, or taking out of, India any goods by land, sea or air;

(f) "Importer-Exporter Code Number" means the Code Number granted under section 7

(g) "Licence" means a licence to import or export and includes a customs clearance permit and any other permission issued or granted under this Act;

(h) "Order" means any order made by the Central Government under section 3; and

(i) "Prescribed" means prescribed by rules made under this Act.

Chapter II: Power of Central Government to make Orders and Announce Export and Import Policy

3. Powers to make provisions relating to imports and exports:

(1) The Central Government may by Order published in the Official Gazette, make provision for the development and regulation of foreign trade by facilitating imports and increasing exports.

(2) The Central Government may also, by Order published in the Official Gazette, make provision for prohibiting, restricting or otherwise regulating, in all cases or in specified classes of cases and subject to such exceptions, if any, as may be made by or under the Order the import or export of goods.

(3) All goods to which any Order under sub-section (2) applies shall be deemed to be goods the import or export of which has been prohibited under section 11 of the Customs Act, 1962 (52 of 1962) and all the provisions of that Act shall have effect accordingly.

4. Continuance of existing Orders: All Orders made under the Imports and Exports (Control) Act, 1947 (18 of 1947), and in force immediately before the commencement of this Act shall, so far as they are not inconsistent with the provisions of this Act, continue to be in force and shall be deemed to have been made under this Act.

5. Export and Import Policy: The Central Government may, from time to time, formulate and announce by notification in the Official Gazette, the Export and Import Policy and may also, in like manner, amend that policy.

6. Appointment of Director General and his functions:

(1) The Central Government may appoint any person to be the Director General of Foreign Trade for the purposes of this Act.

(2) The Director General shall advise the Central Government in the formulation of the Export and Import Policy and shall be responsible for carrying out that policy.

(3) The Central Government may, by Order published in the Official Gazette direct that any power exercisable by it under this Act (other than the powers under sections 3, 5, 15, 16 and 19) may also be exercised, in such cases and subject to such conditions, by the Director General or such other officer subordinate to the Director General, as may be specified in the Order.

Chapter III: Importer-Exporter Code Number and Licence

7. Importer-Exporter Code Number: No person shall make any import or export except under an Importer-Exporter Code Number granted by the Director General or the officer authorised by the Director General in this behalf, in accordance with the procedure specified in this behalf by the Director General.

8. Suspension and Cancellation of Importer-Exporter Code Number :

(1) Where:

(a) any person has contravened any law relating to Central Excise or Customs or Foreign Exchange or has committed any other economic offence under any other law for the time being in force as may be specified by the Central Government by notification in the Official Gazette, or

(b) the Director General has reason to believe that any person has made an export or import in a manner gravely prejudicial to the trade relations of India with any foreign country or to the interests of other persons engaged in imports or exports or has brought disrepute to the credit or the goods of the country. The Director General may call for the record or any other information from that person and may, after giving to that person a notice in writing informing him of the grounds on which it is proposed to suspend or cancel the Importer-Exporter Code Number and giving him a reasonable opportunity of making a representation in writing within such reasonable time as may be specified in the notice and, if that person so desires, of being heard, suspend for a period, as may be specified in the order, or cancel the Importer-Exporter Code Number granted to that person.

(2) Where any Importer-Exporter Code Number granted to a person has been suspended or cancelled under sub-section (1), that person shall not be entitled to import or export any goods except under a special licence granted, in such manner and subject to such conditions as may be prescribed, by the Director General to that person.

9. Issue, suspension and cancellation of Licence :

(1) The Central Government may levy fees, subject to such exceptions, in respect of such person or class of persons making an application for a licence or in respect of any licence granted or renewed in such manner as may be prescribed.

(2) The Director General or an officer authorised by him may, on an application and after making such inquiry as he may think fit, grant or renew or refuse to grant or renew a licence to import or export such class or classes of goods as may be prescribed, after recording in writing his reasons for such refusal.

(3) A licence granted or renewed under this section shall-

(a) be in such form as may be prescribed;

(b) be valid for such period as may be specified therein; and

(c) be subject to such terms, conditions and restrictions as may be prescribed or as specified in the licence with reference to the terms, conditions and restrictions so prescribed.

(4) The Director General or the officer authorised under sub-section (2) may, subject to such conditions as may be prescribed, for good and sufficient reasons, to be recorded in writing suspend or cancel any licence granted under this Act: Provided that no such suspension or cancellation shall be made except after giving the holder of the licence a reasonable opportunity of being heard.

(5) An appeal against an order refusing to grant, or renew or suspending or cancelling, a licence shall lie in like manner as an appeal against an order would lie under section 15.

Chapter IV: Search, Seizure, Penalty and Confiscation

10. Power relating to search and seizure:

(1) The Central Government may, by notification in the Official Gazette, authorise any person for the purposes of exercising such powers with respect to entering such premises and searching, inspecting and seizing of such goods, documents, things and conveyances, subject to such requirements and conditions, as may be prescribed.

(2) The provisions of the Code of Criminal Procedure, 1973(2 of 1974), relating to searches and seizures shall, so far as may be, apply to every search and seizure made under this section.

11. Contravention of provisions of this Act, Rules, Orders and Export and Import Policy:

(1) No export or import shall be made by any person except in accordance with the provisions of this Act, the rules and orders made thereunder and the Export and Import Policy for the time being in force.

(2) Where any person makes or abets or attempts to make any export or import in contravention of any provision of this Act or any rules or orders made thereunder or the Export and Import Policy, he shall be liable to a penalty not exceeding one thousand rupees or five times the value of the goods in respect of which

any contravention is made or attempted to be made, whichever is more.

(3) Where any person, on a notice to him by the Adjudicating Authority, admits any contravention, the Adjudicating Authority may, in such class or classes of cases and in such manner as may be prescribed, determine, by way of settlement, an amount to be paid by that person.

(4) A penalty imposed under this Act may, if it is not paid, be recovered as an arrear of land revenue and the Importer-Exporter Code Number of the person concerned, may, on failure to pay the penalty by him, be suspended by the Adjudicating Authority till the penalty is paid.

(5) Where any contravention of an provision of this Act or any rules or orders made thereunder or the Export and Import Policy has been, is being, or is attempted to be made, the goods together with any package, covering or receptacle and any conveyances shall, subject to such requirements and conditions as may be prescribed, be liable to confiscation by the Adjudicating Authority.

(6) The goods or the conveyance confiscated under sub-section (5) may be released by the Adjudicating Authority, in such manner and subject to such conditions as may be prescribed, on payment by the person concerned of the redemption charges equivalent to the market value of the goods or conveyance, as the case may be.

12. Penalty or confiscation not to interfere with other punishments: No penalty imposed or confiscation made under this Act shall prevent the imposition of any other punishment to which the person affected thereby is liable under any other law for the time being in force.

13. Adjudicating Authority Any penalty may be imposed or any confiscation may be adjudged under this Act by the Director General or, subject such limits as may be specified, by such other officer as the Central Government may, by notification in the Official Gazette, authorise in this behalf.

14. Giving of opportunity to the owner of the goods, etc: No order imposing a penalty or of adjudication or of confiscation shall be made unless the owner of the goods or conveyance or other person concerned, has been given a notice in writing:-

(a) informing him of the grounds on which it is proposed to impose a penalty or to confiscate such goods or conveyance; and

(b) to make a representation in writing within such reasonable time as may be specified in the notice against the imposition of penalty or confiscation mentioned therein, and if he so desires, of being heard in the matter.

Chapter V: Appeal and Revision

15. Appeal:

(1) Any person aggrieved by any decision or order made by the Adjudicating Authority under this Act may prefer an appeal:-

(a) where the decision or order has been made by the Director General, to the Central Government,

(b) where the decision or order has been made by an officer subordinate to the Director General, or the Director General or to any officer superior to the Adjudicating Authority authorised by the Director General to hear the appeal, within a period of forty-five days from the date on which the decision or order is served on such person: Provided that the Appellate Authority may, if it is satisfied that the appellant was prevented by sufficient cause from preferring the appeal within the aforesaid period, allow such appeal to be preferred within a further period of thirty days; Provided further that in the case of an appeal against a decision or order imposing a penalty or redemption charges, no such appeal shall be entertained unless the amount of the penalty or redemption charges has been deposited by the appellant; Provided also that, where the Appellate Authority is of opinion that the deposit to be made will cause undue hardship to the appellant, it may, at its discretion, dispense with such deposit either unconditionally or subject to such conditions as it may impose.

(2) The Appellate Authority may, after giving to the appellant a reasonable opportunity of being heard, if he so desires, and after making such further inquiries, if any, as it may consider necessary, make such orders as it thinks fit, confirming, modifying or reversing the decision or order appealed against, or may send back the case with such directions as it may think fit, for a fresh adjudication or decision, as the case may be, after taking additional evidence, if necessary: Provided that an order enhancing or imposing a penalty or redemption charges or confiscating goods of a greater value shall not be made under this section unless the appellant has been given an opportunity of making a representation, and if he so desires, of being heard in his defence.

(3) The order made in appeal by the Appellate Authority shall be final.

16. Revision: The Central Government, in the case of any decision or order, not being a decision or order made in an appeal, made by the Director General, or the Director General in the case of any decision or order made by any officer subordinate to him, may on its or his own motion or otherwise, call for and examine the records of any proceeding in which a decision or an order imposing a penalty or redemption charges or adjudicating confiscation has been made and against which no appeal has been preferred, for the purposeof satisfying itself or himself, as the case may be, as to the correctness, legality or propriety of such decision or order and make such orders thereon as may be deemed fit Provided that no decision or order shall be varied under this section so as to prejudicially affect any person unless such person-

(a) has, within a period of two years from the date of such decision or order, received a notice to show cause why such decision or order shall not be varied, and

(b) has been given a reasonable opportunity of making representation and, if he so desires, of being heard in his defence.

17. Powers of Adjudicating and other Authorities :

(1) Every authority making any adjudication or hearing any appeal or exercising any powers of revision under this Act shall have all the powers of a civil court under the Code of Civil Procedure, 1908,(V of 1908), while trying a suit, in respect of the following matters, namely:-

(a) summoning and enforcing the attendance of witnesses;

(b) requiring the discovery and production of any document;

(c) requisitioning any public record or copy thereof from any court or office.

(d) receiving evidence on affidavits; and

(e) issuing commissions for the examination of witnesses or documents.

(2) Every authority making any adjudication or hearing any appeal or exercising any powers of revision under this Act shall be deemed to be a civil court for the purposes of sections 345 and 346 of the Code of Criminal Procedure, 1973 (2 0f 1974),

(3) Every authority making any adjudication or hearing any

appeal or exercising any powers of revision under this Act, shall have the power to make such orders of an interim nature as it may think fit and may also, for sufficient cause, order the stay of operation of any decision or order.

(4) Clerical or arithmetical mistakes in any decision or order or errors arising therein from any accidental slip or omission may at any time be corrected by the authority by which the decision or order was made, either on its own motion or on the application of any of the parties:

Provided that where any correction proposed to be made under this sub-section will have the effect of prejudicially affecting any person, no such correction shall be made except after giving to that person a reasonable opportunity of making a representation in the matter and no such correction shall be made after the expiry of two years from the date on which such decision or order was made.

CHAPTER VI: MISCELLANEOUS

18. Protection of action taken in good faith: No order made or deemed to have been made under this Act shall be called in question in any court, and no Suit, prosecution or other legal proceeding shall lie against any person for anything in good faith done or intended to be done under this Act or any order made or deemed to have been made thereunder

19. Power to make rules:

(1) The Central Government may, by notification in the Official Gazette, make rules for carrying out the provisions of this Act.

(2) In particular, and without prejudice to the generality of the foregoing power, such rules may provide for all or any of the following matters, namely:-

(a) the manner in which and the conditions subject to which a special licence may be issued under sub-section (2) of section 8.

(b) the exceptions subject to which and the person or class of persons in respect of whom fees may be levied and the manner in which a licence may be granted or renewed under sub-section (1) of section 9.

(c) the class or classes of goods for which a licence may be granted under sub-section (2) of section 9.

(d) the form in which and the terms, conditions and restrictions subject to which licence may be granted under sub-section (3) of section 9.

(e) the conditions subject to which a licence may be suspended or cancelled under sub-section (4) of section 9.

(f) the premises, goods, documents, things and conveyances in respect of which and the requirements and conditions subject to which power of entry, search, inspection and seizure may be exercised under sub-section (1) of section 10.

(g) the class or classes of cases for which and the manner in which an amount, by way of settlement, may be determined under sub-section (3) of section 11.

(h) the requirements and conditions subject to which goods and conveyances shall be liable to confiscation under sub-section (5) of section 11.

(i) the manner in which and the conditions subject to which goods and conveyances may be released on payment of redemption charges under sub-section (6) of section 11; and

(j) any other matter which is to be, or may be, prescribed, or in respect of which provision is to be, or may be, made by rules.

(3) Every rule and every Order made by the Central Government under this Act shall be laid, as soon as may be after it is made, before each House of Parliament, while it is in session, for a total period of thirty days which may be comprised in one session or in two or more successive sessions, and if, before the expiry of the session immediately following the session or the successive sessions aforesaid, both Houses agree in making any modification in the rule or the Order or both Houses agree that the rule or the Order should not be made, the rule or the Order as the case may be, shall thereafter have effect only in such modified form or be of no effect, as the case may be; so, however, that any such modification or annulment shall be without prejudice to the validity of anything previously done under that rule or the Order.

20. Repeal and savings:

(1) The Imports and Exports (Control) Act, 1947 (18 of 1947) and the Foreign Trade (Development and Regulation) Ordinance 1992 are hereby repealed.

(2) The repeal of the Imports and Exports (Control) Act, 1947 shall, however, not affect, -

(a) the previous operation of the Act so repealed or anything duly done or suffered thereunder; or

(b) any right, privilege, obligation or liability acquired, accrued or incurred under the Act so repealed; or

(c) any penalty, confiscation or punishment incurred in respect of any contravention under the Act so repealed; or

(d) any proceeding or remedy in respect of any such right, privilege, obligation, liability, penalty, confiscation or punishment as aforesaid,

And any such proceeding or remedy may be instituted, continued or enforced, and any such penalty, confiscation or punishment may be imposed or made as if that Act had not been repealed.

(3) Notwithstanding the repeal of the Foreign Trade (Development and Regulation) Ordinance, 1992 (11 of 1992) anything done or any action taken under the said Ordinance shall be deemed to have been done or taken under the corresponding provisions of this Act.

3

Overview of Money Market Instruments

The term *money market* is used to include all short-term financial instruments which are based on an interest rate, whether the interest rate is actually paid (as in a cash deposit) or only implied in the way the instrument is priced and settled (as in an FRA). Longer-term instruments are covered by the term *capital market.*

The underlying instruments are essentially those used by one party (the borrower, seller or issuer) to borrow money and by the other party (the lender, buyer or investor) to lend money.

These instruments have different names in different markets – for example, each country's government issues something equivalent to a Treasury bill in its own market – but the characteristics are essentially the same as described here.

Each of the above instruments represents an obligation on the borrower to repay the amount borrowed at maturity, plus interest if appropriate. As well as these underlying borrowing instruments, there are other money market instruments which are linked to these, or at least to the same interest rate structure, but which are not direct obligations on the issuer in the same way:

The money market is linked to other markets though arbitrage mechanisms. Arbitrage occurs when it is possible to achieve the same result in terms of position and risk though two alternative mechanisms which have a slightly different price. The arbitrage involves achieving the result via the cheaper method and simultane-ously reversing the position via the more expensive method – thereby locking in a profit which is free from market risk (although still prob-ably subject to credit risk). For example, if I can buy one instrument cheaply and simultaneously sell at a higher price another instrument or combination of instruments which has identical characteristics, I am arbitraging. In a completely free market with no other price considerations involved, the supply and demand effect of arbitrage tends to drive the two prices together until the arbitrage opportunity ceases to exist.

For example, the money market is linked in this way to the forward foreign exchange market, through the ability to create synthetic deposits in one currency, by using foreign exchange deals combined with money market instruments. Similarly it is linked to the capital markets (long-term financial instruments) through the ability to create longer-term instruments from a series of short-term instru-ments (such as a 2-year interest rate swap from a series of 3-month FRAs).

The yield curve

If I wish to borrow money for 3 months, the interest rate is likely to be different – possibly higher and possibly lower – from what the rate would be if I wished instead to borrow for 6 months. The *yield curve* shows how interest rates vary with term to maturity. For example, a Reuters screen might show the following rates:

1 month : 9.5%

2 months: 9.7%

3 months: 10.0% 6 months 10.0%

12 months 10.2% 2 years 10.5%

In a free market, these rates show where the market on average believes rates 'should' be, as supply and demand would otherwise tend to move the rates up or down. A yield curve where longer-term rates are higher than shorter-term rates is known as a *normal* or *positive* yield curve; a curve where longer-term rates are lower than shorter-term rates is known as *negative* or *inverted*; a curve where rates are approximately the same across the range of maturities is known as *flat*.

There are in fact an infinite number of yield curves, because yield depends on credit risk as well as maturity. For example, if I am choosing between investing for 6 months in a security issued by the government of a particular country, and a security issued by a medium-risk company in that same country, I would expect the latter to have a significantly higher yield to compensate for the higher risk. A security issued by a government in its own currency is generally considered to represent virtually zero credit risk, because the government can always print its own money to redeem the security if necessary, regardless of the state of the economy. This does not apply to a security issued by a government in a foreign currency.

There are therefore as many different yield curves as there are levels of creditworthiness. In practice, one generally considers a yield curve as referring to either government risk or first-class bank risk.

The yield on any security also depends on liquidity – how easy it is to liquidate a position in that security by selling it if necessary. If there are two securities issued by exactly the same organization but one is more liquid than the other, it should be traded at a slightly lower yield because investors will be more willing to own it.

Liquidity in turn depends partly on creditworthiness. In any domes-tic money market, a Treasury bill (see below) should be the most liquid instrument, since, even in dire circumstances, the government can in theory always print money to redeem its own securities. In the UK market, eligible bills (see below) are also very liquid, as they can be sold to the Bank of England.

There are various factors which influence the shape of the yield curve:

- Economic performance Expectations of future rates, and hence current longer-term rates also, are affected by market expectations of future inflation.
- Central bank operations Intervention in the market by the central bank, involving buying and selling securities, can change the availability of securities of different maturities. If this causes a shortage of supply for investors at a particular maturity, yields will rise at that maturity. If the market believes that the central bank is about to change official 3-month rates, for example, this expectation will already have been factored into the market 3-month rate.
- Borrowing demand An increase or decrease in borrowing in any particular maturity will tend to increase or decrease yields at that maturity. For example, if the government either increases or decreases its borrowing requirement,

this will affect the yield curve at the maturities sought by the government. Similarly if the government shortens or lengthens the maturity of its debt when it rolls over maturing debt, this tends to make longer-term yields lower than shorter-term yields or vice versa.

- Liquidity preference The typical shape for the yield curve, in the absence of other factors, is positive because, if there is no advantage in investing for a longer term, investors would prefer to invest short-term since their investments are then more liquid. Also, the risk of losing money is greater with a longer-term secu-rity than with a shorter-term security, because its price is more sensitive to yield changes. Therefore, an incentive is necessary to attract longer-term investors. This is a supply and demand effect: borrowers prefer long-term and investors prefer short-term, so the price of money is driven up for the long term.
- Market segmentation Bank investors tend to invest short-term and institutional investors like pension funds tend to invest long-term, with fewer investors in the medium-term. In the absence of any other factors, this would tend to encourage a humped yield curve shape.

SOME MORE TERMINOLOGY

- Negotiable security A *security* is a financial asset sold initially for cash by a borrowing organization (the issuer). A security which can be sold and bought again subsequently – i.e. transferred from one party to another – is referred to as *negotiable.*
- Primary market and secondary market When a security is issued, the original purchaser is said to be buying it in the primary market. All subsequent transactions – whether they are on the same day or much later during the life of the security – are said to be secondary market transactions.
- Face value/notional principal For securities, the principal amount is generally known as the *face value* (which can be thought of as the principal amount written on the face of the instrument). It is also sometimes called the *nominal amount*. With some instruments such as an FRA (see Chapter 6), the principal amount is never actually

transferred to either party, but is used as a reference amount for calculation purposes. In this case, it is referred to as a *notional* principal.

- Coupon/yield A certificate of deposit pays interest at matu-rity – sometimes only at maturity but sometimes also during the CD's life – as well as repaying the principal. For example, a CD might be issued with a face value of £1 million, which is repaid on maturity together with interest of say 10% calculated on the number of days between issue and maturity. The 10% interest rate is called the *coupon*. The coupon is fixed once the CD is issued. This should not be confused with the *yield*, which is the current rate of return available in the market when investing, or buying and selling an instrument, and varies continually.

Discount

1 An instrument which does not carry a coupon is a *discount instrument*. Because there is no interest paid on the principal, a buyer will only ever buy it for less than its face value (unless yields are negative!) – i.e. at a discount. For example, Treasury bills are almost always discount instruments.

2 The word discount is also used in the very specialized context of a *discount rate* quoted in the US and UK markets on certain instruments. This is explained in detail below.

3 To *discount* a cashflow means to calculate its present value, as discussed in Chapter 2.

- Bearer/registered A *bearer security* is one where the issuer pays the principal (and coupon if there is one) to whoever is holding the security at maturity. This enables the security to be held anonymously. A *registered security* by contrast is one where the owner is considered to be whoever is registered centrally as the owner; this registration is changed each time the security changes hands.
- LIBOR *LIBOR* means London interbank offered rate– the interest rate at which one London bank offers money as a cash deposit to another London bank of top creditworthiness. *LIBID* means London interbank bid rate – the interest rate at which one London bank

of top creditworthiness bids for money as a cash deposit from another bank. LIBOR is therefore always the higher side of a two-sided interest rate quotation (which is quoted high–low in some markets and low–high in others). *LIMEAN* is the average between the two sides. In practice, the offered rate for a particular currency at any moment is generally no different in London from any other major center, although it is possible for reserve costs, credit considerations etc. to make a slight difference. LIBOR is therefore often just shorthand for offered interest rate.

Specifically, however, LIBOR for a particular currency also means the average offered rate for that currency quoted by a group of banks in London at 11:00 a.m. This is a reference rate, calcu-lated by the BBA (British Bankers' Association) each day, which is used as a benchmark for agreeing rates between two parties for loans, FRAs and other instruments. Similarly, *EURIBOR* refers specifically to the interbank offered rate for euros reported as a reference rate by the ACI and the EBF. There is therefore both a euro LIBOR (for euros at 11:00 a.m. in London) and EURIBOR (for euros at 11:00 a.m. in Europe). *STIBOR* is the reference rate in Stockholm for Swedish kronor, *BUBOR* for forints in Budapest etc.

- Fixed rate or floating rate Many instruments pay a *fixed* rate – that is, an interest rate or coupon which is determined when the instrument is issued and remains fixed throughout its life, regardless of whether the interest is paid only at maturity or on several occasions. Others pay a *floating* rate. This means that the interest rate is changed in line with market conditions at certain predetermined times (for example, refixed each 6 months to the current LIBOR).
- Bid and offer The offered rate, at which a bank wishes to lend funds to another bank of top credit quality, is higher than the bid rate, at which it wishes to take funds. In most markets, the bid rate is quoted first in a two-way price and the offerred rate second – for example, '5.17/5.27%'. In the London market, however,

the quote is traditionally reversed from bid/offer to offer/bid – for example, '5.27/5.17%'. There is no ambiguity in this, since the lower number is always the bid for cash and the higher number is always the offer for cash, regardless of which comes first.

- Basis point When discussing interest rates, a *basis point* is always 0.01% (which is the same as 0.0001). Note that this is not necessarily the same as a *point* in foreign exchange, which can vary according to the size of the exchange rate.

MONEY MARKET INSTRUMENTS

Fixed deposit/loan

A *fixed deposit* is a deposit placed with a bank for an agreed length of time. It is not negotiable, and it is expected therefore to be held to maturity. It is generally possible for the depositor to *break* the deposit – that is, terminate it early – but effectively at a penalty cost. Conceptually, a fixed deposit is exactly the same as a loan or borrowing – the terminology varies only according to circumstance and whether you are borrowing or lending: a company lending money to the bank is making a deposit but a company borrowing money from the bank is taking a loan.

Certificate of deposit (CD)

A certificate of deposit is a security issued to a depositor by a bank or building society, to raise money in the same way as a time deposit. A CD is, however, negotiable. This gives the investor flexibility in two ways. Firstly, he can liquidate the CD if he needs the cash back sooner than anticipated. Secondly, it allows him to take a view on how interest rates will move, which is linked to the price at which the CD can be bought and sold. For example, if he buys a 6-month CD at 5% and one week later interest rates have fallen to 4.5%, he can then sell the CD and make a capital profit.

Bill of exchange

A bill of exchange is used by a company essentially for trade purposes. It is an unconditional order in writing from one party to another, requiring the second party to pay an amount on a future date. The party originating the bill (this is the party to whom the money is owed) is called the *drawer* of the bill. The party to whom the bill requires the money to be paid (usually the same as the drawer) is the *payee*. The party owing the money is the *drawee* of the bill. When the drawee accepts liability to pay the amount, it becomes the *acceptor*. If a bank stands as guarantor to the drawer, it is also said to accept the bill by endorsing it appropriately. A bill accepted in this way is a *bankers' acceptance (BA)*.

A commercial or finance company can also address a bill directly to a bank, rather than to a trading partner, and discount it immediately at the bank, in order to raise funds for general purposes rather then to finance a specific sale of goods. A repo is also known as a *repurchase agreement, RP, classic repo* or *US-style repo*. A variation on the structure which achieves essentially the same result is a sell/buy-back.

Throughout the book, 'days' means the number of days in the period, including the first date but not the last date; in the money markets, this generally means the number of actual calendar days in the normal way. 'Year' means the number of days in a conventional year, which in the money markets is generally 360 or 365.

DEPOSITS AND COUPON-BEARING INSTRUMENTS

Quoting for fixed deposits with delayed interest settlement

A fixed deposit for longer than 1 year conventionally pays interest at the end of each year and then at maturity. Sometimes a customer asks for all the interest to be paid at maturity instead but for the interest rate to be quoted on a simple basis. Effectively in this case, the bank is keeping the interim interest payments, reinvesting them until maturity, and then giving them to the customer. In quoting to the customer in such a case, account must therefore be taken of the rate at which it is possible to reinvest the interim cashflows. The calculation for the interest rate to be quoted to the customer in this case is considered in Chapter 6.

TAKING A POSITION

A company borrows money because it needs to finance its operations. An investor deposits money in a bank because he wishes to earn interest on it. To some extent, a bank will also have similar underlying requirements - funding its operations and investing surpluses. To a large extent, however, a money market trader borrows and lends money as an activity in itself, in order to make a profit from doing so. This can be through fixed deposits and repos, or through negotiable securities.

To earn profit from dealing, the dealer's objective is to borrow (i.e. take in deposits, issue securities or sell securities) at a lower interest rate and lend (i.e. make deposits, lend money or buy securities) at a higher interest rate. A dealer who has been borrowing and lending in one particular maturity needs to know his net position, average interest rate and profit or loss in that maturity.

The net position is therefore long of USD 3 million at an average rate of 4.563%. The dealer can compare this average rate with the current market rate to determine whether he is running a profit or a loss; in this example, he is running a profit. To calculate the profit, assume that he closes out his position by lending USD 3 million at the current rate of 4.71% (the bid side because he will be hitting someone else's bid rate). This would give a profit of 0.147% (=4.71% — 4.563%) for 31 days on USD 3 million:

The exact average rate and profit or loss will depend on whether the transactions are all for exactly the same maturity. It may be that the dealer has grouped together on his book various deals which have slightly differentmaturities, but are all within 1 month. For someone trading in repos rather than deposits, the calculation is the same since repos can be seen as secured deposits.

As discussed below, when a dealer is trading in negotiable securi-ties, a change in interest rates appears as a change in the value of the security. When interest rates rise, the value of a security falls and vice versa. Therefore a dealer hoping that interest rates will rise is the same as a dealer hoping that prices will fall.

Suppose that a dealer effectively borrows by selling security A at a lower interest rate and effectively lends by buying security B (with the same term and coupon as security A) at a higher interest rate. This means that when he sells security A, he receives a higher price for it than he pays when he buys security B. His profit therefore appears as a capital gain.

THE PRICE OF A CD

When a CD is issued, the original purchaser in the primary market pays the face value for it. In this way, if the original purchaser holds it until maturity, it is the same as a fixed deposit - he pays the principal amount at the start and receives back the principal amount plus coupon at the end.

If the CD is sold again to someone else during its life, however, the amount paid will depend on its value at that time. For an instrument such as a CD which pays a coupon, that value in the market depends on both the coupon rate, because the coupon rate affects the size of the cashflow received at maturity, and the current yield which varies from time to time.

For any security, the price an investor is prepared to pay is essentially the present value of the future cashflow which he will receive at matu-rity because he owns it. This is the same as the cash investment needed now, at the current market yield, to achieve this amount at maturity. This present value depends, as explained in Chapter 2, on the yield he expects to earn, the time to the cashflow and the size of the cashflow.

Suppose that l buy a CD and then sell it again later. The yield that I have earned over this period of holding the CD can be calculated in this way. The cashflow at the start is the amount I pay for the CD when I buy it. The cashflow at the end is the amount I receive for the CD when I sell it.

The dealer in Example 3, having purchased the CD as described in that example, then sells it again a week later, when it has only 23 days left to maturity, when yields are quoted as 5.07/5.17%. This time, assuming that he is again the price-taker, he will deal on the other side of the price at 5.17% (the same rate at which he purchased the CD originally) - as a price-taker, he deals at the higher yield, which implies the lower price.

MONEY MARKET YIELD OF A BOND IN ITS LAST COUPON PERIOD

The same idea we have used to value a CD can be used to value any security where there is only one cashflow left. Suppose, for example, that a dealer wishes to invest for 5 months in a security issued by Bank A. This could be because he considers that Bank A represents both a good yield and an acceptable credit risk.

Suppose that the dealer is able to choose between a CD previously issued by that bank which now has 5 months left to maturity and a bond issued by that bank several years ago, but which also now has 5 months left to maturity. From the investor's point of view, assuming that the two securities are equally liquid, he might be indifferent to whether he buys the first or the second. They both represent a single cashflow in 5 months' time. Therefore in valuing the bond, he could value it in exactly the same way as the CD, on the basis of a money market yield. There is more than one way of doing this. Our approach here is to calculate a money market yield which is exactly comparable with the yield on a money market instrument.

The bond market is outside the scope of this book. It is worth noting, however, that the normal convention for expressing the yield of a bond is slightly different from this. A bond price is also normally quoted excluding *accrued coupon* (a *clean price),* unlike a CD price which includes everything (a *dirty price).*

Example : An investor purchases a bond, face value EUR 10 million, which pays an annual coupon of 7%. The price he pays, including accrued coupon, is 104.98326 per 100 face value. There are 158 days left until maturity of the bond.

Almost all fixed-rate bonds pay a coupon which is calculated as a round amount, rather than on the basis of the exact number of calendar days in the coupon period. Therefore the coupon paid by the issuer of this bond at maturity will be exactly EUR 700,000 (=EUR 10 million x 7%), regardless of exactly how many days there have been since the last coupon was paid, or the effect of any non-business days at either end of the coupon period.

A fixed deposit is expected to be held to maturity. It is gener-ally possible, however, for the depositor to break the deposit – that is, terminate it early – although the bank will usually charge the customer a penalty for this.

The bank wishes to make sure that it is not losing by repaying the deposit early. This can be achieved as follows:

- First, calculate the amount (principal plus interest) which it would have expected to repay on the normal maturity date of the deposit.
- Second, calculate how much the bank will need to borrow at current market rates, from now until that original

maturity date, in order to repay that same amount as originally expected.

If the bank repays this amount to the depositor, it will be neither losing nor gaining. This amount is in fact the present value of the original maturing principal and interest. The rate of discount to be used is the rate at which the bank believes it could borrow new money, taking into account any spread over LIBOR which it typically pays.

You would therefore repay a total (including interest) of GBP 999,934.30 because, if you borrow this amount from a different source now at current rates, you will need to repay GBP 1,025,670.14 – i.e. the same amount that you originally expected to repay. You are therefore left in the same position as if the deposit had not been broken.

In practice, you might wish to protect yourself by taking a more pessimistic view on the rate at which you can refund yourself in the market, and therefore use an interest rate higher than 6.14% to discount to a present value.

The customer in this example receives back a total of less than he deposited. If interest rates had fallen rather than risen since the deposit had been made, the repayment amount calculated in this way would be rather higher, to the customer's advantage. However, in order to discourage customers from breaking deposits, the bank might agree to do so only on condition that the interest rate used for the calculation is unrealistically high.

The calculation used here is in fact the same as calculating the price of a CD – it is the present value of the maturing amount.

To calculate the total amount repayable when a fixed deposit is broken

First, calculate the principal plus interest due on the normal maturity date.

Second, calculate the present value of this, using the bank's funding rate.

CDS PAYING MORE THAN ONE COUPON

Most CDs are short-term instruments paying interest only at matu-rity. Some CDs, however, are issued with a maturity of several years. In this case, interest is paid periodically - generally every 6 months or every year. The price for a CD paying more than one coupon will therefore depend on all the intervening coupons before maturity, valued at the current yield.

Suppose that a CD has several more coupons yet to be paid, the last of which will be paid on maturity together with the face value of the CD.

The pricing method is first to discount the final cashflow - the final coupon payment plus the face value of the CD - back to the previous coupon payment date, using the current yield as the rate of discount.

The result is then added to the coupon payment actually made on that date and the combined total is then discounted back again to the previous coupon payment date, also using the current yield as the rate of discount.

This new result is then again added to the coupon payment actually made on that date and the combined total again discounted back.

This process continues until the nearest coupon payment outstand-ing. The value thus reached is finally discounted back to the trans-action settlement date.

Throughout the process, both the calculation of each coupon payment and each discounting are performed using the exact number of days in the relevant coupon period.

To value a CD with more than one coupon payment outstanding:

DISCOUNT INSTRUMENTS

Instruments which pay no coupon are known as discount instru-ments, because the amount paid for them is always less than the face value. This is so because, otherwise, the investor would earn a negative return. Commercial paper, for example, is a discount instrument.

In the last example, the yield earned over the holding period of 7 days was calculated as shown in the section on 'Calculating the yield on an investment or the cost of a borrowing' in Chapter 2. An alternative, as in the previous chapter, is to use the following formula:

With a yield, the investor in a security asks the question: "If

I invest a certain amount at the beginning, how much extra will I receive by the end?'' The answer is his yield on the investment, expressed as a proportion of the amount invested. For example, if he invests GBP 100 for one year and receives back a total of GBP 110 at the end of a year, he has earned GBP 10 extra. This represents 10% of the GBP 100 originally invested.

With a discount rate, however, the investor asks instead: ''If I receive a certain amount back at the end, how much less will I need to invest at the beginning?'' The answer is the discount amount on the investment. With the same investment as above, if he will receive back GBP 110 at the end of the year but only invests GBP 100 at the beginning, there is a discount amount of GBP 10. This represents 9.091% of the GBP 110 received at the end.

In this example, therefore, the yield is 10% but the discount rate is 9.091%. In general, the discount rate is the amount of discount expressed as a percentage per year of the face value, rather than as a percentage per year of the original amount paid.

The discount rate is always less than the corresponding yield. Any investment could be expressed either in terms of yield or in terms of discount rate. In practice, however, the market convention is to use yield in almost all financial markets worldwide, but to use discount rate in just five instruments. These are listed below.

Terminology can be confusing. What we are calling 'discount rate' is also known in the USA as 'discount yield' or even just 'yield'. When we use the term 'yield' in this book, we always mean yield as we have described – also known as 'true yield', or 'investment yield'; we never mean discount rate.

Since the difference between the start amount and the end amount can in theory be expressed as either a yield or a discount rate, it is possible to express one in terms of the other. This is useful when it is necessary to compare an instrument quoted with a yield (for example, US dollar commercial paper issued internationally) with an instrument quoted with a discount rate (for example, US dollar commercial paper issued domestically in the USA).

Instruments quoted on a discount rate include Treasury bills, domestic CP and trade bills/BAs in the USA, and sterling Treasury bills and trade bills/BAs in the UK. However, all loans/fixed deposits and CDs in dollars and sterling are quoted on a yield.

Note that domestic CP in the UK, and US dollar CP issued in the Euromarket (i.e. dollar Euro-commercial paper) are all quoted on a yield. Note also that while the Treasury-bills issued by the UK government in sterling are quoted on a discount rate, the Treasury-bills it issues in euros are quoted on a yield, as are other international instruments in euros.

In Example 1, the dealer originally purchased at a yield of 5.17%. However, when he sold the investment at the same yield of 5.17%, it turned out that the yield he earned over the holding period was in fact 5.15%. It is always true that if you buy at a particular yield and then sell later at the same yield, then the yield earned is less.

In Example 2, however, the dealer originally purchased at a dis-count rate of 5.17%, which was equivalent to a yield of 5.19%. In this case, when he sold the investment at the same discount rate of 5.17%, it turned out that the yield he earned over the holding period was the same 5.19% at which he had originally invested. It is always true that if you buy at a particular discount rate and then sell later at the same discount rate, then the yield earned is the same as the original equivalent yield.

If you buy at particular discount rate and later sell at the same discount rate, the yield earned over the holding period is the same as the purchase yield.

BOND-EQUIVALENT YIELDS FOR US TREASURY BILLS

For trading purposes, a government Treasury bond which has less than a year left to maturity may be just as acceptable to a money market trader as a Treasury bill with the same remaining maturity. As the method used for quoting yields generally differs between the two instruments, the rate quoted for Treasury bills in the USA is often converted to a bond-equivalent yield for comparison.

The bond-equivalent yield of a Treasury bill is defined as the coupon of a theoretical US Treasury bond, trading at par, with the same maturity date, which would give the same return as the bill.

We show below the formulas for calculating this. If the bill has 182 days or less until maturity, the calculation is the same conversion from discount rate to yield as we have already seen above, except that it is also then converted to a 365-day year. If the bill has more than 182 days until maturity, however, the calculation must take account of the fact that the equivalent bond would pay a coupon during the period as well as at the end.

In either case, if 29 February falls in the 12-month period starting on the purchase date, 365 is conventionally replaced by 366.

FORWARD INTEREST RATES, FRAS AND INTRODUCTION TO FUTURES

Forward-forwards, forward rate agreements (FRAs) and futures are very closely linked instruments, all relating to an interest rate applied to some period which starts in the future. We shall outline them first and then examine each more closely.

- A forward-forward is a cash borrowing or deposit which starts on one forward date and ends on another forward date. The term, amount and interest rate are all fixed in advance. Someone who expects to borrow or deposit cash in the future can use this to remove any uncertainty relating to what interest rates will be when the time arrives.
- An FRA is an *off-balance sheet* instrument which can be used to achieve the same economic effect as a forward-forward. Someone who expects to borrow cash in the future can buy an FRA to fix in advance the interest rate on the borrowing. When the time to borrow arrives, he borrows the cash in the usual way. Under the FRA, which remains quite separate, he receives or pays the difference between the cash borrowing rate and the FRA rate, so that he achieves the same net effect as with a forward-forward borrowing.

Similarly, an investor or other lender can use an FRA to protect the return on a future investment.

There is of course no need to have any underlying borrowing or investment when trading an FRA. In this way, an FRA an be used speculatively, to take a view on whether interest rates will rise or fall, and also in arbitrage strategies.

A futures contract is similar to an FRA. Futures are, however, traded only on an exchange, and differ from FRAs in a variety of technical ways.

PRICING A FORWARD-FORWARD

The dollar interest rate now for 2 months (61 days) is 5.6/5.7% and the rate for 5 months (153 days) is 5.3/5.4%.

If I borrow now for 5 months at 5.4% and simultaneously deposit the cash borrowed at 5.6% for 2 months, the position over the first 2 months is a net zero one. I have therefore synthet-ically created a net borrowing which begins in 2 months and ends in 5 months - that is, a forward-forward borrowing. All the cashflows are known in advance, so it must be possible to calcu-late the cost of borrowing over the 3-month forward period. This rate is in fact given by the formula below.

If I am a bank customer, I could more simply ask the bank to provide the forward-forward loan from 2 months to 5 months at an agreed rate, rather than construct it myself as in Example 1. However, the bank would be able to construct it in exactly the same way and then present it to me as a forward-forward loan: the bank borrows for 5 months, lends the cash in the interbank market for 2 months and then has the cash available to lend to me for the forward period from 2 months to 5 months.

Forward-forwards and FRAs are referred to by the beginning and end dates of the forward period, compared with the dealing date or *spot* value date. Thus the forward-forward described here is a '2v5' (or '2x5', or 2/5, or 'twos against fives'), meaning that the forward period starts 2 months from now and ends 5 months from now.

Break-even on a forward position

If a dealer has borrowed for a longer period than he has lent– for example, he has borrowed USD 10 million for 8 months and lent USD 10 million for two months – he is said to be *over-borrowed*, because at a future point (in 2 months' time in this case), his borrowing will be greater than his lending. He will therefore need to lend again in the future to square his book. Similarly, a dealer who has lent for a longer period than he has borrowed is said to be *over-lent*. The forward-forward formula is useful for calculating the break-even rate which a dealer needs to achieve to cover such an unmatched position, because the forward-forward rate is exactly the rate which is consistent with the rate for the shorter period and the rate for the longer period.

FORWARD RATE AGREEMENT (FRA)

An FRA is an off-balance sheet agreement to make a settlement in the future which, when combined with a cash borrowing in the future, can be used to have the same economic effect as a forward-forward. It is an agreement to pay or receive, on an agreed future date, the difference between a fixed interest rate agreed at the outset and the interest rate actually prevailing at that future date, calculated on an agreed notional principal amount. The principal itself is not transferred in either direction.

Pricing

In calculating a theoretical FRA price, we can apply exactly the same ideas as in the forward-forward calculation earlier. As we are not actu-ally borrowing cash with the FRA, however, we could calculate using middle rates for both the 5-month and 2-month periods – rather than separate bid and offered rates. This calculation produces a theoretical FRA rate which is comparable to LIMEAN. By conven-tion, however, FRAs are always settled against LIBOR rather than LIMEAN. We therefore need to add the difference between LIMEAN and LIBOR – generally around 0.05% – to this theoretical rate. An alternative approach is to base the theoretical price calculation on LIBOR for both periods, rather than LIMEAN. The result is different, but generally only very slightly.

In practice, a dealer generally prices an FRA from the futures market (see below) rather than from cash forward-forwards, because futures are very liquid and cash is expensive on the balance sheet. However, futures pricing theory still comes back to forward-forward pricing and in any case, FRAs in minor currencies where there is no futures market do need to be priced from, and hedged by, cash forward-forwards.

Having established a theoretical FRA price, a dealer would then build a spread round this price to give a two-way price with a bid and an offer. Based on this two-way price, a customer or bank wishing to pay the fixed FRA rate (as in Example 3) would pay the offer (the higher rate). This is known as buying an FRA. A customer wishing to receive the fixed FRA rate would receive the bid (the lower rate). This is known as selling an FRA. The terminology of buying or selling an FRA has nothing to do with the customer/bank relationship; it is merely a way of distinguishing who is the fixed rate payer from who is the fixed rate receiver.

Settlement

The settlement on an FRA – of the difference between the FRA rate and LIBOR at the beginning of the period – is in fact settled net rather than gross. That is, the difference is paid in one direction or the other, rather than having two payments, one in each direction. By convention, this difference is paid or received at the beginning of the forward period to which it relates, rather than at the end as is normal for interest payments. It is therefore discounted to a present value (see Chapter 2) in order to calculate the actual settlement amount paid. Taking this into account, the settlement amount is as follows:

The LIBOR used to calculate the settlement amount depends on the currency. With a sterling FRA, it is generally the LIBOR for the forward period that prevails on the *effective* date of the FRA - that is, the first day of the forward period. LIBOR is therefore fixed on the settlement date itself. This is also sometimes the case with Canadian dollars and Hong Kong dollars.

With an FRA in other currencies, it is generally the LIBOR that prevails two business days earlier. This is because the LIBOR for a currency other than sterling is for value spot. In domestic markets in other currencies, as opposed to the international market, FRAs can be traded for settlement against a same-day value reference, as with sterling.

Suppose that an FRA is traded for a regular period - for example, 7 months against 10 months. In the case of foreign currency FRAs, both the effective date (7 months) and the end date (10 months) are generally taken from the spot date. Because of non-business days, however, it might be that, when LIBOR is fixed, the period between the two dates turns out not to be a regular period. The following example demonstrates this.

It is now Thursday 13 March 2003. I will need to borrow USD 1 million for a 3-month period, starting in 2 months' time. I purchase a 2v5 FRA at 5.22% on a notional amount of USD 1 million.

Spot value date is Monday 17 March. The 2-month value date is Monday 19 May (because 17 and 18 May are non-business days). The 5-month value date is Monday 18 August (because 17 August is a non-business day). I have therefore purchased an FRA from 19 May to 18 August (a 91-day period).

LIBOR on 15 May for the period from 19 May to 18 August is not exactly the 3-month LIBOR fixing on that day, because 3-month LIBOR would be from 19 May to 19 August. It is there-fore necessary on 15 May to interpolate between the 2-month LIBOR and 3-month LIBOR fixings, although the difference would be rather slight. Assume that the LIBOR so calculated for the period 19 May to 18 August is 5.05%..

Assuming that on 15 May, I arrange a 3-month borrowing of USD 1 million, this would normally be from 19 May to 19 August, so that, as well as being based on a slightly different LIBOR from the FRA settlement, the borrowing would be for one day longer than the FRA. It would have been possible instead to have arranged the FRA originally for the exact dates I wanted.

FRA periods longer than one year

If the period of the FRA is longer than one year, the corresponding LIBOR rate used for settlement relates to a period where interest is conventionally paid at the end of each year as well as at maturity. A 6v24 FRA, for example, covers a period from 6 months to 24 months and will be settled against an 18-month LIBOR rate at the beginning of the FRA period.

An 18-month deposit would, however, typically pay interest at the end of one year and again after 18 months. As FRA settlements are paid at the beginning of the period on a discounted basis, each of these amounts needs to be discounted separately. Strictly, the net settlement payment calculated for the end of 18 months should be discounted at an appropriate compounded 18-month rate and the net settlement amount calculated for the end of the first year should be discounted at 1-year LIBOR. In practice, the FRA settlement LIBOR is generally used for both.

INTRODUCTION TO FUTURES

In general, a *futures* contract in any market is a contract in which the commodity being bought and sold is considered as being delivered (even though this may not physically occur) at some future date rather than immediately – hence the name. The significant differences between a futures contract and a *forward* arise in two ways.

Firstly, a futures contract is traded on a particular exchange (although two or more exchanges might trade identically specified contracts). A forward, however, which is also a deal for delivery on a future date, is dealt *over the counter* (*OTC*) – a deal made between any two parties, but not on an exchange.

Secondly, futures contracts are generally standardized, while forwards are not. The specifications of each futures contract are laid down precisely by the relevant exchange and vary from instrument to instrument and from exchange to exchange. Some contracts, for example, specifically do not allow for the instrument to be delivered; although their prices are calculated as if future delivery does take place, the contracts must be reversed before the notional delivery date, thereby capturing a profit or a loss. Short-term interest rate futures (*STIR* futures), for example, cannot be delivered.

The theory underlying the pricing of a futures contract depends on the underlying instrument on which the contract is based. For a futures contract based on 3-month interest rates, the pricing is therefore based on the same forward-forward pricing theory explained earlier.

3-month EURIBOR futures contract traded on LIFFE:

Exchange: LIFFE (London International Financial Futures and Options Exchange).

Underlying: The basis of the contract is a 3-month deposit of EUR 1 million based on an ACT/360 year.

Delivery: It is not permitted for this contract to be delivered; if a trader buys such a contract, he cannot insist that, on the future delivery date, his counterparty makes arrangements for him to have a deposit for 3 months from then onwards at the interest rate agreed. Rather, the trader must reverse his futures contract by delivery, thereby taking a profit or loss.

Delivery months: The nearest 3 months following dealing and March, June, September and December thereafter.

Delivery day: First business day after the Last Trading Day.

Last trading day: 10.00 a.m. 2 business days prior to the third Wednesday of the delivery month.

Settlement price: On the last day of trading - usually the third Monday of the month - LIFFE declares an 'exchange delivery settlement price' (EDSP) which is the closing price at which any contracts still outstanding will be automatically reversed. The EDSP is 100 minus the European Bankers Federation/ACI 3-month offered rate (EURIBOR) at 11:00 a.m. Brussels time.

Price: The price is determined by the free market and is quoted as an index rather than an as interest rate. The index is expressed as 100 minus the implied interest. Thus a price of 94.52 implies an interest rate of 5.48% *(100 — 94.52 = 5.48).*

Price movement: Prices are quoted in units of 0.005. This minimum movement is called a tick.

There are relatively minor differences between futures exchanges, and even between different STIR contracts on the same exchange:

Underlying The typical contract specification for short-term interest rate futures is for a 3-month interest rate, although 1-month contracts also exist in some currencies on some exchanges (for example, US dollar and euro futures contracts). The precise specification varies from exchange to exchange but is in practice for exactly one quarter of a year (or exactly one twelfth of a year for 1-month contracts). Thus settlement on the sterling 3-month interest rate futures contract traded on LIFFE, is effectively equivalent to 91 $^{1}{}_{4}$ days' settlement because sterling is based on a year of 365 days:

The size of the contract varies. For example, the US dollar and euro 3-month contracts are USD 1 million and EUR 1 million, the US dollar and euro 1-month contracts are USD 3 million and EUR 3 million, the sterling 3-month contract is GBP 500,000 and the yen 3-month contract is JPY 100 million.

In the case of sterling futures, both the last trading day and the LIBOR fixing used for settlement are the third Wednesday of the delivery month (or the next following business day), rather than two business days earlier.

- Trading Trading times vary. Some contracts are traded by open outcry (see below) - notably on the *IMM* (the International Monetary Market, the financial sector of the Chicago Mercantile Exchange *(CME))* - and some are traded electronically.

- Price movement Tick sizes, and hence tick values, vary. For example, the minimum price movement on sterling is 1 basis point. The minimum price movement for US dollars varies from 4 basis point for the nearest-dated futures contact, through $^{1}{}_{2}$ basis point for subsequent ones, to 1 basis point for later ones.
- Settlement price The settlement price varies according to both currency and exchange.

A dealer expects interest rates to fall (futures to rise) and takes a speculative position. He therefore buys 20 EUR 1-month futures contracts at 95.27. He closes them out subsequently at 95.20. What is his profit or loss? The price has fallen, so he makes a loss of EUR 3,500:

Market participants

The users of an exchange are its members and their customers. An exchange also has *locals*, private traders dealing only for their own account. Each member may enter into transactions either on his own account or, if he is a *public order member*, also on behalf of customers. Certain members may also act as floor dealers executing transactions on behalf of other members.

Open outcry versus screen-trading

There are two methods of dealing. The first, traditional, method is *open outcry*, whereby the buyer and seller deal face to face in public in the exchange's trading pit. This should ensure that a customer's order is always transacted at the best possible rate and ensures complete transparency of all dealing. The second method is electronic screen-trading, designed to simulate open outcry but with the advantage of lower costs and wider access. Some exchanges use only screen-based trading and there is a general trend away from open outcry because of its higher costs.

Clearing

The futures exchange is responsible for administering the market, but all transactions are cleared through a clearing house, which may be separately owned. On LIFFE, for example, this function is performed by the London Clearing House (LCH). Following confirmation of a transaction, the clearing house substitutes itself for each counter-party and becomes the seller to every buyer and the buyer to every seller. Only clearing members of an exchange are entitled to clear their transactions directly with the clearing house. In order to become a clearing member, certain conditions set by the exchange and the clearing house have to be satisfied, including a minimum net worth requirement. Non-clearing members have to clear all their transactions through a clearing member.

Margin requirements

In order to protect the clearing house, clearing members are required to place collateral with it for each deal transacted. This collateral is called *initial margin.*

Members are then debited or credited each day with *variation margin* which reflects the day's loss or profit on contracts held. Customers, in turn, are required to pay initial margin and variation margin to the member through whom they have cleared their deal. The initial margin is intended to protect the clearing house for the short period until a position can be revalued and variation margin called for if necessary. As variation margin is paid each day, the initial margin is relatively small in relation to the potential price movements over a longer period.

The calculation of variation margin is equivalent to *marking to market* – that is, revaluing a futures contract each day at the closing price. The variation margin required is the tick value multiplied by the number of ticks price movement since the close the previous day. For example, if the tick value is EUR 12.50 on each contract, and the price moves from 94.730 to 94.215 (a fall of 103 ticks), the loss on a long futures contract is EUR (12.50 × 103) = EUR 1,287.50. Depending on the size of initial margin already placed with the exchange, and the exchange's current rules, a variation margin may not be called for below a certain level. Initial margin requirements need to be funded by members for as long as positions are held open. It is therefore in the interests of promoting market liquidity to keep this margin as low as possible while maintaining adequate protection for the clearing house. For example, the LCH's system for calculating margin, known as SPAN (standard portfolio analysis of risk), recognizes that a combination of futures (and options) may have less risk than the sum of the risks attached to each element of the position individually, and therefore require less margin.

Closing out

A futures position can be closed out by means of an exactly offset-ting transaction. Contracts which are not settled before maturity are required to be reversed automatically at maturity and the price difference paid or received.

All contracts are completely *fungible;* once a purchase of a certain quantity of a particular contract is added to an existing holding of the same contract, there is no distinction whatever between the two purchases; they simply become a single, larger holding of the contract.

Limit up/down

Some markets impose limits on trading movements in an attempt to prevent wild price fluctuations and hence limit risk to some extent.

Basis

In practice, the actual futures price trading in the market is unlikely to be exactly the same as the fair theoretical value which can be calculated according to the underlying cash market forward-forward. The difference between the actual price and the theoretical fair price is termed the *value basis.*

Basis is the difference between what the futures price would be, based on the current cash interest rate, and the actual futures price. This difference should tend towards zero on the last trading day for the futures contract.

Basis risk is the risk arising from the basis on a futures position. Suppose, for example, that on 2 April a futures trader sells a 1v4 FRA to a customer which will settle on 4 May and that he hedges this by selling futures contracts for delivery on 18 June.

The trader cannot be perfectly hedged because on 4 May the cash market 3-month LIBOR against which the FRA will be settled will not necessarily have moved since 2 April to the same extent as the futures price. He thus has a basis risk.

Value basis = theoretical futures price – actual futures price

Basis = implied cash price – actual futures price

Basis risk is the risk arising from the basis

FUTURES COMPARED WITH FRAS

It is worth summarizing the differences between an FRA and a futures contract:

- Standardization versus flexibility For each futures contract, the amount, delivery date and period are all standardized. With an FRA, they are entirely flexible.
- Margin versus credit risk Dealing in futures requires the payment of collateral (initial margin) as security. In addition, variation margin is paid or received each day to reflect the day's loss or profit on contracts held. The margin system ensures that the exchange clearing house is generally fully protected against the risk of default. There is therefore usually virtually no credit risk in dealing futures. When trading OTC, however, professional traders usually deal on the basis of credit lines, with no security required.
- Settlement An important practical difference between FRAs and futures is in the settlement mechanics. An FRA settlement is paid at the beginning of the forward period, and the settlement formula incorporates discounting to a present value. The futures settlement – the profit or loss on the contract – is also all settled by the same date, via the variation margin payments made during the period from transaction until the futures delivery date. However, in most futures markets, this settlement is not discounted. A 90-day FRA is not therefore exactly matched by an offsetting futures contract even if the amounts and dates are the same.
- Liquidity and spread Standardization and transparency gener-ally ensure a liquid market in futures contracts, together with narrower spreads between bid and offer than in FRAs. For delivery dates far in the future, on the other hand, there may be insuffi-cient liquidity in the futures market, whereas an FRA price might be available.
- Underlying commodity Futures contracts are not available in all currencies, whereas an FRA might be available, albeit at an unattractive price.
- Taking a position FRAs and futures are in opposite directions. A buyer of an FRA will profit if interest rates

rise. A buyer of a futures contract will profit if interest rates fall. If a trader sells an FRA to a counterparty, he might therefore also sell a futures contract to cover his position.

THE YIELD CURVE

Rather than this normal yield curve, a more useful curve to look at might be one that shows what the market expects rates to be at certain times in the future. For example, what is the 3-month rate now, what will the 3-month rate be after 1 month, after 2 months, after 3 months etc.? Given enough such rates, it is in fact possible to work backwards to construct the normal yield curve. Suppose, for example, that the 3-month rate now is 5.0% and the market expects that rates will fall slightly during the next 3 months - so that at the end of 3 months, the new 3-month rate will be 4.94%. Given these data, what should the 6-month rate be now? The answer must be the rate achieved by taking the 3-month rate now, compounded with the expected 3-month rate in 3 months' time; otherwise there would be an expected profit in going long for 3 months and short for 6 months, or vice versa, and the market would tend to move the rates. In this way, the 6-month rate now can be calculated using a strip (see Chapter 2): This shows that a flat short-term yield curve – in our example, the 3-month and 6-month rates are the same at 5.00% – does not imply that the market expects interest rates to remain stable. Rather, it expects them to fall. An important point here is to consider the question of which comes first. Are forward-forward rates (and hence FRA rates and futures prices) the mathematical result of the yield curve? Or are the market's expectations of future rates (i.e. forward-forwards, FRAs and futures) the starting point, and from these it is possible to create the yield curve? The question is a circular one to some extent, but market traders increasingly look at constructing a yield curve from expected future rates for various periods and maturities - in other words, the futures market is the driving force.

APPLICATIONS OF FRAS AND FUTURES

As with any instrument, FRAs may be used for hedging, speculating or arbitrage, depending on whether they are taken to offset an existing position or taken as new positions themselves.

Hedging

As we have discussed above, a future borrower wishing to hedge against the possibility of higher interest rates would buy an FRA or sell futures. A future investor or lender wishing to hedge against the possibility of lower interest rates would sell an FRA or buy futures.

In this case, the result is not known exactly because FRAs are always priced and settled against LIBOR but the rollover will be at LIBID. The dealer can estimate, however, what the spread is likely to be.

In practice, the amount of the FRA dealt will probably be USD 3 million. If the dealer wishes to hedge the position exactly however, he can calculate the maturing amount of the lending at the end of 1 month, including principal and interest. This is the amount which he will have available to relend at that time, and is therefore the amount to be protected by the FRA if he wishes to be precise.

In Chapter 2 we used a strip to calculate a borrower's overall cost when he rolls over a loan. We have repeated the strip formula below. Exactly the same approach works when using FRAs or futures, as in the next example.

It is now mid-September and an investor wishes to deposit USD 1 million for nine months. Given the following rates, and assuming that he can always place cash at LIBID, what is the best way of doing so?

3 months (91 days)	5.23/5.33%
6 months (181 days)	5.25/5.35%
9 months (273 days)	5.25/5.35%
3v6 FRA	5.28/5.33%
6v9 FRA	5.24/5.29%
December futures	94.68/94.69
March futures	94.77/94.78

If the 3v6 period is covered separately, it is better to buy December futures at 94.69 (implied interest rate 5.31%) than to sell an FRA at 5.28%.

If the 6v9 period is covered separately, it is better to sell an FRA at 5.24% than to buy March futures at 94.78 (implied interest rate 5.22%).

It is important to remember that, even for an investor, an FRA or a futures contract is still settled against LIBOR, not LIBID. If the investor covers the 3v6 period with futures at 5.31%, for example, his return for that period will not be 5.31% but rather 5.31% less the LIBID/LIBOR spread. If this is 10 basis points, his return will be only 5.21% for that period. Similarly, if he covers the 6v9 period with an FRA, his return would be say 5.14%, not 5.24%

The choices are therefore reduced to:

- Deposit 9-month cash at 5.25%.
- Deposit 3-month cash at 5.23%, buy December futures at 5.31%, sell a 6v9 FRA at 5.24% and roll over the deposit at LIBID after 6 months and again after 9 months, to give a compound return of 5.262%:

Of these, the last is the best, although the difference is so small that the administrative burden, and uncertainty of cashflow timing, arising from the futures trade might well make the strategy not worth while. On the other hand, there could be an advantage from the reduced credit risk and capital adequacy requirements compared with a straightforward 9-month deposit.

Hedging an FRA position with futures

We have already mentioned that a trader is likely to generate an FRA price from futures prices rather than from cash forward-forwards. Similarly, he is likely to hedge the resulting position by buying or selling futures.

If the FRA period coincides exactly with one futures period, then the dealer can hedge the FRA with that futures contract - if he is long of FRAs, then he buys futures to hedge; if he is short of FRAs then he sells futures to hedge. He can price the FRA as the interest rate implied by the futures price, together with an appropriate bid/offer spread.

A dealer sells an FRA for GBP 12 million for a 3-month period from mid-March to mid-June.

The number of futures contracts used for the hedge should be such that a 1 basis point change has equal but opposite effects on the FRA position and the futures hedge. Ignoring exact day counts and the present value component of the FRA settlement formula, the profit or loss on the FRA arising from a 1 basis point change in rates would be: If the FRA period coincides with a strip of futures, then he hedges with a strip of futures.

Example: *A* dealer buys from a customer a GBP 12 million FRA for the 9-month period from mid-September to mid-June. Futures prices at the time are:

September: 95.36 (implied rate 4.64%)

December: 95.43 (implied rate 4.57%)

March 95.65 (implied rate 4.35%)

The interest rate implied by the strip of futures is 4.57%:

The dealer will therefore quote a rate for the FRA of 4.59% less a spread. He hedges the position by buying 24 September contracts, 24 December contracts and 24 March contracts). When the FRA is settled in mid-September, the September futures contract expires at the same time and he closes out the December and March contracts.

If the FRA period does not coincide exactly with futures periods, however, the dealer must use overlapping futures contracts. Suppose, for example, that the FRA is for GBP 12 million for a 6-month period from mid-April to mid-October. This could be hedged by a combina-tion of some March futures, some June futures and some September futures (see Figure 6.1).

This period overlaps 2 months out of 3 of the March futures contract (i.e. mid-April to mid-June, 3 months out of 3 of the June contract (mid-June to mid-September) and 1 month out of 3 of the September contract (mid-September to mid-October). For each futures contract where the overlap is complete, the hedge should be complete - i.e. 24 contracts. For each end where the overlap is not complete, the hedge should be pro-rata. Therefore the hedge should be 16 March contracts, 24 June contracts and 8 September contracts.

The total number of futures contracts used for the hedge in this case should still be such that a 1 basis point change has equal but opposite effects on the FRA position and the futures hedge.

Example : In January, a dealer buys a 4v9 FRA from a customer for the 5-month period from 12 May to 12 October for EUR 10 million and needs to hedge this with futures.

If the FRA were for a 3-month period, the approximate value of a 1 basis point change on the FRA would be EUR 250:

The value of a 1 basis point change on a single EUR futures contract is EUR 25. Therefore 10 contracts would be required. However, the FRA period is in fact 5 months and overlaps approximately 5 weeks out of 12 of the March futures period, all of the June futures period and approximately 3 weeks out of 12 of the September futures period (see Figure 6.2).

As futures must be traded in round amounts, the dealer there-fore buys 4 March contracts, 10 June contracts and 3 September contracts.

In mid-March, the hedge must be adjusted because the March futures contracts expire. They are therefore replaced by 4 more June contracts. This creates a bias, however. The FRA is for a period starting in mid-May but the futures strip is for a period starting in mid-June. The hedge is satisfactory if the forward yield curve moves up or down in parallel. However, if it also twists anti-clockwise, the loss on the FRA position could be greater than the profit on the futures hedge (or the profit on the FRA less than the loss on the futures). In order to reduce this risk, the dealer could superimpose a further hedge, by buying a further 4 June contracts and selling 4 September contracts. This is essentially the same strategy as a spread - see below. He would then be left with a hedge of long 18 June contracts and short 1 September contract.

On 10 May, when LIBOR is fixed for the FRA settlement, all the futures contracts are closed.

The hedge in the previous example is not perfect, for various reasons:

- Futures contracts are for standardized notional amounts only.
- Futures profit/loss is based on exactly $\frac{3}{12}$ year, rather than 90, 91 or 92 calendar days etc.
- FRA settlements are discounted but futures settlements are not and also the timing of the futures variation margin cashflows is unknown.
- There is basis risk because the futures dates do not coincide with the FRA date.

Quoting for fixed deposits with delayed interest settlement

A fixed deposit for longer than 1 year conventionally pays interest at the end of each year and then at maturity. Sometimes a customer asks for all the interest to be paid at maturity instead. Effectively in this case, the bank is keeping the interim interest payments, rein-vesting them until maturity, and then giving them to the customer. In quoting to the customer in such a case, account must therefore be taken of the rate at which it is possible to reinvest the interim cashflows. Since this reinvestment rate can be fixed in advance by using FRAs or futures, the FRA or futures rates can be used for the calculation.

Example : You are a dealer. You quote a customer 5.13% for a deposit of GBP 1 million for 18 months, with interest paid at the end of 1 year and again at maturity. The customer asks to have all the interest paid at the end and asks for a quote on that basis instead. What rate do you quote? 12v18 FRAs are currently quoted at 4.55/4.65%. The 1-year period has 365 days and the 18-month period has 548 days. Effectively, you will need to take the interest amount at the end of 1 year and invest it for 6 months - which you can protect at the FRA bid rate of 4.55% - and then add it to the remaining interest due at the end of 18 months.

The most basic trading strategy is to speculate on whether the cash interest rate when the forward period begins is higher or lower than the FRA rate or implied futures rate. If the trader expects interest rates to rise, he buys an FRA or sells a futures contract; if he expects rates to fall, he sells an FRA or buys a futures contract. In example 6, we considered speculation using futures contracts. Here is the same strategy using FRAs:

Strip trading

In the same way, if a trader is using futures and wishes to speculate on a longer-term rate than the 3-month rate, he would sell or buy a strip of futures.

Example : It is now February. A dealer with no position expects 12-month interest rates to rise. He therefore sells a strip of March, June, September and December futures. If he is correct and the 12-month rate rises above the 12-month interest rate implied by stripping these four prices together, he will be able to reverse the four contracts at an overall profit.

Calendar spread

A spread is a strategy whereby the trader buys a shorter-dated FRA or futures contract and sells a longer-dated one, because he expects the difference between them to change - a twist in the shape of the yield curve - but does not necessarily have any expectation about the whole yield curve moving up or down.

CALENDAR SPREAD

A dealer expecting the yield curve to twist anti-clockwise sells a shorter-date FRA and buys a longer-dated FRA (or buys a shorter-dated futures and sells a longer-dated futures).

A dealer expecting the yield curve to twist clockwise buys a shorter-date FRA and sells a longer-dated FRA (or sells a shorter-dated futures and buys a longer-dated futures).

A longer-term spread can be taken if a trader has a view on short-term yields compared with bond yields – for example, a spread between a 3-month Eurodollar futures and long-term USD bond futures. In this case an adjustment has to be made for the difference in maturity of the underlying instrument. Settlement on the short-term futures relates to a 90-day instrument, while settlement on the bond futures relates to a notional 15-year bond. For a given change in yield therefore, there will be a far greater profit or loss on the bond futures than on the short-term futures. To balance this, the trader would buy or sell a much smaller notional amount of the bond futures than of the short-term futures.

Cross-market spread

A spread can similarly be taken on the difference between two markets. For example, if sterling interest rates are above dollar rates and a trader believes that the spread between them will narrow, he could sell sterling FRAs and buy dollar FRAs, or buy sterling futures and sell dollar futures.

Arbitrage

Because FRAs and futures are essentially the same instrument traded in different ways, there is a straightforward arbitrage between them if prices move out of line - either buy a FRA and buy futures, or sell a FRA and sell futures.

Because of the close link between the two instruments, and the fact that dealers will hedge positions in one against the other, FRAs are often dealt to coincide with futures dates - that is, with effective dates on the third Wednesday of March, June, September or December and a forward period of 3 months. These futures dates are known as IMM dates, after the IMM, the oldest financial futures exchange.

Example : It is mid-March and rates for US dollars are as follows:

3v6 FRA: 4.75/4.80%

June futures: 95.17/95.18

A dealer buys a USD 1 million 3v6 FRA at 4.80% and at the same time he buys 1 futures contract at 95.18. The implied interest rate of the futures contract is 4.82%. The dealer has therefore locked in a profit of 2 basis points.

There are at least two possible problems for the dealer, even if the effective date of the FRA exactly matches the futures date. Firstly, if interest rates rise at all significantly, he will make a profit on the FRA and a loss on the futures contract. The profit will be discounted to a present value but the loss will not be. The loss will also arise earlier (because of the mechanics of variation margin payments), which effectively increases the value of the loss even further.

Secondly, if interest rates fall, he will make a loss on the FRA and a profit on the futures. If the FRA is for a 3-month period of, say, 92 days, this would magnify the loss compared to the futures profit which is based effectively on 90 days.

Either of these effects could offset his apparent profit of 2 basis points.

Arbitraging and creating FRAs

It is possible to make use of FRAs and futures in covering forward FX positions, and also to construct synthetically an FRA in one currency from an FRA in another. These topics are covered in the FX section, in Chapter 9.

Exercises

1. Based on the following cash market rates for Swedish kronor, what is the theoretical rate at which a dealer would take a 6v9 forward-forward deposit from a customer?

3 months (91 days): 4.87/5.00%

6 months (182 days): 5.12/5.25%

9 months (273 days): 5.00/5.12%

2. On Friday, you lend EUR 10 million for 1 week at 4.3% and borrow the same amount overnight at 4.25%. What is the break-even rate for the remaining period?

3. You sold a 2v5 GBP 2,000,000 FRA when rates were quoted to you as 7.30/7.40%. Settlement is now due and 3-month (91 days) GBP LIBOR is 7.15%. What amount do you pay or receive?

4. You are a dealer. You are given a deposit of EUR 7 million at 4.9% for 9 months (273 days). You also lend EUR 7 million at 4.9% for 3 months (92 days). You cover the mismatch with a 3v9 FRA, quoted to, you as 4.80/4.85%.

a. Do you buy or sell the FRA?

b. At what price do you deal?

c. What notional principal amount do you deal for the FRA, assuming that you wish to match your exposure as closely as possible and that you can deal exactly the right amount?

d. When the time comes to settle the FRA, the 6-month interest rate is 4.95%/5.05%. What is the settlement amount on the FRA, and who pays whom?

e. You always borrow at LIBOR and lend at LIBID. What is your overall cash profit or loss in euros at the end of nine months?

5. You sell 10 December euro futures contracts at 95.32. In which direction do you expect euro interest rates to move? You buy them back at 95.43. What is your profit or loss?

6. It is now the middle of March. You fund yourself at LIBOR flat and need to borrow euros for 9 months. What is the cheapest way of achieving this, given the following rates?

3-month cash: 5.10/5.20%

6-month cash: 5.25/5.35%

9-month cash: 5.35/5.45%

3v6 FRA: 5.34/5.39%

3v9 FRA: 5.42/5.47%

6v9 FRA: 5.40/5.45%

June futures: 94.60/94.61

September futures: 94.57/94.58

7. It is now the middle of October. You are a dealer and sell

a 7v12 FRA to a customer. Which futures contracts might you use to hedge your position?

8. You have taken a deposit from one customer for 6 months and lent to another for 3 months. Assuming all the dates match, what is the best hedge for the mismatched position, given the following prices available to you?

3v6 FRA: 6.51/6.56%

futures: 93.50/93.51

9. It is now the middle of April. What is the theoretical 2v8 FRA rate in US dollars consistent with the following futures prices?

March: 95.23

June: 95.61

September: 95.84

December: 95.93

10 It is now March and the yield curve is negative. You expect it to become less negative over the next few months but have no view on whether interest rates will rise or fall overall. What might be an appropriate trading strategy?

4

Foreign Exchange

SPOT FOREIGN EXCHANGE

A *spot* transaction is a straightforward purchase or sale of one currency against another. For an end-user, such a transaction is generally used simply for converting one currency to another. For example, if an industrial company in the UK has received US dollars for its exports to the USA, it probably needs to convert them to sterling, which it will do using a spot transaction.

Banks and other financial institutions, however, often use the spot market for *speculation* – that is, deliberately taking a risk in the hope of making a profit. For example, a German bank (with the euro as its domestic currency) might believe that the Japanese yen will strengthen during the day. It will therefore undertake a spot transaction to buy yen against euros. As it does not actually need the yen, it will sell them back again into euros later the same day, so that there is no net inflow or outflow of yen, other than possibly a profit or loss between the two transactions.

Some banks present themselves to the market as *market makers*. This means that they are prepared to quote a spot price for buying and selling, to anyone who asks (as long as they are creditworthy) – both customers and other financial institutions.

In practice, the market is of course less segmented than this. Individ-uals and corporate users also take speculative positions. Conversely, banks also use spot transactions to convert cash into another currency other than for speculation. Also, a bank which deals with a customer at the customer's request – for example, selling Australian dollars to the customer – has created a risk for itself. If it wishes to remove this risk, it will *close* the position by buying the same amount of Australian dollars from another bank, in another transaction.

The value date

A *spot* transaction is for delivery two working days after the dealing date (the date on which the contract is made). This allows time for the necessary paperwork and cash transfers to be arranged. Normally therefore, if a spot deal is contracted on Monday, Tuesday or Wednesday, delivery will be two days after (i.e. Wednesday, Thursday or Friday respectively). If a spot deal is contracted on a Thursday or Friday, the delivery date is generally on Monday or Tuesday respec-tively, as neither Saturday nor Sunday are working days in the major markets.

There are, however, some exceptions. For example, a price for the US dollar against the Canadian dollar in the professional interbank market generally implies delivery on the next working day after the dealing day. This is referred to as *funds* rather than spot. A spot price (value two working days after the dealing day, as usual) can generally be requested as an alternative. The rate for the US dollar against the Hong Kong dollar is also often traded for value the next working day. The US dollar/ Turkish lira rate is generally traded for value on either the same day as the deal is done, or the next day. A problem arises in trading Middle East currencies where the relevant markets are closed on Friday but open on Saturday. A spot deal on Wednesday between the US dollar and the Saudi riyal, for example, would need to have a split settlement date: the dollars would be settled on Friday, but the riyals on Saturday.

If the spot date falls on a public holiday in one or both of the centers of the two currencies involved, the next working day is taken as the value date. For example, if a spot deal between sterling and the US dollar is transacted on Thursday 31 August, it would normally be for value Monday 4 September. If this date is a holiday in the UK or the USA, however, all spot transactions on Thursday 31 August are for value Tuesday 5 September. If the intervening day (between today and spot) is a holiday in one of the two centers, the spot value date is again usually delayed by one day. The recognized opening and closing times for the foreign exchange market each week are 5:00 a.m. Monday, Sydney time and 5:00 p.m. Friday, New York time.

HOW SPOT RATES ARE QUOTED

Base currency and variable currency

Throughout this book, we have generally used ISO codes (also used by the SWIFT system) to abbreviate currency names. You can find a list of the codes in Appendix C.

Spot foreign exchange

In the spot market, a variable number of units of one currency is quoted per one unit of another currency. In this book, we have used the usual convention that, for example, the US dollar/ Japanese yen exchange rate is written as 'USD/JPY' if it refers to the number of yen equal to 1 US dollar but as 'JPY/USD' if it refers to the number of US dollars equal to 1 yen. The currency code written on the left is the *base* currency; there is always 1 of the base unit.

The currency code written on the right is the *variable* currency (or *counter* currency or *quoted* currency); the number of units of this currency equal to 1 of the base currency varies according to the exchange rate.

When quoting against the euro, it is the practice in the interbank market to quote all currencies in terms of a varying number of units of that currency per 1 euro. In other words, the euro is, by convention, always the base currency if it is one of the two currencies involved. Similarly, apart from the euro, it is the interbank convention to quote all currencies against sterling using sterling as the base currency. Again, apart from the euro, sterling, Australian dollar and New Zealand dollar, all rates against the US dollar are always quoted interbank with the US dollar as the base currency.

The Canadian dollar is generally quoted as the variable currency against the US dollar, although the other way round is possible.

In the currency futures markets, as opposed to the interbank market, quotations against the USD usually have USD as the variable currency.

In other cases, there is not a universal convention for which way round to quote a cross-rate – that is, which is the base currency and which the variable currency.

Cross-rates

Although dealing is possible between any two convertible curren-cies – for example, New Zealand dollars against euros or Swiss francs against Japanese yen – the interbank market has historically quoted mostly against US dollars, so reducing the number of individual rates that needed to be quoted. The exchange rate between any two non-US dollar currencies could then be calculated from the rate for each currency against US dollars. Such a rate between any two currencies, neither of which is the dollar, is known as a cross-rate.

Some of these cross-rates (for example, euro/sterling, euro/yen, euro/Swiss franc) have, however, increasingly been traded between banks in addition to the dollar-based rates. This sometimes reflects the importance of the relationship between the pair of currencies. The economic relationship between the Swiss franc and the euro, for example, is closer than the relationship between the Swiss franc and the dollar. It is therefore more true nowadays to say that the dollar/franc exchange rate is a function of the euro/dollar rate and the euro/franc rate, rather than that the euro/franc rate is a function of the euro/dollar rate and the dollar/franc rate. The principle of calculating one rate from two others remains the same, however. The calculations are explained below.

Bid and offer rates

As in other markets, a bank normally quotes a two-way price, whereby it indicates both at what level it is prepared to buy the base currency against the variable currency (the *bid* for the base currency - a cheaper rate), and at what level it is prepared to sell the base currency against the variable currency (the *offer* of the base currency - a more expensive rate). For example, if a bank is prepared to buy 1 US dollar for 1.6375 Swiss francs, and sell 1 US dollar for 1.6385 Swiss francs, the USD/CHF rate would be quoted as '1.6375/1.6385'.

In the spot market, the price is always quoted so that the quoting bank buys the base currency on the left. This is the quoting bank's bid for the base currency, which is the lower number. Similarly, the quoting bank always sells the base currency - its offer for the base currency, which is the higher number - on the right. If the bank quotes such a rate to a company or other counterparty, the counterparty would sell the base currency on the left, and buy the base currency on the right - the opposite of how the bank itself sees the deal. The universal rule is that the party quoting the price deals on the side which is more advantageous to it, while the party asking for the price - if it decides to deal - is obliged to deal on the side which is less advantageous to it.

As the market moves very quickly, dealers need to deal with great speed and therefore abbreviate when dealing. For example, if one dealer wishes to buy USD 5 million from another who is quoting him a USD/CHF price, he will say simply "5 mine"; this means "I wish to buy from you 5 million of the base currency and sell the other currency, at your offered price". Similarly, if he wishes to sell USD 5 million, he will say simply "5 yours", meaning "I wish to sell you 5 million of the base currency and buy the other currency, at your bid price".

Spot foreign exchange

Bank A wishes to buy EUR 5 million. The quoting bank will therefore be selling EUR, the base currency. If Bank A chooses to deal on either of these prices, it will therefore deal on the right side. Bank A is therefore looking for the most attractive right side price, which in this case is Bank B's price at 0.9354.

Bank B therefore replies "Nothing thanks." to Bank C and replies "5 mine" to Bank B. He has then bought EUR 5 million from Bank B at 0.9354.

The difference between the two sides of the quotation is known as the *spread* and represents the dealer's profit for being willing to take the risk of quoting prices to other parties. Historically, a two-way price in a cross-rate would have a wider spread than a two-way price in a dollar-based rate, because the cross-rate constructed from the dollar-based rates would combine both the spreads. Now, however, the spread in say a euro/Swiss franc price might be proportion-ally narrower than a dollar/franc spread, because it is more the euro/franc price that is driving the market, as noted above, than the dollar/franc price.

Dealers generally operate on the basis of small percentage profits but large turnover. These rates will be good for large, round amounts. For very large amounts, or for smaller amounts, a bank would normally quote a wider spread. The amount for which a quotation is *good* (i.e. a valid quote on which the dealer will deal) will vary to some extent with the currency concerned and market conditions.

Rates are often quoted to 1/100th of a cent etc. (known as a *point* or a *pip*). For example, the US dollar/Swiss franc rate would usually be quoted to four decimal places - for example, "1.5375/1.5385". This depends on the size of the number, however, and in the case of USD/JPY, for example, which might be quoted say "105.05/105.15", "15 points" means 0.15 yen. One point is thus one unit of the last decimal place quoted.

As the first three digits of the exchange rate (known as the *big figure*) do not change in the short term, dealers generally do not mention them when dealing in the interbank market. In the example above (1.6375/1.6385) the quotation would therefore be given as simply "75/85". However, when dealers are quoting a rate to a corpo-rate client they will often mention the big figure also. In this case, the quotation would be "1.6375/55".

If the bid and offer prices are close to a round number, it can sometimes appear that the right side is smaller than the left side. For example, the price might be abbreviated as "1.6395/05". This in fact means "1.6395/1.6405" and might be expressed as "Ninety-five/o five, around one sixty-four". Similarly, a price of "1.6390/00" means "1.6390/1.6400" and might be expressed as "One sixty-three, ninety/the figure", where "the figure" means "00".

Some more terminology

A *long* position is a surplus of purchases over sales of a given currency – i.e., a position which benefits from a strengthening of that currency. Similarly, a *short* position is a surplus of sales over purchases of a given currency, which benefits from a weakening of that currency. A *square* position is one which is neither long nor short – i.e. one in which the sales and purchases are equal.

A *yard* of a currency is an American billion units of that currency (i.e. 1,000,000,000 units).

Cable is a nickname for the sterling/US dollar exchange rate.

If one party asks another for a two-way price and then chooses to deal on the bid side of the price, he is said to *hit* the bid. If he chooses to deal on the offer side of the price, he is said to *lift* the offer. Occasionally a dealer will narrow the bid/offer spread to zero – i.e. he will quote a single price and the party asking for the price can choose whether he will buy or sell at that price. This is known as a *choice* price.

If a dealer quoting puts his price *under reference,* it means that the counterparty must ask again for a reconfirmation of the price before dealing on it.

If a party who has asked for a price says "My risk", he is acknowl-edging that the price may change before he has accepted it – generally because he knows that he may not be able to respond immediately as to whether or not he will choose to deal on the price. If a dealer says "Off!", he means that the last price he quoted is no longer valid.

POSITION-KEEPING

To earn profit from dealing, the bank's objective is clearly to sell the base currency at the highest rate it can against the variable currency and buy the base currency at the lowest rate.

Example : You are a dealer and are long of USD 4 million against CHF at 1.6612. You want to close this position because you expect the dollar to weaken.

You therefore ask another bank for a USD/CHF price and are quoted 1.6610/15. You decide that you will deal on this price. You need to sell US dollars, so that the quoting dealer is buying dollars, the base currency. You therefore hit his bid at 1.6610. You have a net loss of CHF 800:

Example : You have the same original situation as in the previous example. This time, however, another bank calls you to ask for a price. The market is currently 1.6610/15. What price should you quote in order to encourage the other bank to buy dollars from you, so that your position will be squared up, which is what you want?

You hope that the other dealer will lift your offer and not hit your bid. You should therefore show him a two-way price with a more attractive offer than the market generally, but an unattractive bid. You might therefore quote, say, 1.6608/13 to encourage him to deal at 1.6613.

At any time, a dealer needs to know what is his position resulting from the net of all the deals he has undertaken during the day so far. He also needs to know what is the average exchange rate of this net position, so that he can compare it with the current market rate to see whether or not the position is profitable. At the end of the day, he might not close out the position, but will in that case need to *mark to market* the position – i.e. calculate the unrealized profit or loss on the position so far. This is achieved by calculating what the profit or loss would be if he did in fact close out the position out at the current rate (i.e. the end-of-day closing market rate).

The position is therefore long USD 2 million. The average rate is 1.67425. The loss is CHF 2,500. This loss could be expressed in US dollars by converting it into US dollars at the spot rate, or in any other currency by converting it at the appropriate spot rate.

RECIPROCAL RATES

Any quotation with a particular currency as the base currency can be converted into the equivalent quotation with that currency as the variable currency by taking its reciprocal. Thus a USD/CHF quotation of 1.4375/1.4385 can be converted to a CHF/USD quotation of (1 -*i*- 1.4375)/(1 -*i*- 1.4385). However, this would still be quoted with a smaller number on the left, so that the two sides of the quotation are reversed: 0.6952/0.6957. In every case, the bank buys the base currency against the variable currency on the left, and sells the base currency against the variable currency on the right.

CROSS-RATE CALCULATIONS

As mentioned earlier, it is often necessary to calculate an exchange rate between two currencies from two other rates, because only a small proportion of possible currency pairs are regularly traded interbank. Frequently, but not always, it is the dollar-based rates which serve as the starting point for these calculations.

Example : Given the following rates, what is the CAD/CHF rate?

USD/CHF: 1.6348/53

USD/CAD: 1.5497/02

The left side (i.e. the bid side) of the resulting CAD/CHF rate is where the quoting bank buys CAD and sells CHF. The bank's USD/CAD dealer buys CAD (the same as selling USD) on the right side of his own price - i.e. 1.5502. The banks USD/CHF dealer sells CHF (the same as buying USD) on the left side of his own price - i.e. 1.6348.

Each USD 1 is worth CAD 1.5502 and is also worth CHF 1.6348. Therefore the rate between CAD and CHF is the ratio between these two numbers:

1.6348 -*i*- 1.5502 = 1.05457

1.0546 is therefore the left side of the resulting CAD/CHF price. Similarly, the right side is derived from the right side of the USD/CHF price and the left side of the USD/CAD price:

1.6353 -*i*- 1.5497 = 1.05524

The CAD/CHF price is therefore 1.0546/52. Note that in prac-tice a dealer would probably round down the left price (to 1.0545 in this example) and round up the right price (to 1.0553) to ensure that he does not make a loss. For simplicity however, we have used normal rounding rules in this book.

In summary, to calculate a spot rate from two other rates which share the same base currency (in our example this was USD), divide opposite sides of the exchange rates. Following the same logic shows that to calculate a spot rate from two other rates which share the same variable currency (in the following example this is also USD), we again need to divide opposite sides of the exchange rates:

Example : Given the following rates, what is the GBP/NZD rate?

GBP/USD: 1.4320/25

NZD/USD: 0.4460/65

The left side (i.e. the bid side) of the resulting GBP/NZD rate is where the quoting bank buys GBP and sells NZD. The bank's GBP/USD dealer buys GBP on the left side of his own price - i.e. 1.4320. The banks NZD/USD dealer sells NZD on the right side of his own price - i.e. 0.4465.

Each GBP 1 is worth USD 1.4320. Each NZD 1 is worth USD 0.4465. Therefore the rate between GBP and NZD is the ratio between these two numbers:

1.4320 -*i*- 0.4465 = 3.2072

3.2072 is therefore the left side of the resulting GBP/NZD price. Similarly, the right side is derived from the right side of the

GBP/USD price and the left side of the NZD/USD price:

1.4325 -*i*- 0.4460 = 3.2119

The GBP/NZD price is therefore 3.2072/19

Finally, to calculate a cross-rate from two rates where the common currency is the base currency in one quotation but the variable currency in the other, following the same logic through shows that we multiply the same sides of the exchange rates:

Example : Given the following rates, what is the GBP/CHF rate?

GBP/USD: 1.4320/25

USD/CHF: 1.6348/53

The left side (i.e. the bid side) of the resulting GBP/CHF rate is where the quoting bank buys GBP and sells CHF. The bank's GBP/USD dealer buys GBP on the left side of his own price - i.e. 1.4320. The banks USD/CHF dealer sells CHF (the same as buying USD) on the left side of his own price - i.e. 1.6348.

Each GBP 1 is worth USD 1.4320. Each of these USD is worth CHF 1.6348. Therefore the rate between GBP and CHF is the product of these two numbers:

1.4320 x 1.6348 = 2.3410

2.3410 is therefore the left side of the resulting GBP/CHF price. Similarly, the right side is derived from the right side of the GBP/USD price and the right side of the USD/CHF price:

1.4325 x 1.6353 = 2.3426

The GBP/CHF price is therefore 2.3410/26

To calculate an exchange rate by combining two others

From two rates with the same base currency or the same variable currency: divide opposite sides of the exchange rates. See the next box for deciding which exchange rate to divide by which

From two rates where the base currency in one is the same as the variable currency in the other: multiply the same sides of the exchange rates.

The construction of one exchange rate from two others in this way can be seen algebraically:

Given two exchange rates *A/B* and *A/C*, they can be combined as follows:

$B/C = A/C + \% A/B$

Given two exchange rates B/A and C/A, they can be combined as follows:

$B/C = B/A + C/A$

Given two exchange rates B/A and A/C, they can be combined as follows:

$B/C = B/A \times A/C$

and $C/B = 1$ -^ $(B/A \times A/C)$

When dividing, use opposite sides. When multiplying, use the same sides.

The examples above all construct exchange rates from two other rates involving the US dollar (which is often the case). The same approach applies when constructing any rate from any other two rates. Considering the way in which each of the two separate dealers will deal to create the combined rate, gives the construction:

THE MARKET ENVIRONMENT

It is useful to have an idea of the size of the foreign exchange market. The total average daily volume of transactions worldwide is around USD 1,200 billion. Of this total, only a tiny proportion represents deals to convert the cashflows of international commercial trade; the vast majority represents position-taking and financial flows.

Around 32% of the total is spot transactions and 68% is forward swaps and outrights (covered in the next chapter). By far the largest turnover – around one third of the total world volume – takes place in the London market, followed by New York in second place and Tokyo in third place. Around 57% of the total volume involves cross-border transactions – i.e. deals where the two banks are in different countries.

As has been the case historically, around 90% of all transactions involve the US dollar as one of the two currencies. Other important traded currencies, in decreasing order of volume, are the euro, the yen and sterling. The Swiss franc, Canadian dollar and Australian dollar are also traded in reasonable volume.

5

Forward Outrights and Swaps

At the end of this chapter, we have summarized the uses of the various instruments described in it. You might find it useful to glance through this summary before reading the rest of the chapter.

FORWARD OUTRIGHTS

Although *spot* is settled 2 working days in the future, it is not considered in the foreign exchange market as 'future' or 'forward', but as the baseline from which all other dates (earlier or later) are considered.

An *outright* is an outright purchase or sale of one currency in exchange for another currency for settlement on a fixed date other than the spot value date. Rates are quoted in a similar way to those in the spot market, with the quoting bank buying the base currency on the left side and selling it on the right side. The term *short date* (see later in this chapter) is used for settlement on a date other than spot but less than 1 month after spot, and the term *forward outright* is therefore generally reserved for settlement later than that- i.e. at least one month after spot - although short dates are really only a particular range of forward outrights.

The spread (the difference between the bank's buying price and the bank's selling price) is wider in the forward outright quotation than in the spot quotation. Also, in this example, the dollar is worth less for delivery in the future than for delivery on the spot date. USD 1 buys CHF 1.7144 in 3 months' time, as opposed to CHF 1.7166 spot. In a different example, the dollar might be worth more for delivery in the future than on the spot date.

Where does the forward outright rate come from?

The forward outright rate may be seen both as the market's assess-ment of where the spot rate will be in the future and as a reflection of current interest rates in the two currencies concerned.

Consider, for example, the following round-trip transactions, all undertaken simultaneously: (i) Borrow Swiss francs for 3 months starting from spot value date. (ii) Sell the Swiss francs and buy dollars for value spot. (iii) Deposit the purchased dollars for 3 months starting from spot value date. (iv) Sell forward now the dollar principal and interest which mature in 3 months' time, into Swiss francs; use these Swiss francs to repay the borrowing in (i).

In general, the market will adjust the forward price for (iv) so that these simultaneous transactions generate neither a profit nor a loss. When the four rates involved are not in line (Swiss franc interest rate, USD/CHF spot rate, dollar interest rate and USD/CHF forward rate), there is in fact opportunity for making a profit by round-tripping. That is, either the transactions as shown above will produce a profit, or exactly the reverse transactions (borrow dollars, sell dollars spot, deposit Swiss francs and sell Swiss francs forward) will produce a profit. The supply and demand effect of this arbitrage activity is such as to move the rates back into line. If in fact this results in a forward rate which is out of line with the market's average view, supply and demand pressure will tend to move the spot rate or the interest rates until this is no longer the case.

Forward outright prices can be quoted as two-way prices in the same way as other prices. One could use the bank's bid rate for the spot, its offered rate for sterling (5.20%) and its bid rate for dollars (4.30%) in the above example, to calculate the price where the bank buys sterling from the customer against dollars for delivery in 6 months' time, and use the bank's offered rate for spot, its bid rate for sterling (5.10%) and its offered rate for dollars (4.40%) to determine the other side of the price, as in the following example.

In minor markets where the price does need to be constructed and hedged in this way, this calculation might be necessary. In a well-established market, however, this would generally produce a rather larger bid/offer spread than is realistic. In this case, it might be better to use middle prices throughout to calculate a middle price, as in Example 2, and then to spread the two-way price around this middle price. In practice, a dealer does not recalculate forward prices continually in any case, but takes them from the market just as the spot dealer takes spot prices.

FORWARD SWAPS

Forward outrights are an important instrument because they enable a bank's customer to lock in an exchange rate for the future. However, trading banks generally do not deal between themselves in forward outrights, but rather in forward *swaps,* where a forward swap is the difference between the spot and the forward outright. The reason for not dealing in outrights will become clear later. The forward outright rate can therefore be seen as a combination of the current spot rate and the forward swap rate added together.

Forward outright = spot + forward swap

It is important to note that the forward swap is sometimes positive and sometimes negative. As we shall see, this depends on which of the two currencies involved has higher interest rates. As with spot prices and outright prices, swap prices are quoted as two-way prices.

Discounts and premiums

When the base currency interest rate is lower than the variable currency rate, the forward outright exchange rate is always greater than the spot rate. That is, the base currency is worth more units of the variable currency for delivery forward than it is for delivery spot. This can be seen as compensating for the lower interest rate: if I deposit money in the variable currency rather than the base currency, I will receive more interest. However, if I sell forward the maturing deposit amount, in an attempt to lock in this advantage, the forward exchange rate is correspondingly worse so I lose the advantage. In this case, the base currency is said to be at a *premium* to the variable currency, and the forward swap price must be positive. At the same time, the variable currency is said to be at a *discount* to the base currency.

The reverse also follows. In general, given two currencies, the currency with the higher interest rate is at a discount (worth fewer units of the other currency forward than spot) and the currency with the lower interest rate is at a premium (worth more units of the other currency forward than spot). When the base currency is at a premium to the variable currency (and the variable currency is at a discount to the base currency), the forward swap price is positive; when the base currency is at a discount (and the variable currency is at a premium), the forward swap price is negative.

When the swap price is positive, and the forward dealer applies a bid/offer spread to make a two-way swap price, the left price is smaller than the right price as usual. When the swap price is negative, he must similarly quote a more negative number on the left and a more positive number on the right in order to make a profit. This can be seen in Example 5 above, where the swap price was -0.0058/-0.0044.

However, the minus sign '-' is generally not shown. The result is that, when the swap price is negative, the larger number appears to be on the left. As a result, whenever the swap price appears larger on the left than the right, it is in fact negative, and must be subtracted from the swap rate rather than added.

Swap prices are generally quoted as points, in such a way that the last digit of the swap points coincides with the same decimal place as the last digit of the spot price. For example, if the spot price is quoted to 4 decimal places - say 1.7166 - and the swap price is 120 points, this means a swap price of 0.0120. If the spot price is quoted to 2 decimal places - say 171.66 - and the swap price is 120 points, this means a swap price of 1.20.

The currency with the higher interest rate is at a discount and the currency with the lower interest rate is at a premium.

When the base currency is at a premium and the variable currency is at a discount, the forward swap points are positive and the left price appears smaller than the right price. When the base currency is at a discount and the variable currency is at a premium, the forward swap points are negative and the left price appears bigger than the right price.

Example

euro interest rate: 4%

dollar interest rate: 5%

yen interest rate: 1%

The euro is at a premium to the dollar The dollar is at a discount to the euro The forward swap points for EUR/USD are positive The dollar is at a discount to the yen The yen is at a premium to the dollar The forward swap points for USD/JPY are negative

If a forward swap price includes the word *par* it means that the spot rate and the forward outright rate are the same: par in this case represents zero. *A/P* is *around par*, meaning that the left-hand side of the swap must be subtracted from spot and the right-hand side added. This happens when the two interest rates are the same or very similar.

The swap price in Example 9 would often be written as -6/+4, which means the same as 6/4 A/P but indicates the price more clearly.

It is important to be careful about the terminology regarding premiums and discounts. The clearest terminology, for example, is to say that "the euro is at a premium to the dollar" or that "the dollar is at a discount to the euro"; there is then no ambiguity. If, however, a London dealer says that "the EUR/USD is at a discount", he generally means that the variable currency, the dollar, is at a discount and that the swap points are to be added to the spot. Similarly, if he says that "the GBP/JPY is at a premium", he means that the variable currency, the yen, is at a premium and that the points are to be subtracted from the spot. If there is no qualification, he is generally referring to the variable currency, not the base currency. This is not the same in all countries, however, so beware! It is better to avoid this terminology and always explain which of the two currencies is meant when referring to premiums and discounts.

What is a forward swap deal?

In order to see why a bank trades in forward swaps rather than forward outrights, consider how the following swap and outright rates change as the spot rate and interest rates.

Amovement of 100 points in the exchange rate from 1.7100 to 1.7200 has affected the forward swap price only slightly (by 1 point). A change in the interest rate differential from 3.0% to 2.5%, however, has changed it significantly. Essentially, a forward swap is an interest rate instrument rather than a currency instrument: when a bank takes a forward swap position, it is taking an interest rate view rather than a currency view. If bank dealers traded outrights, they would be combining two related but different markets in one deal, which is less satisfactory.

So far, we have seen what the swap price is only as a number to be added to or subtracted from the spot rate in order to achieve the outright rate. However, the forward swap is also an instrument in its own right. The swap deal itself is an exchange of one currency for another currency on one date, to be reversed on a given future date. A swap deal is therefore always a deal to 'sell and buy' or 'buy and sell' a currency - i.e., to sell it for settlement spot and buy it back forsettlement forward, or vice versa. The following example shows how this fits into the construction of a forward outright. Then we consider what the swap is on its own.

Example: A bank sells dollars 3 months forward outright to a counterparty, against Swiss francs.

The customer in the example above thinks of the deal as a single deal, with a single price, for a single settlement and receives only one confirmation, for the forward outright settlement. However, internally, the deal is split between the spot dealer's trading book and the forward dealer's trading book.

When a bank quotes a swap rate, it quotes in a similar manner to a spot rate: the bank's forward dealer buys the base currency forward on the left (at the same time as selling it spot), and sells the base currency forward on the right (at the same time as buying it spot).

The quoting bank always 'sells and buys' (in that order) the base currency on the left and 'buys and sells' the base currency on the right.

A forward foreign exchange swap viewed on its own, rather than as part of an outright, is therefore a temporary purchase or sale of one currency against another. An equivalent effect could be achieved by borrowing one currency for a given period, while lending the other currency for the same period. This is why the approximate formula shown earlier for the swap points reflects the interest rate differential (generally based on Eurocurrency interest rates rather than domestic interest rates) between the two currencies, converted into foreign exchange terms.

Suppose that a forward dealer has undertaken a similar deal to the one above - bought and sold dollars (in that order) - but as a speculative position, rather than in order to provide an outright to a customer. In this case, what interest rate view has he taken? He has effectively borrowed dollars and lent Swiss francs for the period. He probably expects US interest rates to rise (so that he can relend them at a higher rate) and/or Swiss rates to fall (so that he can reborrow them at a lower rate). In fact the important point is that the interest differential should move in the dollar's favour. For example, even if US interest rates fall rather than rise, the dealer will still make a profit as long as Swiss rates fall even more than dollar rates.

Although only one single price is dealt (the swap price), the swap transaction has two separate settlements: (i) A settlement on the spot value date (ii) A settlement on the forward value date

There is no net outright position taken, and the spot dealer's spread will therefore not be involved, but some benchmark spot rate will nevertheless be needed in order to arrive at the settlement rates. As the swap is a representation of the interest rate differential between the two currencies quoted, as long as the near and far sides of the swap settlement preserve this differential, it does not generally make a significant difference which exact spot rate is used as a base for adding or subtracting the swap points. The rate must, however, generally be a current rate. This is discussed further below - see the section on 'Historic rate rollovers' and also Chapter 10.

Example : At the moment, 3-month dollar interest rates are higher than 3-month sterling rates. You expect this difference to narrow. Rates are quoted to you as follows:

GBP/USD spot: 1.4752/58

3-month swap: 80/86.

You 'buy and sell' GBP 5 million (which is also selling and buying dollars), spot against 3 months. This is equivalent to borrowing sterling and at the same time lending dollars. This will make you a profit if rates move as you expect: for example, if sterling rates rise, you could lend out the sterling at a higher rate, or if dollar rates fall, you could borrow the dollars at a lower rate.

You therefore deal at 80 points because the bank quoting the price 'sells and buys' the base currency on the left. You agree a settlement rate for spot as say 1.4755 (the mid-rate). Therefore the two legs of the swap are settled at 1.4755 and 1.4835 (=1.4755 + 0.0080):

However, this does not take account of the time value of money (see Chapter 2). Assuming that there are 91 days in the 3-month period and that the 3-month dollar interest rate is 5%, the NPV. A dealer expecting the interest rate differential to move in favour of the base currency (for example, base currency interest rates to rise or variable currency interest rates to fall) will 'buy and sell' the base currency. This is equivalent to borrowing the base currency and depositing in the variable currency. And vice versa.

Valuation of a swap book

In Example 11, we valued the result of two swaps, where the second swap neatly offset the first. In practice, a dealer will have many swaps on his book, resulting in many cashflows in different currencies on different dates. The entire book can be valued by calculating the present value of each cashflow separately and then adding up all the present values - some positive and some negative - including those of the cashflows in the dealer's home currency, to calculate a *net present value (NPV).*

Historic rate rollovers

We have mentioned above that the settlement rates (spot and forward) for a forward swap deal must generally be based on a current market spot rate. This is because many central banks require that banks under their supervision use only current rates, except in occasional and well-documented circumstances. The following example illus-trates why a corporate customer might wish to use a historic rate rather than a current rate, and the effect.

Example: In June, a US company sells USD 1 million forward outright for value 15 August against Swiss francs, at a forward outright rate of 1.7250. This deal is done to cover the cost the company expects to pay for Swiss imports. On 13 August, the company realizes that it will not need to pay the Swiss francs to its supplier until a month later. It therefore rolls over the foreign exchange cover by using a forward swap - buying and selling dollars, spot against one month. On 13 August, the exchange rates are as follows:

USD/CHF spot: 1.8166/71

31-day swap: 20/22

The company therefore buys and sells dollars at 1.8168 (spot) and 1.8168 + 0.0020= 1.8188 (forward). The company's cashflows will then be:

15 August	15 September
sell USD 1,000,000	
buy CHF 1,725,000	
buy USD 1,000,000	sell USD 1,000,000
sell CHF 1,816.800	buy CHF 1,818,800
Net:	sell USD 1,000,000
sell CHF 91,800	buy CHF 1,818,800

The overall net result is that the company sells USD 1 million against CHF 1,727,000 (=CHF 1,818,800 — CHF 91,800) - an all-in rate of 1.7270, which is effectively the original rate dealt of 1.7250 adjusted by the swap price of 20 points. The company might, however, have a cashflow problem on 15 August, because there is a cash outflow then of CHF 91,800.

The company might therefore prefer to request the bank to base the swap on the historic rate of 1.7250 - dealing instead at 1.7250 spot and 1.7270 forward. The cashflows would then be:

15 August	15 September
sell USD 1,000,000	
buy CHF 1,725,000	
buy USD 1,000,000	sell USD 1,000,000
sell CHF 1,725,000	buy CHF 1,727,000
Net:	sell USD 1,000,000
buy CHF 1,727,000	

The overall net result is the same as before, but there is no cashflow problem.

Underlying this arrangement, however, is an effective loan from the bank to the company of CHF 91,800 for 31 days. If the bank is, exceptionally, prepared to base the swap on a historic rate in this way, it needs to charge the company interest on this hidden loan. This interest would normally be incorporated into a less favourable swap price.

The reason many central banks discourage historic rate rollovers is that they might help a bank's customer to conceal foreign exchange losses. If a customer has taken a speculative position which has made a loss, a historic rate rollover enables it to roll the loss over to a later date rather than realize it.

As a result, if a bank does agree to a historic rate rollover, it must generally insist that the reasons be agreed between senior manage-ment of the customer and the bank, with appropriate documentary evidence of this.

SHORT DATES

For convenience, we have repeated here a short part of the intro-ductory chapter. Value dates earlier than 1 month are referred to as *short dates.* There are certain regular dates usually quoted, and the terminology used is the same as in the deposit market, as follows:

Overnight (O/N): a deposit or foreign exchange swap from today until tomorrow

Tom-next (T/N): a deposit or foreign exchange swap from tomorrow until the next day (spot)

Spot-next (S/N): a deposit or foreign exchange swap from spot

until the next day *Spot-a-week (S/W)*: a deposit or foreign exchange swap from spot until a week later

'Tomorrow' means the next working day after today and 'next' means the next working day following (i.e. spot).

Outright deals (as opposed to swaps) are referred to as 'value today', 'value tomorrow', etc.

Deals cannot always be done for value today. For example, when London and European markets are open, Japanese banks have gener-ally closed their books for today, so deals in yen can only be done for value tomorrow. Similarly in London, most European currencies can only be dealt early in the morning for value today, because of the time difference and the mechanical difficulties of ensuring good value. For many currencies, even the market for value tomorrow generally closes during the morning.

In considering swaps and outrights for short dates later than the spot date, exactly the same rules apply as in calculating longer dates. However, confusion can arise in considering outrights for dates earlier than spot-i.e., outright value today and outright value tomorrow. The rules are still the same in that the bank always 'sells and buys' (in that order) the base currency on the left and 'buys and sells' the base currency on the right - regardless of whether it is before or after spot. The confusion can arise because the spot value date - effectively the baseline date for calculation of the outright rate - is the near date when calculating most forward prices. For value today and tomorrow, however, the spot date becomes the far date and the outright date is the near date.

Example : *A* bank sells dollars for outright value tomorrow to a counter-party, against Swiss francs. The bank can be seen as creating the outright in the following way:

{bank's forward dealer sells dollars tomorrow and bank's forward dealer buys dollars spot

spot deal: bank's spot dealer sells dollars spot

net effect: bank sells dollars outright tomorrow

It is useful to compare this with Example 10. Importantly, notice that, because tomorrow is earlier than spot, the tom-next deal in Example 13 is 'sell and buy', whereas in Example 10 the swap deal was 'buy and sell'. In Example 10, the spot dealer and the forward dealer both dealt on the right side of the quote. In Example 13, however, the spot dealer still deals on the right side of the price but the forward dealer deals on the left side of the price.

Swap prices for very short periods like O/N, T/N and S/N are very small numbers. The forward points are therefore often less than 1 point and it is important to line them up correctly when they are being added to or subtracted from the spot. Sometimes they are quoted as fractions - for example, a price of "11/11" means "one and a half points/one and a quarter points" - and sometimes as decimals - for example, a price of "1.5/1.25" again means "1.5 points/1.25 points". In this case, that part of the price which is immediately before the decimal point should be lined up with the final digit of the spot price.

(i) Suppose a customer wishes to sell dollars for outright value one week after spot. The bank spot dealer buys dollars for value spot on the left at 1.7505. The bank forward dealer 'sells and buys' dollars also on the left at a swap difference of 7 points. Therefore the bank buys dollars outright one week after spot at 1.7505 —

0.0007= 1.7498. The other side of the one week outright price is 1.7510 — 0.0005 = 1.7505.

(ii) Suppose the customer wishes to sell dollars for outright value tomorrow. This is equivalent to selling dollars for value spot and, at the same time, undertaking a swap to sell dollars for value tomorrow and buy dollars back for value spot.

Again, the bank spot dealer buys dollars for value spot on the left at 1.7505. However, the bank forward dealer 'buys and sells' dollars tomorrow against spot on the right at a swap difference of $^{1}{}_{4}$ point. Furthermore (because Swiss interest rates are lower than dollar rates), the dollar is at a discount to the Swiss franc: the 'bigger number' $^{1}{}_{2}$ is on the left. The dollar is therefore worth less on the far date (i.e. spot) and more on the near date (i.e. tomorrow). The swap difference is therefore added to the spot rate, rather than subtracted, to give an outright value tomorrow price of 1.7505 + 4 = 1.750525.

A simple rule to remember for the calculation of dates earlier than spot is 'reverse the swap points and proceed exactly as for a forward later than spot'. In the above example, this would mean reversing because the 'bigger' swap number is now on the right. However, it is important always to remember to make this reversal in your head only! Never actually quote the price in reverse!

O/N prices are the only regular swap prices not involving the spot value date - i.e., the O/N swap is from today until tomorrow, not from today until spot. To calculate an outright value today price, it is therefore necessary to combine the spot with both the overnight price and the tom-next price:

(iii) Suppose the customer wishes to sell dollars for outright value today. This is equivalent to three separate transactions: selling dollars for value spot, undertaking a swap to sell dollars for value tomorrow and buy dollars back for value spot (tom-next swap) and undertaking another swap to sell dollars for value today and buy dollars back for value tomorrow (overnight swap). The price is therefore 1.7505 + 4 + 3 = 1.7506.

The rules can be thought of in terms of premiums and discounts, which apply in the same way as with forwards after spot. The swaps in the previous example show a dollar discount because Swiss franc interest rates are lower than dollar interest rates. Consequently, if the customer sells dollars value today and not value spot, he will receive the currency with the lower interest rate two days early. The extra point which he receives from the bank reflects this

FORWARD-FORWARDS

A forward-forward swap is a swap deal between two forward dates rather than from spot to a forward date - for example, to sell US dollars 1 month forward and buy them back 3 months forward. In this case, the swap is for the 2-month period between the 1-month date and the 3-month date. A company might undertake such a swap because it has previously bought dollars forward but wishes now to defer the transaction by a further two months, as it will not need the dollars as soon as it thought.

As with forward-forward interest rates, FX forward-forwards are referred to by the beginning and end dates of the forward period, compared with the spot value date. Thus the forward-forward described here is a '1v3', meaning that the forward period starts 1 month from now and ends 3 months from now.

From the bank's point of view, a forward-forward swap can be seen as constructed from two separate swaps, each based on spot.

Example :

USD/CHF spot rate: 1.7325/ 35

1-month swap: 65/ 61

3-month swap: 160/155

If our bank's counterparty wishes to sell dollars 1 month forward, and buy them back 3 months forward, this is the same as under-taking one swap to buy dollars spot and sell dollars 1 month forward, and another swap to sell dollars spot and buy dollars 3 months forward.

As swaps are always quoted as how the quoting bank 'sells and buys' the base currency on the left, and 'buys and sells' the base currency on the right, the counterparty can 'buy and sell' dollars spot against 1 month at a swap price of -65, with settlement rates of spot and (spot -0.0065). He can simultaneously 'sell and buy' dollars spot against 3 months at a swap price of -155 with settlement rates of spot and (spot -0.0155). He can therefore do both – 'sell and buy' dollars 1 month against 3 months – at settlement rates of (spot -0.0065) and (spot -0.0155), which implies a difference between the two forward settlement rates of (-155) - (-65) = -90 points.

Conversely, the counterparty can 'buy and sell' dollars 1 month against 3 months at a swap price of (-160) - (-61) = -99 points. The two-way price is therefore -99/-90, quoted as usual without the '-' signs, as 99/90.

As with a swap from spot to a forward date, the two settle-ment prices in a forward-forward must be based on a current market rate. In the above example, using the middle spot rate, for example, the settlement rates could be 1.7265 (= 1.7330 - 0.0065) for 1 month forward and 1.7175(= 1.7330 - 0.0155) for 3 months forward.

These settlement rates would enable our forward dealer to cover his position exactly with another bank. We could, for example, ask another bank for a 1-month swap price to cover the first leg of the forward-forward. Assuming prices have not moved, we could deal at -65 points with settlement rates of 1.7330 (spot) and 1.7265 (1 month). We could then cover the second leg with a 3-month swap at another bank's price of -155, with settlement rates of 1.7330 (spot) and 1.7175 (3 months). The spot settlements would offset each other and the forward settlements would exactly offset the settlements with our own counterparty.

In practice, however, forward dealers often base the settlement rate for the first leg on a middle rate for spot and also a middle rate for the near forward date. In the example above, this would give a settlement rate of 1.7330 (middle) - 0.0063 (middle) = 1.7267. The settlement rate for the second leg would then be 1.7267 - 0.0090 = 1.7177. The difference between the two settlement rates is still the -90 points agreed, but the settlement rates are slightly different.

If the yield curves of the two currencies cross over at some point between the two forward dates, the forward points will show a premium for one period but a discount for the other. In this case, it is important to make sure that the '+' and '-' signs are correctly shown before constructing the forward-forward price, and also to remember that two negatives make a positive.

Forward-forward price after spot

First, insert'—' signs where necessary. Then:

left side = (left side of far-date swap) — (right side of near-date swap) right side = (right side of far-date swap) — (left side of near-date swap)

The bid-offer spread of the resulting price is the sum of the two separate bid-offer spreads.

Example : Given the following prices, you need to 'sell and buy' sterling against euros forward-forward 2v5.

EUR/GBP spot: 0.6235/45

2-month swap: 17/13

5-month swap: 25/31

The 2-month price is —17/—13 (a euro discount) but the 5-month price is +25/+31 (a euro premium). The 2v5 price is therefore:

25 — (—13) = 38 on the left

and 31 — (—17) = 48 on the right

On this forward-forward price of 38/48, you deal at 38 (the quoting bank always 'sells and buys' the base currency on the left).

The middle rate for 2 months forward is 0.6225 (=0.6240 — 0.0015). You therefore agree to settlement rates of 0.6225 for 2 months and 0.6263 (=0.6225 + 0.0038) for 5 months.

Care needs to be taken with swaps from before spot until after spot.

Example :

USD/CHF spot rate: 1.7325/35

T/N swap: 3/2

3-month swap: 160/155

If a counterparty requests a price to 'sell and buy' dollars tomorrow against 3 months after spot, this can be seen as a price to sell tomorrow and buy spot at (—2) points with settlement rates of (spot + 0.0002) and spot, and a price to sell spot and buy 3 months later at (—155) points, with settlement rates of spot and (spot — 0.0155). The total price is there-fore the difference between (spot — 0.0155) and (spot+ 0.0002), which is (—155) — (+2) = —157. The other side of the price is (—160) — (+3) = —163. The 2-sided price is therefore 163/157.

Forward-forward price from before spot until after spot First, insert'—' signs where necessary. Then: left side = (left side of far-date swap) + (left side of T/N or T/N and O/N) right side = (right side of far-date swap) + (right side of T/N or T/N and O/N)

The bid-offer spread of the resulting price is the sum of the separate bid-offer spreads.

A forward-forward from before spot might be for a regular period from the start date, rather than until a regular date after spot. For example, a swap for '3 months out of today' would mean that the end date is not 3 months after the spot date but 3 months after today. The regular 3-month price is therefore too long a period to use, and the correct period must be interpolated (see Chapter 2) from the 2-month price and the 3-month price.

Example : Today is 15 April, spot is 17 April, 2 months from spot is 17 June and 3 months from spot is 17 July. You need to quote to customer a swap price for 3 months out of today which is from 15 April to 15 July.

GBP/USD spot rate: 1.4325/35

O/N swap: 4/3

T/N swap: 3/2

2-month swap (61 days): 100/95

3-month swap (91 days): 160/155

The period from spot until 17 June is 61 days. The period from spot until 15 July is 89 days. The period from spot until 17 July is 91 days.

To calculate the swap we need, we therefore add the following prices:

O/N swap: —4/ —3

T/N swap: —3/ —2

swap from spot to 15 July: —156/—151 —163/—156

CALCULATION SUMMARY

It might be helpful to collect together here the various rules which apply to calculating forwards:

The currency with higher interest rate (=the currency at a discount) is worth less in the future. If this is the base currency, the points are negative.

The currency with lower interest rate (=the currency at a premium) is worth more in the future. If this is the base currency, the points are positive.

The bank quoting the price always 'sells and buys' the base currency on the left and 'buys and sells' the base currency on the right. If the swap price appears larger on the right than the left, it is positive. If the swap price appears larger on the left than the right, it is negative.

For outright forwards later than spot: The left swap price is added to (or subtracted from) the left spot price.

The right swap price is added to (or subtracted from) the right spot price.

For outright deals earlier than spot: Calculate as if the swap price were reversed.

Forward-forwards: First, insert'—' signs where necessary. Then:

after spot: left side = (left side of far-date swap)

— (right side of near-date swap)

right side = (right side of far-date swap)

— (left side of near-date swap)

from before spot until after spot: left side = (left side of far-date swap)

+ (left side of T/N or T/N and O/N) right side = (right side of far-date swap)

+ (right side of T/N or T/N and O/N)

In general: Of the two prices available, the customer gets the worse one.

Thus if the swap price is 3/2 and the customer knows that the points are in his favour (the outright will be better than the spot), the price will be 2. If he knows that the points are against him (the outright will be worse than the spot), the price will be 3.

The bid-offer spread of the resulting price is the sum of the separate bid-offer spreads.

CROSS-RATE CALCULATIONS

A forward cross-rate is calculated in a similar way to a spot cross-rate as explained in the previous chapter, but using outrights.

The same is true for any outright calculated from two other outrights and is true for short dates as well as any other outrights:

- To calculate an outright from two exchange rates with the same base currency (for example, the dollar), divide opposite sides of the individual outrights.
- To calculate an outright from two exchange rates with the same variable currency, again divide opposite sides of the individual outrights.
- To calculate an outright from two rates where the common currency is the base for one but the variable for the other, multiply the same sides of the individual outrights.

To calculate cross-rate forward swaps, the process above must be taken a step further:

(i) calculate the spot cross-rate as usual

(ii) calculate the two individual forward outrights as above

(iii) from (ii) calculate the forward outright cross-rate

(iv) subtract (i) from (iii) to give the cross-rate swap

Example : Based on the following prices, what is the EUR/GBP 6-month swap?

EUR/USD spot:	0.8734/39
6 months:	23/19
GBP/USD spot:	1.4237/42
6 months:	63/67
EUR/USD spot:	0.8734/ 0.8739
6 months:	-0.0023/-0.0019
outright:	0.8711/ 0.8720
GBP/USD spot:	1.4237/ 1.4242
6 months:	0.0063/ 0.0067
outright:	1.4300/ 1.4309

0.8734 ÷ 1.4242 = 0.6133 0.8711 ÷ 1.4309 = 0.6088

0.8739 ÷ 1.4237 = 0.6138 0.8720 ÷ 1.4300 = 0.6098

EUR/GBP 6-month outright:	0.6088/ 0.6098
EUR/GBP spot:	0.6133/ 0.6138
EUR/GBP 6-month swap:	-0.0045/-0.0040 i.e. 45/40

The same approach can be used for calculating a USD-based rate from two cross-rates, and also for calculating short-date swaps.

Example : Based on the following prices, what is the USD/SEK O/N swap?

EUR/USD spot:	0.8734/39
O/N:	0.6/0.4
T/N:	0.7/0.5
EUR/SEK spot:	8.3975/95
O/N:	2.4/2.6
T/N:	2.3/2.5
EUR/USD spot:	0.8734 / 0.8739
T/N:	-0.00007/-0.00005
outright tomorrow:	0.87345/ 0.87397
O/N	-0.00006/-0.00004
outright today:	0.87349/ 0.87403
EUR/SEK spot:	8.3975 / 8.3995
T/N:	0.00023/ 0.00025
outright tomorrow:	8.39725/ 8.39927
O/N:	0.00024/ 0.00026
outright today:	8.39699/ 8.39903

8.39699 ÷ 0.87403 = 9.607210 8.39903 ÷ 0.87349 = 9.615485

8.39725 ÷ 0.87397 = 9.608167 8.39927 ÷ 0.87345 = 9.616200

USD/SEK outright tomorrow: 9.608167/9.616200

USD/SEK outright USD/SEK O/N swa

today: 9.607210/9.615485

p: 0.000715/0.000957 i.e. 7.1/9.6

Remember that in calculating the outright today and outright tomorrow rates above for EUR/USD and EUR/SEK, each spot price is combined with the opposite side of the swap price and the sign is 'reversed'. Similarly, in the final calculation of the O/N swap price for USD/SEK, the swap price appears to be 'reversed' for the same reason.

In order to calculate a cross-rate forward-forward, extend the process: calculate the cross-rate swap for the near date of the forward-forward and also the cross-rate swap for the far date, and then combine them as usual.

It might be possible to use cross-rates to construct an outright in a more cost-efficient way if prices are out of line, as in the following example.

Example : Based on the following prices available to you in the market, what is best price at which you can buy euros against sterling, 6 months forward outright?

EUR/GBP spot: 0.6132/37

6 months: 44/39

EUR/USD spot: 0.8734/39

6 months: 23/19

GBP/USD spot: 1.4237/42

6 months: 63/67

The outright EUR/GBP must be constructed from a spot and a swap. We are dealing on the right-hand side.

For the spot, the straightforward EUR/GBP price of 0.6137 is better than the price of 0.6138 which can be constructed via the cross-rate calculation (see Example 20, which is based on the same market prices).

For the swap, the price of -40 points which can be constructed via the cross-rate calculation (again see Example 20, which is based on the same market prices) is better than the straightfor-ward EUR/GBP price of -39 points.

Therefore an outright price of 0.6097 (=0.6137 - 0.0040) can be achieved by: buying euros against sterling directly at 0.6137 and selling and buying euros against dollars at -19 points and buying and selling sterling against dollars at +63 points

NON-DELIVERABLE FORWARDS (NDFS)

A *non-deliverable forward (NDF)* is a forward outright where, instead of settling the outright amounts at maturity, the two parties agree at the outset that they will settle only the change in value between the forward rate dealt and the spot rate two working days before maturity. The economic effect is the same as if a normal forward outright had been dealt and then closed out two days before maturity by an offsetting spot deal.

One advantage of an NDF is that it can be used to trade non-convertible currencies. In this case, the settlement at maturity of the NDF is necessarily made in a convertible currency - generally one of the pair of currencies being traded. An NDF also reduces the counterparty credit risk, as the risk is limited to the settlement amount and does not involve the usual settlement risk of the whole principal amount of the deal.

An NDF is a contract for differences, analogous to an FRA for interest rates.

Example : It is now 15 April. A company needs to buy TWD 100 million against sterling for settlement in 3 months (17 July). It buys this amount 3 months forward using an NDF, at a rate of 49.06.

On 15 July, the company and the bank agree a GBP/TWD spot rate of 48.43 for settlement.

$$\frac{100,000,000}{49.06} = 2,038,320.42$$

$$\frac{100,000,000}{48.43} = 2,064,835.85$$

The profit or loss is settled as if the company had bought TWD 100 million at 49.06 and then sold again at 48.43. As this is an NDF, there is no need to transact an actual spot deal on 15 July.

buyTWD 100,000,000, sell GBP 2,038,320.42

sell TWD 100,000,000, buy GBP 2,064,835.85

profit GBP 26,515.42

The company therefore receives a settlement of GBP 26,515.42 from the bank on 17 July.

If this were a speculative transaction, nothing further would be required. However, the company physically needs the TWD 100 million. Therefore, it buys TWD 100 million spot on 15 July for value 17 July at 48.43 in the normal way. This will cost GBP 2,064,835.85. The net effect for the company is therefore a cost of GBP 2,038,320.42 (=GBP 2,064,835.85 — GBP 26,515.42), leaving the company in the same position as if it had been able to buy the TWD 100 million 3 months forward in the first place.

In practice, the net effect might be slightly worse than this because the NDF would be settled against a middle reference rate but the spot deal would be at bid rate. However, if the company had been able to transact a normal forward outright in the first place, that also would have involved the bid side of the spot rate.

A source must be agreed for the reference spot rate to be used for calculating the settlement amount if the NDF is left open until maturity. The conventional source will vary from currency to currency and could, for example, be a central bank fixing rate or a rate published on Reuters or Telerate.

If the NDF is used speculatively, an alternative is for the NDF to be closed out early and for the settlement amount to be based on the difference between the two rates dealt. In this case, the settlement can be paid at maturity date of the two NDFs or discounted to a present value and settled early.

Example : It is now 15 April. A dealer takes a speculative 3-month position by buying TWD 100 million against sterling for value 17 July, using an NDF, at a rate of 49.06.

On 22 April, the dealer closes out the position with another NDF for value 17 July at 48.43.

As in the last example, the dealer is due a profit of GBP 26,515.42 for settlement on 17 July:

buyTWD 100,000,000, sell GBP 2,038,320.42

sell TWD 100,000,000, buy GBP 2,064,835.85

profit GBP 26,515.42

There are 84 days from 24 April to 17 July. Assuming that the sterling interest rate for the period is say 5%, the present value of this amount could be settled instead on 24 April.

TIME OPTIONS

When a bank makes a forward outright deal with a company, it quotes a rate for a fixed date, which means the company must deliver one currency and receive another on that date.

If the company has a commitment in the future but does not know the exact delivery date required, it has an alternative means of covering this exposure in the traditional foreign exchange market, using a *time option* (also known as an *option forward).* This allows the company to deal now, but to choose the maturity date later within a specified period. There is, however, no choice about whether to deliver - delivery must take place at some point during the agreed period, for the amount and rate agreed.

It is important not to confuse time options in this sense with currency options. A currency options entails the up-front payment of an 'insurance premium', in return for which the customer has the right to choose whether or not to deal at all.

In pricing a time option, the bank will always assume that the company will take delivery of the currency at the worst possible time for the bank. Therefore the company will always be charged the worst possible forward rate within the period of the time option.

Example: The bank's customer wishes to transact a forward deal in dollars against Swiss francs, with a flexible delivery date of between 2 and 3 months. Given the following market prices, what rate does the bank quote?

USD/CHF spot rate: 1.7325/35

2-month swap: 130/125

3-month swap: 160/155

The 2-month outright would be 1.7195/1.7210:

1.7325/1.7335 130/125

1.7195/1.7210

The 3-month outright would be 1.7165/1.7180:

1.7325/1.7335 160/155

1.7165/1.7180

If the customer is selling dollars, the worse price is the 3-month price of 1.7165. If the customer is buying dollars, the worse price is the 2-month price of 1.7210. Therefore the time option price is a swap price of 160/125, or an outright price of 1.7165/1.7210.

The advantage to a company of a time option is its flexibility. The company can lock in a fixed exchange rate at which it knows it can deal. There is no exposure to interest rate changes which would affect it if commitments were covered with a forward outright which subsequently needed to be adjusted by means of forward swaps. The disadvantage is the cost, given the wide bid/offer spread involved, particularly if the time period of the option is a long one. A time option price is the best for the bank/worst for the customer over the time option period

LONG-DATED FORWARDS

These were derived from the assumption that the interest on a deposit or loan is paid on a simple basis as described in Chapter 2. For deposits and loans over 1 year, the interest must be compounded because interest is normally paid at the end of each year.

The interest rates in this case are bond basis rates - quoted on the basis of a true calendar year rather than a 360-day year. These theoretical formulas are not precise in practice for two reasons. Firstly, this compounding does not take account of reinvestment risk. This problem is overcome by using zero-coupon yields for the interest rates. More importantly, the market in long-dated forwards is not very liquid and spreads are very wide. The prices available in practice therefore depend partly on banks' individual positions and hence their interest in quoting a price.

Example : What are the theoretical GBP/USD 3-year outright and forward swap, based on the following?

GBP/USD spot: 1.4123

GBP 3-year interest rate: 5.15%

USD 3-year interest rate: 4.35%

SYNTHETIC AGREEMENTS FOR FORWARD EXCHANGE (SAFES)

SAFES are used very little now, but we have included them here for completeness. A SAFE is an off-balance sheet forward-forward foreign exchange swap. There are two versions of a SAFE – an *FXA* and an *ERA*.

An FXA (*forward exchange agreement*) exactly replicates the economic effect of a forward-forward in the cash market which is reversed at the first settlement date of the forward-forward in order to take a profit or loss. A price for an FXA is quoted in the same way as a forward-forward price, and is dealt in the same way. A forward-forward swap results in two cash settlements, each for the whole amount of the deal. An FXA, however, is settled in a manner analogous to the way an FRA is settled. On the nearer of the two forward dates, a settlement amount is paid from one party to the other to reflect the movement in rates between dealing and settlement, using an agreed settlement rate.

The settlement formula ensures that the result is economically the same as the profit or loss would be with a cash forward-forward. To do so, it takes account of the movement in the spot rate from dealing to settlement, as well as the movement in the forward swap points.

This is because, although a forward dealer takes a position on the basis of his expectations of swap movements, his profit or loss is also affected to some extent by spot rate movements. The reason for this is discussed in Chapter 10.

As with an FRA, the settlement formula involves an element of discounting, because the settlement is made at the beginning of the forward-forward period.

An FXA can have equal or unequal notional base currency amounts at each end of the swap.

An ERA (*exchange rate agreement*) price is exactly the same as an FXA price, and allows for a discounted settlement to be made at the beginning of the forward-forward period in the same way as an FXA.

The ERA settlement, however, deliberately takes no account of the movement in the spot rate, and the settlement formula is correspond-ingly simpler. The settlement amount is simply the notional amount of the contract multiplied by the change in the swap rate. With an ERA, only one notional base currency amount is involved. The two instruments can therefore be compared as follows:

An FXA replicates exactly the economic effect of a cash forward-forward. In a trading strategy that requires a forward-forward, an FXA is an alternative.

An ERA may be used to trade movements in forward swap prices when the trader specifically wishes the result to be unaffected by movements in the spot rate. This does not exactly replicate a forward-forward.

Advantages of SAFEs

The advantages of a SAFE lie in the problems which arise on credit lines and balance sheet utilization. In the absence of an appropriate netting agreement, when a bank deals forward-forward, its credit lines to and from the counterparty are generally utilized to the extent of twice the notional credit amount applied to the deal - once for each leg of the forward-forward. Between dealing date and the first settlement date, however, the real risk might be far less than this, because the two legs of the deal largely offset each other.

The credit exposure allocated to a SAFE, as a contract for differences, will be far less.

The capital utilization requirements (see Chapter 12) are similarly reduced. Rather than having two deals on the balance sheet, there are none.

A further advantage of an ERA arises if a forward trader wishes to trade the forward swap points without needing to hedge the effect of potential spot rate movements (although this does not avoid the effect that a significant spot rate movement has on the swap price itself).

The settlement amount is paid by the seller of the FXA or ERA to the buyer (or vice versa if it is a negative amount), where the buyer is the party which 'buys and sells' the base currency.

In the above settlement formulas:

- 'First amount' is the base currency amount transacted at the beginning of the swap.
- 'Second amount' is the base currency amount transacted at the end of the swap.

  (These amounts can be the same but do not need to be.)
- 'Outright exchange rate' is the outright, to the near date of the forward-forward period, when the FXA is transacted.
- 'Settlement spot rate' is the reference spot agreed 2 working days before the swap period.
- 'Settlement swap price' is the reference swap price agreed 2 working days before the swap period.
- 'LIBOR is for the swap period, agreed 2 working days before the swap period.

Example : At the moment, dollar interest rates are lower than sterling rates. You expect this difference to narrow and therefore decide to sell a 1v3 SAFE for GBP 5 million. The 1v3 month period is 61 days. Rates are quoted to you as follows:

GBP/USD 1-month outright: 1.4675

1v3 swap: 86/80.

You sell the SAFE at —80 points. Two business days before the 1-month settlement date, rates are as follows:

GBP/USD spot: 1.4915

2-month swap: -76.

USD 2-month LIBOR: 4.23%.

If you have used an FXA, the settlement amount will be a profit of USD 1131.79 (the settlement formula gives a negative amount so it is payable by the buyer to the seller).

Speculation

A dealer wishing to take a strategic (i.e. medium-term) speculative position in a currency, will use a forward outright, rather than a spot deal which would continually require rolling over with swaps.

Forward swaps are essentially interest rate instruments. A dealer wishing to speculate on the interest rate differential between two currencies will 'buy and sell' or 'sell and buy'. Frequently, a dealer will establish forward-forward positions, either directly for this purpose, or as a result of two or more swap deals he has transacted with customers in different maturities.

Arbitrage

The relationship between interest rates and swap prices allows for the possibility of arbitrage. This is considered in Chapter 9.

6

Hedging Swaps with Deposits, FRAs and Futures, Covered Interest Arbitrage and Creating Synthetic FRAs

The link between interest rates and forward swaps explained in the previous chapter allows dealers and end-users of the market to take advantage of opportunities in different markets, in two ways.

Firstly, it enables a dealer with a forward swap position to hedge this position by using money market borrowings and deposits, if it turns out to be cheaper or easier to do so.

Secondly, it enables a borrower or investor to borrow or invest in a different currency from that in which he originally intended to deal, and then to convert this transaction to the intended currency by using a swap.

Again, he would do so if the result were a better all-in rate, or if it were easier to arrange.

These two strategies are in fact essentially the same idea, viewed from different angles; the second strategy is known as *covered interest arbitrage*. Both depend on the fact that an FX swap is broadly equiv-alent to a borrowing plus a deposit.

Both these ideas can be extended from forwards to forward-forwards. This means that a forward-forward swap position can be hedged by using FRAs and futures, and an FRA in one currency can be created from, or arbitraged against, an FRA in another currency by using forward-forward swaps.

HEDGING FX FORWARDS USING BORROWINGS AND DEPOSITS

Hedging a forward swap

When a dealer buys and sells one currency against another, he is taking a position economically very similar to borrowing the first currency and lending the second. Therefore, he can hedge the swap position by doing the opposite - i.e. lending the first currency and borrowing the second.

Example : *A* dealer buys and sells USD 10 million against yen, spot against 3 months (91 days) at 118.50 and 117.25.

He hedges the position by lending USD 10 million for 3 months at 4.8% and borrowing JPY 1,185,000,000 for three months at 0.5%. The total proceeds due back from the lending, and the repayment amount on the borrowing, are as follows:

$$\text{Interest} = \text{USD } 10{,}000{,}000 \times 0.048 \times \frac{91}{360} = \text{USD } 121{,}333$$

Principal + interest = USD 10,000,000 + USD 121,333 = USD 10,121,333

$$\text{Interest} = \text{JPY } 1{,}185{,}000{,}000 \times 0.005 \times \frac{91}{360} = \text{JPY } 1{,}497{,}708$$

Principal+ interest = JPY 1,185,000,000 + JPY 1,497,708 = JPY 1,186,497,708

Hedging swaps

The cashflows from the deal and the cover are therefore as follows:

spot

USD 10,000,000	JPY	1,185,000,000
USD 10,000,000	JPY	1,185,000,000
USD 10,000,000	JPY	1,172,500,000
USD 10,121,333	JPY	1,186,497,708
		121,333 13,997,708

If the dealer is dollar-based, for example, he could then remove the remaining small risk by buying JPY 13,997,708 3 months forward outright. If the rate for this forward outright is 117.25, this would give additional cashflows. The dealer is now hedged, as the result measured in dollars is unaffected by any subsequent change in rates. The result is a small profit, rather than zero, because the rate of the original swap deal (-125 points) is not exactly the same as the rate implied by the borrowing and lending interest rates – see 'Why bother?' below.

The small forward outright purchase of JPY 13,997,708 in the previous example is intended to 'tidy up' the position by removing any residual currency risk. In practice, this amount might be left unhedged. For completeness however, we will continue to assume in our examples here that the bank does want to hedge this completely.

If this amount is to be hedged, using a forward outright as a hedge is rather messy. An alternative would be to use a small spot hedge rather than a small forward outright hedge. In this case, however, in order to hedge completely, the amounts of the borrowing and lending would need to be slightly different. It would be necessary to calculate the amount of dollars it is necessary to lend at the beginning, in order to achieve proceeds of exactly USD 10,000,000 after 3 months. Similarly, it would be necessary to calculate the amount of yen it is necessary to borrow at the beginning, in order to achieve a repayment of exactly JPY 1,172,500,000 after 3 months. This is effectively the same as calculating present values and can be seen in the following example.

Example: With the same original deal as in the previous example, the dealer hedges by matching the 3-month FX cashflows exactly with a borrowing and a deposit, and then doing a spot hedge for the small unmatched amount of yen, which can be seen to be JPY 13,980,039.

This second example gives the dealer a net profit of USD 1,904, rather than the USD 1,950 in the first example. The difference arises in two ways. Firstly, the USD 1,904 profit is value spot, whereas the USD 1,950 profit is in 3 months' time.

Secondly, the forward swap price and interest rates in the examples are slightly out of line. That is, the dollar rate of 4.8% and the yen rate of 0.5% do not correspond exactly to the swap price of -125 points (the difference between 118.50 and 117.25). Indeed, this might be the reason why the dealer is using the borrowing and deposit (rather than a swap) to hedge the position in the first place. The sizes of the borrowing and deposit are slightly greater in the first example than in the second example, so that slightly greater advantage is taken of this discrepancy, leading to a slightly greater profit.

Why bother?

The dealer could have hedged his original forward swap position by using another swap. How did he know that he would benefit by using a borrowing and deposit instead? He could calculate the effective swap price achieved via the borrowing and deposit by using exactly the same formula as in the previous chapter for deriving swap points from interest rates.

The forward swap achieved synthetically is therefore -1.2726, which is -127.26 points. Presumably, therefore, the dealer has chosen to hedge via the borrowing and deposit because the straightforward swap price available for hedging is not as good as -127.26 points. In practice, a bank would need to take account also of the balance sheet and capital adequacy implications of hedging by using deposits in this way – see Chapter 12.

The original deal was transacted at -125 points. If the borrowing and deposit hedge is used, the dealer expects a profit after 3 months of 2.26 points (the difference between -125 points and -127.26 points).

This is JPY 226,000, which has a present valueA foreign exchange swap position to buy and sell one currency against another can be hedged by lending the first currency and borrowing the second currency, plus small spot or outright hedges to bring net foreign currency cashflows to zero.

Hedging a forward outright

A forward outright can be hedged in the same way. A forward outright is constructed from - and normally hedged by - a spot deal and a swap deal. The swap hedge can be replaced by a borrowing and a deposit as above.

A foreign exchange dealer sells USD 10 million 3 months outright to a customer, against yen at 117.25. The US dollar deposit dealer in his own bank is short of dollars and is prepared to pay the foreign exchange dealer 4.8% to borrow dollars from him. The foreign exchange dealer therefore covers his forward outright position by buying dollars spot in the market at 118.50, lending dollars to his colleague, and borrowing yen from the market at 0.5%. His cashflows are as follows:

Exactly as in Examples 1 and 2, the remaining USD/JPY risk can be hedged by a spot or forward deal.

A forward outright position to sell one currency against another can be hedged by buying the first currency spot, lending the first currency and borrowing the second currency, plus small spot or outright hedges to bring net foreign currency cashflows to zero.

HEDGING FX FORWARD-FORWARDS WITH FRAS OR FUTURES

In running a forward book, a dealer will normally have forward-forward positions. Suppose, for example, that a dealer does only two deals, each in response to a customer. In the first deal, he buys and sells USD 10 million against yen, spot against 1 month. In the second deal, he sells and buys USD 10 million against yen, spot against 4 months. The dealer now has a net forward-forward position in USD 10 million, 1 month against 4 months. Alternatively, the dealer might have established the same forward-forward position without any customer-related business, purely as a speculative position.

If the dealer wishes to hedge this position, he could do so simply by buying and selling USD 10 million, 1 month against 4 months. Alternatively, he could hedge the position by borrowing and lending, as in the examples above. Because it is a forward-forward position rather than a spot-to-forward position, however, the borrowing and lending must also be forward-forward, to match the cashflow timings.

Another approach, which uses the balance sheet less, is to use FRAs or futures, because these are exactly off-balance sheet equivalents of cash forward-forward borrowings. These instruments are covered in Chapter 6.

The following example is parallel to Example 2, with the same exchange rates, but with the cashflows in the future rather than based on spot.

A dealer buys and sells USD 10 million against yen, 1 month against 4 months (91 days) at 118.50 and 117.25.

He hedges the position by selling a 1v4 FRA for USD 9,880,121 at 4.8% and buying a 1v4 FRA for JPY 1,171,019,961 at 0.5%.

As in Example 2, there is another small FX risk to be hedged. Consider what the cashflows would be if, instead of using a yen FRA, the dealer used a cash forward-forward yen borrowing. There would be a cash inflow of 1,171,019,961 after 1 month and a cash outflow of JPY 1,172,500,000 after 4 months, similar to the flows in Example 2. The dealer therefore also buys JPY 13,980,039 (the difference between JPY 1,171,019,961 and JPY 1,185,000,000) 1-month forward outright. This is the amount which would make the yen cashflows net to zero if we were using cash forward-forward borrowings.

Also, as the FRAs are in fact contracts for differences rather than cash instruments, the dealer will still need to reverse the swap cashflows when the first leg of the forward-forward swap settles after one month. This can be done using either a 3-month swap again, or a borrowing and a deposit. We will assume here that the dealer simply uses a swap.

After 1 month, US dollar LIBOR is set at 4.95% and yen LIBOR is set at 0.6%, and the USD/JPY spot rate is 125.00. Assuming that the USD/JPY 3-month FX swap at the same time is exactly in line with these interest rates, the 3-month outright rate is 123.6425 (this is unrealistically precise, but helps to clarify the figures in this example).

As covered briefly in Chapter 6, futures are the exchange-traded equivalent of FRAs. The last example could therefore have used futures as a hedge, instead of FRAs. In major currencies at least, futures have the advantage of being liquid and finely priced. The drawbacks for hedging, however, include the mechanical complexity of margin calls and the inflexibility regarding periods and dates. The following example is parallel to the last one, using futures instead of FRAs.

Today is 5 March, spot is 7 March, the 1-month date is 7 April and the 4-month date is 7 July. A dealer buys and sells USD 10 million against yen, 1 month against 4 months (91 days) at 118.50 and 117.25.

He hedges the position by buying 10 March dollar futures contracts at 95.30 (representing USD 10 million at 4.70%) and selling 12 March yen futures contracts at 99.55 (representing JPY

1,200 million at 0.45%). As in Example 4, there is another small FX risk to be hedged. Again, consider what the cashflows would be if, instead of using yen futures, the dealer used a cash forward-forward yen borrowing for 90 days at 0.45%. There would be a cash inflow of 1,200,000,000 after 1 month and a cash outflow of JPY 1,201,350,000 after 4 months. The dealer therefore also sells JPY 15,000,000 (the difference between JPY 1,200,000,000 and JPY 1,185,000,000) 1 month forward outright and also buys JPY 28,850,0000 (the difference between JPY 1,201,350,000 and JPY 1,172,500,000) 4 months forward outright.

On 17 March (the last trading day for March futures), the futures positions are closed out and rolled into June futures - i.e. the March futures are reversed and replaced by new June futures positions. The closing prices for the March futures are 95.25 for dollars (representing a dollar interest rate of 4.75%) and 99.52 for yen (representing a yen interest rate of 0.48%). The June futures prices at the same time are 94.90 for dollars and 99.40 for yen.

On 5 April, the dealer closes out the June futures contracts. The futures prices are then 94.80 for dollars and 99.35 for yen. As in Example 4, the USD/JPY spot rate is 125.00 and the 3-month outright rate is 123.6425.

The net profit of USD 1,562 in the above example is a little different from the USD 1,904 in the previous example, because futures are a less exact hedge. In particular:

- The amount of the hedge is restricted to a round number – USD 10 million and JPY 1,200 million in this case.
- The futures contract period does not coincide exactly with the swap period. In this case, it was also necessary to roll over the futures when they expired in March.
- The profit and loss on these futures contracts is calculated using a 90-day period, whereas there are in fact 91 days in this particular 3-month period.
- There is a basis risk. That is, the movements in the futures prices do not necessarily match exactly the movement in the interest rates underlying the swap price. In this example, there was a total gain on the yen futures contract of 8 basis points (3 basis points gained on the March contract from 99.55 to 99.52, plus 5 basis points gained on the June contract, from 99.40 to 99.35) However, the

movement in the forward interest rate underlying the swap was 10 basis points, from 0.5% to 0.6%. It is possible to improve slightly the hedge against this basis risk, but the detailed use of futures strategies is really outside the scope of this book.

- The timing of the cashflows on the futures also affects the result, because part of the loss on the dollar futures and the profit on the yen futures arose in March – although we did not take account of this timing complication above, assuming instead that all the profit and loss on the futures arose in April. A forward-forward FX position to buy and sell one currency against another can be hedged by selling an FRA (or buying futures) in the first currency and buying an FRA (or selling futures) in the second currency, plus small spot or outright hedges to bring the notional net foreign currency cashflows to zero.

COVERED INTEREST ARBITRAGE

Borrowing or investing via a different currency

Suppose that an organization needs to fund itself in one currency but can borrow relatively more cheaply in another; it can choose deliberately to borrow in that second currency and use a forward swap to convert the borrowing to the first currency. This might be done, for example, if the resulting all-in cost of borrowing were slightly less than the cost of borrowing the first currency directly. It might also be done if borrowing in the original currency of choice were for some reason unavailable.

Even if it does not need to borrow, a bank can still borrow in the second currency, use a forward swap to convert the borrowing to the first currency and then make a deposit directly in the first currency; a reason for doing this would be that a profit can be locked in because the swap price is slightly out of line with the interest rates.

Taking advantage of such a strategy is known as covered interest arbitrage.

Covered interest arbitrage is synthetically creating a loan (or deposit) in one currency by combining a loan (or deposit) in another currency with a forward foreign exchange swap.

The simplest approach would be to borrow sterling directly at 6.1%. An alternative is to borrow dollars at 4.1% and swap them to sterling as follows.

The dealer borrows enough dollars so that when converted to sterling for value spot, he receives exactly GBP 1 million. Based on a spot rate of 1.4250 (see below for why we have chosen the left side of the spot rate), the amount to borrow is USD 1,425,000.

He transacts a foreign exchange swap to buy and sell sterling against dollars, spot against 6 months. The dollar amount transacted for value spot is the amount of dollars borrowed (USD 1,425,000); the dollar amount transacted for value 6 months is the amount of dollars repaid (USD 1,454,699.38). The swap deal is transacted on the left side of the price (because the market-maker who has quoted the price is selling and buying the base currency) at —133 points. Therefore if the settlement rate for spot is set at 1.4250, the settlement rate for 6 months must be set at 1.4117 (= 1.4250 — 0.0133). Applying these settlement rates, the cashflows are as follows:

The net result is effectively a borrowing of GBP 1,000,000 with a total repayment after six months of GBP 1,030,459.29 - i.e. an effective interest cost of GBP 30,459.29.

This rate achieved of 6.075% is slightly cheaper than the 6.1% cost of borrowing sterling directly. It is therefore worthwhile to create a synthetic sterling borrowing via dollars in this way.

Three points to notice in the above Example are:

- The Example assumes that the dealer is taking another bank's rates to borrow dollars at 4.1% and another bank's rates to swap at -133 points. If he were able to trade on his own prices, the result would be even better.
- When a swap is dealt, the amount of the deal (for example, GBP 1,000,000) is usually the same at both ends of the deal, spot and forward. In the example above, however, the amounts are mismatched, with GBP 1,030,459.29 at the far end in order to match the swap cashflows exactly with the underlying flows arising from the borrowing. It is generally acceptable in the market to use mismatched amounts in this way as long as the mismatch is not great.
- When dealing a forward swap rather than a forward outright, it is the swap price that is dealt rather than the

spot price; the spot price is needed only for settlement. The spot dealer is not involved and the spot spread is not involved. In general, therefore, the spot and forward settlement prices could be 1.4250 (the bid side of the spot price, as used in the example above) and 1.4117, or 1.4256 (the offer side of the spot price) and 1.4123, or something between such as 1.4253 and 1.4120. The important point is that the spot rate must be a current market rate and the difference between the spot and forward settlement prices must be the correct swap price of -133 points.

Conventionally for a swap, an approximate mid-price is taken for the spot. In an example such as this where the amounts are mismatched, however, it is common to use, for the whole deal, whichever side of the spot price would normally be used for the mismatch amount.

The mismatch in this example is a forward purchase of GBP 30,459.29 (= 1,030,459.29 - 1,000,000). For an outright alone, the quoting bank would wish to deal on the left for this, based on a spot of 1.4250, so that the settle-ment rates would be 1.4250 and 1.4117; commonly therefore, it would choose to deal on these same rates for the whole mismatched swap.

Although this approach is common, it does not necessarily benefit the quoting bank. In the example above, the quoting bank does indeed benefit by using a spot of 1.4250, as we have done. In general, however, this depends on whether the forward points are positive or negative. Specifically in the case of a mismatched swap for covered interest arbitrage, it is usually the case that:

- if the points are negative, the quoting bank benefits slightly by using the spot rate on the same side as the swap: if the left swap price is used (as in the example above), the quoting bank benefits by using the left side of the spot price; if the right swap price is used, the quoting bank benefits by using the right side of the spot price.
- if the points are positive, the quoting bank benefits slightly by using the spot rate on the opposite side from the swap: if the left swap price is used, the quoting bank benefits by using the right side of the spot price; if the right swap price is used, the quoting bank benefits by using the left side of the spot price.

MANAGING THE SPOT RISK ON A FORWARD FX POSITION

It may be helpful to explain why we have included this chapter here, rather than including it within the 'Bank risk management' chapter later in the book. Although it is important for dealers to understand the wide range of risks faced by a bank, most of these risks fall to be controlled largely by someone other than the dealer. The particular risk discussed in this chapter, however, requires continual positive action by the dealer which forms an essential part of his day-to-day trading activity.

When a forward dealer takes a position, he is taking a risk delib-erately because he is hoping to make a profit out of changes in the forward swap price, which depends essentially on interest rates as discussed in an earlier chapter. However, also as mentioned earlier, for each forward foreign exchange position, there is another risk, which arises out of potential spot exchange rate movements. This risk is known as the *tail* of the forward position.

HEDGING A FORWARD SWAP POSITION

The valuations, and calculations of profit and loss, in this chapter, as well as the calculation of the hedge required, depend on the concept of *present value*. This is covered in Chapter 2.

CURRENCY RELATIONSHIPS

In considering exchange rate movements, both historical and prospec-tive, it is useful to see different currencies within some structure. This is not an exact science, but broadly speaking there are at least two major currency blocs – the US dollar bloc and the euro bloc – and several major currency pairs which are traded in great volume and around which other relationships revolve – USD/EUR, USD/JPY and EUR/JPY. For many exchange rates other than these, it is often helpful to consider these few rates as central and other rates as satellites around them.

Consider, for example, the exchange rate between the Canadian dollar and the Danish krone. In practice, the market tends to think in terms of the Canadian dollar relative to the US dollar. This does not imply that the USD/CAD rate is, or is expected to be, stable but rather just that dealers tend to focus on changes in the USD/ CAD rate when they think about the Canadian dollar. This is not surprising, given the close historical and economic relationship between the USA and Canada. Similarly, when considering the Danish krone, the market tends to focus on its rate against the euro, rather than against the dollar. Therefore in analysing the CAD/DKK rate, one would tend to analyse separately 3 rates – USD/CAD, EUR/DKK and EUR/USD. The movement in the CAD/DKK rate is in practice a combination of these three.

In the same way, the dollar generally serves as a convenient bench-mark for considering currencies in Latin America, the Middle East, Africa and the Far East, such as the Brazilian real, the Saudi Arabian riyal, the Somalian shilling and the Singapore dollar. As with the Canadian dollar, this does not imply stability against the dollar – often quite the contrary – but merely gives a starting point. The euro bloc is composed not only of the other currencies in the EU (Danish krone, Swedish krona and to some extent sterling) but also of such other European currencies as the Swiss franc and Norwegian krone.

The yen, the most important currency outside these 2 groupings, is likely to become increasingly the centre of a third major bloc.

EXCHANGE RATE REGIMES

Government policy with regard to how it chooses to manage or not manage the exchange rate of its currency, is clearly important to exchange rate movements. Again, distinctions between the following categories are in practice generally not clear-cut, but they neverthe-less offer a helpful framework:

Fixed-rate regime Under a fixed-rate system, the exchange rate of a currency is fixed by the government for the foreseeable future with respect to some other currency.

The Hong Kong dollar, for example, is fixed against the US dollar at 7.80, although in practice it generally trades slightly stronger than this. The monetary authorities try to correct it if it moves significantly away from this level. The Saudi Arabian riyal is fixed very tightly to the dollar at 3.75. The CFA franc is fixed against the euro, following its former link to the French franc.

Floating-rate regime Under a freely floating system, the value of a currency is determined by the market, with no government intervention. Exchange rates are determined entirely by forces of supply and demand. The three major currencies, the US dollar, euro and yen, for example, essentially float freely against one another. Although there is occasionally intervention by central banks to put a limit to, or even reverse, very large changes in these rates, this is comparatively rare.

A problem with such a regime is that the free-market exchange rate at any moment might not be consistent with longer-term equi-librium. In practice therefore, governments sometimes intervene to smooth movements in the foreign exchange market. This is a *dirty floating* or *managed floating* system. Although there is no official rate between the Swiss franc and euro, for example, the exchange rate has in practice remained within a range of 1.40 to 1.80 (or the previous equivalent against the Deutschemark) for very many years.

Crawling peg/adjustable peg Under a crawling peg system, the par value of a currency relative to some other currency is adjusted regularly – often monthly. The par value and rate of adjustment are determined with reference to some measure of the external strength of a currency such as inflation differentials with other countries. The policy on exchange rate adjustments is announced in advance, so that it provides some measure of certainty.

An adjustable peg is similar to a crawling peg, except that the adjustments are on more of an *ad hoc* basis, rather than predetermined. The Egyptian pound is managed on an adjustable peg against the US dollar.

The European ERM (see below) has been in practice a hybrid between a dirty floating system and an adjustable peg, whereby the exchange rates have been maintained by the governments within limits around par values value with respect to each other.

Basket arrangements Some currencies are managed under a fixed regime or on a crawling peg, but against an average basket of currencies rather than against a single currency, where the currencies in the basket are weighted according to their importance in the country's international transactions.

The *SDR* (*special drawing right*) – the artificial accounting currency of the IMF – is itself a basket currency, composed of fixed amounts of US dollars, euro, sterling and yen. Dual rates One means of controlling speculation against a currency is a system of multiple exchange rates, whereby the rate for the currency is differentiated according to the type of transaction.

EUROPEAN MONETARY UNION

The European monetary system

The *European monetary system* (*EMS*), launched on 13 March 1979, grouped together the currencies of eight European countries. The EMS included a mechanism for enabling currency adjustments to take place in an orderly way – the *exchange rate mechanism* (*ERM*). This was built around the *ECU*, a basket currency composed of different weightings of the national currencies.

The EMS also represented the initial phase of European monetary and economic integration. The system's original goals were:

- To facilitate exchange rate stability in order to foster monetary and price stability as well as intra-European trade and thereby to promote economic integration within the European Union (EU).
- To put the responsibility for correcting policies on governments asking for changes in exchange rate parities. For example, a government seeking a devaluation of its currency was obliged to tighten monetary and/or fiscal policies to reduce economic imbalances.
- To facilitate the eventual creation of a European currency – now the euro.

In line with these aims, each member country had to reduce pres-sure on its currency when it became apparent that its economic pattern was diverging from other members' economies and creating problems in the foreign exchange market. The action might be increased intervention in the foreign exchange market, a change in economic policies, or a devaluation or revaluation of the currency.

From January 1987 to 1992, there were no revaluations or devalu-ations of any member currencies except for devaluations of the lira. This was essentially because no government wished to be seen as having a weak economy and currency. There were nevertheless signif-icant economic divergences between the economies and pressures therefore built on the ERM. By September

1992, market specula-tion was sufficient to force the lira and sterling to leave the ERM (the alternative would have been to devalue massively) – although the lira rejoined in November 1996. By August 1993, speculation forced a more general readjustment of the currencies. The governments concerned still did not wish to be seen as giving in to the markets, however. The EU chose to avoid the issue by widening the ERM bands from ±2.25% as they then were for most currencies (±6% for ESP and PTE) to ±15% for all currencies. The result was bands so wide that there was little incentive for the market to speculate against any member currency. This begged the question of whether a system with such tolerant limits was in fact a system at all, and remained the situation until *European Monetary Union* (*EMU*) in 1999.

EMU and the euro

The Maastricht Treaty of 1991 set out a three-stage path towards monetary union. The first stage, already begun in mid-1990, involved the easing of restrictions on capital movements and closer economic policy co-ordination. The second stage, started at the beginning of 1994, established a European Monetary Institute (EMI) in Frank-furt to pave the way for transition to the final stage through closer alignment or convergence of the economic policies and the economies of the member states. The EMI was replaced in July 1998 by the establishment of a European Central Bank (ECB).

The third and final stage was the introduction of a single currency, the euro, at the beginning of 1999. In order to provide benchmarks for economic soundness, there were five convergence criteria which should have been met or approached in 1997 by countries intending to participate:

(i) The country's general government budget deficit should be no more than 3% of GDP.

(ii) The country's total general government debt outstanding should be no more than 60% of GDP, or approaching that level satis-factorily.

(iii) Consumer price inflation should be no more than 1.5% higher than the average of the inflation in the three countries with the lowest inflation.

(iv) Long-term government bond yields should be no more

than 2.0% higher than the average of the long-term interest rates of the same three countries as in (iii).

(v) The country's exchange rate must have been maintained within the 'normal fluctuation bands' for 2 years prior to joining.

The 12 EMU currencies

Following this process, it was determined on 2 May 1998 which eleven currencies would join the euro on 1 January 1999, and at what fixed exchange rates against each other. These rates were in fact the same central ERM cross-rate parities then prevailing. On 31 December 1998, the rates were announced at which each of these currencies was then fixed irrevocably against the euro. This rate depended partly on the 2 non-EMU components of the ECU – sterling and the Danish krone (the drachma and the Swedish krona were not in the ECU basket).

The Greek drachma joined the euro subsequently, on 1 January 2001.

The 12 *national currency units* or *legacy currencies* continued to exist, but only as units of the euro, until early 2002.

The irrevocably fixed rates of the legacy currencies against the euro were set at the following:

	Fixed rate against the euro
Austrian Schilling	13.7603
Belgian franc	40.3399
Finnish markka	5.94573
French franc	6.55957
Deutschemark	1.95583
Irish pound	0.787584
Italian lira	1936.27
Luxembourg franc	40.3399
Dutch guilder	2.20371
Portuguese escudo	200.482
Spanish peseta	166.386
Greek drachma	340.750

ERMII

The EU countries not joining EMU in 1999 were Denmark, Greece, Sweden and the UK. Of these currencies, the Danish krone and the Greek drachma transferred from the former ERM to a new ERMII.

Under the rules of ERMII, the member currencies (now only the krone) must be kept within an agreed band around an agreed central rate against the euro. In the case of the krone, the band is ±2.25%.

As with the original ERM, once a currency is in danger of breaching its bands, the government concerned is obliged to do one of the following:

- Intervene directly in the foreign exchange market to strengthen or weaken the currency. All governments may support the interven-tion, but the onus is on the government of the currency involved.
- Adjust economic policy to affect currency market perceptions. For example, the government of a weak currency might raise interest rates to make the currency more attractive.
- Revalue or devalue the central rate against the euro.

7

Analysing Currency Movements

OVERVIEW

This book does not attempt to provide a recipe for forecasting exchange rates. Rather, this is a very brief look at the framework in which forecasts are developed. There are essentially 2 very different approaches.

Technical analysis

One approach is *technical analysis* or *charting*. In its purest form, this depends entirely on examining past price movements and ignoring any outside factors which the forecaster may anticipate. An important principle of technical analysis is that the current price already reflects all known factors, as they have been absorbed into past price move-ments by market participants. There is no value in superimposing further factors and the chartist's forecast is therefore generated entirely from past price patterns.

By careful observation of price, volume and open interest and mathematical analysis of patterns in the price movement, the chartist constructs a picture that reflects existing investor sentiment and psychology and hence how investors view the market. On this basis, future price movements are forecast.

Fundamental analysis

The second approach is to assume that the forecaster can validly anticipate changes in outside factors and that he should do so and base his forecast on these. This is termed *fundamental* or *judgmental* forecasting. The forecaster must use his judgement in assessing which factors are important, how these factors will develop, and what effect they will have on the price being forecast.

For example: are world political developments likely to have an effect on the EUR/USD exchange rate? If so, what are these developments expected to be? Will these developments have a positive or negative effect on the exchange rate? The answers to these questions can all change over time. Rising US interest rates, for example, have, at different times in the past, had a strongly negative effect on the US dollar, a strongly positive effect, and no effect at all. The fundamental approach can be considered in several stages – long-term, medium-term and short-term.

Technical analysis assumes that the current price already reflects all known factors and that future price movements can be forecast on the basis of past price patterns.

Fundamental analysis assumes that the forecaster can validly anticipate changes in outside factors and that future price move-ments can be forecast on the basis of these changes.

The long-term view – purchasing power parity

Fundamentally, in a free market, an exchange rate is the mecha-nism by which prices of goods in different countries are equated. Assume that identical goods, freely tradeable, are obtainable from either country A or country B. If I am in country C, I am concerned only with the price to me in my own currency of buying from either A or B. If the prices are the same when converted into my own currency, then the exchange rate between A and B is at a fair level in relation to these goods. Suppose that over the next ten years, inflation in country A is much higher than in country B, so that the price of the goods rises much faster in A than in B. If the A/B exchange rate does not change, I will buy only from B, not from A. To overcome this lack of competitiveness in country A, the exchange rate must move over the ten years in such a way as to take account of the inflation differential. This is the *purchasing power parity* (*PPP*) concept.

PPP is the idea that a currency's exchange rate must move, in the long term, to adjust for inflation differentials against other countries.

This theory can sometimes be seen to function reasonably well in the very long run. In the short and medium term, however, it is generally a poor indicator of currency movements. There are several difficulties with it:

- Many goods are not internationally tradeable. The prices of a haircut, a mortgage or local fresh food may be important parts of inflation as measured, but have no bearing on international trade. Ideally, a measure of inflation is needed which only measures internationally traded goods.
- In practice, most goods are not identical in different countries. Even when they are, other factors such as product quality, delivery time, credit terms, prestige, after-sales service, reliability, preju-dice etc. may affect the extent to which one country can sell its goods more easily than another.
- Price differentials may be maintained by tariff and trade controls, transportation costs, different national resources, or technological innovations.
- Price equalization cannot, in practice, hold for individual goods. One test is to compare a country's domestic prices for a range of goods with a weighted average of prices for similar imported products.
- Once a country has a balance of payments deficit, its exchange rate may need to be even weaker than implied by purchasing power parity in order to redress the balance. This gives rise to the concept of a *Fundamental Equilibrium Exchange Rate* (*FEER*). This is the rate which is necessary in order to achieve a sustainable balance in the country's external current account.

In both cases, the infla-tion differential used is based on producer price indexes (German PPI ÷ US PPI and German PPI ÷ UK PPI respectively). The GBP/DEM demonstrates a reasonably good long-term correlation between the curves. The USD/DEM is reasonable in the very long term but dramatically wrong in the short term. In the case of Germany, the exchange rate has been expressed against the Deutschemark rather than the euro, as the Deutschemark was the currency for most of the period. From 1999 onwards, the euro rate has been converted at the fixed EUR/DEM parity.

The medium-term view

There are very many factors which can affect an exchange rate in the medium term including, for example, economic growth, monetary policy, fiscal policy, political developments, natural disasters and changes in sentiment, as well as the balance of payments and infla-tion. The forecaster's skill arises in selecting the appropriate factors from time to time, as well as in forecasting those factors themselves.

Short-term influences - market forces

Attitudes towards the foreign exchange market shift strongly from time to time, as different participants place different emphasis on particular factors which influence market behaviour. In the early and mid-1970s, relative monetary growth became fashionable as a currency indicator. In 1980, it was the turn of nominal and real interest rates. During much of 1987/88, the focus was more on trade imbalances. In 1988/89 attention turned more to interest rates again. In 1995, the biggest single emphasis was possibly on economic growth expectations. From the introduction of the euro in 1999 onwards, the EUR/USD rate has been dominated by a rather intangible disen-chantment with the strength and direction of European Central Bank (ECB) policy.

No matter how irrelevant a factor may appear, potential changes in market focus makes that factor an essential element in exchange rate forecasting. The market is therefore often characterized by sudden shifts of sentiment which may violently distort supply and demand relationships.

Expectations also have a crucial role in exchange rate determina-tion. A discrepancy between a previous expectation of a particular economic event and the actual outcome of that event may well move an exchange rate. For example, a currency may strengthen in anticipation of a good economic announcement but then weaken perversely when the announcement is made, even if it is as good as expected. Hence, there is a market saying: "Buy the rumour; sell the fact".

It is not possible to suggest a recipe for forecasting. The essence of fundamental forecasting is that it is judgemental and the forecaster's judgement may call for widely differing ingredients from time to time.

The forward rate

The forward outright exchange rate is, in one sense, strictly the mathematical result of combining the spot rate with interest rates, as we have seen in Chapter 2. In this sense, it cannot be a forecast of anything. Assuming free financial markets, however, this is a circular argument. If the current forward rate differs from the average expectation of market participants, then those participants will tend to move the forward rate towards that expectation by buying or selling the currency. This will move the spot rate and/or the two interest rates involved. The result will be that the forward rate will tend to reflect this average market expectation; in this sense, it is a forecast.

Effective exchange rates

An *effective exchange rate* measures a currency's average experience against other currencies which are important to that country for trade purposes. This average measure serves as a summary indicator of the currency's performance and is therefore a useful basis for foreign exchange market intervention by the government.

A *real effective exchange rate* measures the effective exchange rate, after adjustment for inflation differences between countries. This is useful for judging the country's competitive position in international markets.

An effective exchange rate measures a currency's average expe-rience against other currencies.

A real effective exchange rate adjusts this for inflation.

BANK RISK MANAGEMENT

In this chapter, we focus mostly on the risks arising from the instru-ments discussed in this book. We do not, for example, consider the risks arising specifically from trading options.

There are different ways of categorizing risks. The risks we describe here might therefore be grouped together slightly differently in another book. This is unimportant to the understanding of the risks and their management. The list is also not exhaustive – the reader will no doubt come across other examples.

The first two categories – market risk and credit risk – are risks which the bank often takes deliberately, in return for potential reward, in the normal course of its business – although it will be selective in this, choosing to hedge against some of the risks from time to time. The remaining risks – operational risk, fraud, systemic risk, legal and regulatory risk and business risk – are risks which arise because of the mechanics of doing business, but which the bank seeks to avoid, or at least minimize.

Many risks have a knock-on effect and affect more than 1 category. For example, failure to send a deal confirmation (an operational risk) can lead to both market risk and credit risk. We have given examples below of such knock-on effects.

Market risk

The risks

Market risk is the risk that the value of a position falls due to changes in market rates or prices. This is generally a major source of risk for the bank.

As mentioned, this is a risk which the bank might take on deliber-ately, to the extent that it seeks to make a profit by taking a position in a particular market. However, there are also situations where a market risk arises either unintentionally or unknowingly, possibly as a result of a credit or operational failure.

Movements in any market can be relevant. In general, there are four broad categories of market prices which are usually considered - FX, interest rates, equities and commodities.

Foreign exchange

A currency movement affects a spot dealer's position in an obvious way. However, it also affects a forward swap dealer's position; it is possible for a forward dealer to take a position which correctly anticipates a market move in the forward swap rates, but which causes the bank a loss because of spot rate movements. This risk (the *tail* of the position) might not be correctly recognized by the dealer or correctly hedged. This is covered fully in Chapter 10.

Example: *A* dealer buys USD 10 million against CHF. For each 1 point fall in the exchange rate, the bank would lose CHF 1,000.

Currency risks might in fact be less significant than they appear when measured against the base or reporting currency, because of cross-rate implications. For example, a yen-based organization might report two positions, the first long EUR 10 million against yen and the second short DKK 75 million against yen. The net exposure of long euros against kroner is likely to be a much less significant one than the two JPY exposures viewed separately, because of the relationship between the euro and the krone.

Interest rates

The value of many securities traded, including the ones discussed earlier in this book, is dependent on interest rates. If the bank holds a short-term security to maturity, the cashflows are not vulnerable to interest rate movements because there are no interim cashflows to be reinvested. However, the bank is still vulnerable because it cannot assume that the security will be held to maturity. Although that might be the intention, changing circumstances might force an early sale of the security at a time of high interest rates (and hence low prices).

A bank which buys or sells an FRA is also exposed to interest rates, as the settlement amount depends directly on the change in the rate between transaction and settlement.

Example : *A* dealer buys a 182-day US Treasury bill with face value USD 10 million, at a discount rate of 5.00%, for which he pays USD 9,747,222.22. He funds the position at a day-to-day cost of 5.20%.

Other market risks

There are clearly markets other than currency and interest rates which can affect the bank's position. Positions held in securities related to commodity markets or equities will clearly be affected by movements in those markets. The risks might also be interrelated. For example, a rise in interest rates might weaken the equity market, so that a long position in interest rate securities might possibly be partly relieved by a short position in equities. Currency movements similarly might affect some commodity prices, and commodity price movements might affect some equity prices.

Market movements can also affect the value of collateral which the bank is holding against credit extended to its customers and counterparties. This collateral is not part of the banks positions but, if the collateral value falls sharply, the bank becomes vulnerable to a credit risk which was previously secured.

Basis risk

Basis risk is the risk that two instruments do not move exactly in line as anticipated. Suppose, for example, that the bank has an FRA position which is matched by a futures position. The net position should be invulnerable to interest rate movements. There is, however, a basis risk, as the two markets might in fact not move exactly together. A similar basis risk might arise in any position, so that the actual price change is less favorable than the expected change.

The hedge has not matched the original exposure, because the June futures price has not moved to the same extent as the difference between the original FRA price and the LIBOR fixing on 17 May.

Liquidity risk

Liquidity risk is related to market risk. It is the risk of being unable to find a liquid market for a particular instrument, when the time comes to close out a position. An extreme example of lack of liquidity occurred following 11 September 2001 when the New York stock exchange was closed for several days, making it impossible to liqui-date positions. A less extreme example is the common problem of a particular stock or bond in which there is very little trading.

Example: A dealer sells an FRA to a customer in a minor currency, intending to hedge this using futures. He then finds that the futures market is not liquid enough to provide the hedge requi-red, so that he must keep the risk uncovered for the moment.

Model risk

Model risk is the risk that a computer model used by a dealer to price and value an instrument is wrong. This can also be considered as forming a part of operational risk rather than market risk.

RISK MEASUREMENT AND CONTROLS

Measurement

Risks are measured in various ways, some of which are appropriate to different instruments and in different situations.

- Firstly, positions are netted for market risk. For example, if a US dollar-based bank has only two deals, one of which is a spot purchase of JPY 1 billion and the other of which is a spot sale of JPY 1 billion, then there is zero market risk – although there is likely to be credit risk.
- Banks continually *mark-to-market* trading positions. This means that the position is revalued by calculating the profit or loss which would be realized if the position were closed out at current rates. This unrealized profit or loss is taken into the accounts daily.
- Risk on positions in interest rate instruments can be estimated using *modified duration*. This is a factor measuring the sensitivity of a position to changes in interest rates. For example, if a partic-ular long position in a security has a modified duration of 4, then an immediate increase of 0.01% in all interest rates would cause an immediate loss of approximately 0.04% of the value of the position.
- *Gap analysis* – see below – is also used to measure risk on interest rate positions and forward FX positions.
- Increasingly, banks use *value at risk (VaR)* to measure risk over all their positions. This is considered later in the chapter.

Limits

An essential control is to set maximum limits on the size of positions and the extent of market risk which dealers are allowed to take, and to ensure that management procedures are in place to keep positions strictly within these limits. Limits are set in various ways:

- Position limits are set for each trading position, depending on both the instrument concerned and the experience and expertise of the dealer.
- Limits might be set on the maximum size of a single transaction.
- Limits are set for the maximum size of a forward dealer's or deposit dealer's gap exposure.
- Limits are set for both intra-day positions (*daylight limit*) and positions left open overnight (*overnight limit*).

- *Stop loss* and *take profit* levels are set. These are prices or rates which, if touched in the market, will trigger the closing of a position, in order to avoid any further loss or to ensure that an existing profit is captured.
- Limits are set for overall risk across various positions in different securities or currencies.
- Limits are set for overall risk across the bank's worldwide opera-tions, as well as in each center.
- Limits are set on the level of VaR.

Gap analysis

Gap analysis is a measure of the difference in exposures to interest rates in different periods. Clearly a portfolio consisting of a USD 1 million asset and a USD 1 million liability both of exactly 1 year maturity, and a USD 2 million asset and a USD 2 million liability both of exactly 2 years' maturity is not at risk to interest rate changes in general, although it might of course involve basis risk. If, however, the portfolio consists of the following net positions:

1 year maturity short USD 3 million

10 years' maturity: long USD 3 million

then there is a risk to general changes along the yield curve, even if there is no basis risk.

Suppose, for example, that interest rates rise by 0.5% for 1-year yields and 0.8% for 10-year yields (a steepening positive yield curve, or a flattening negative one). Broadly speaking, the effect will be a gain of USD 15,000 per annum for 1 year on the assets but a much greater loss of USD 24,000 per annum for 10 years on the liabilities. In order to control this risk, gap analysis considers a portfolio broken down by period. In a major portfolio, this cannot conveniently be done in great detail, so that periods will be grouped, with more subdivision of shorter time periods, where yield curve changes are likely to be more pronounced. Thus, for example, maturities might be split as follows:

0–7 days 7–30 days 1–3 months 3–6 months 6–12 months 1–2 years 2–5 years 5–10 years

Analysis in this way forces consideration of maturity imbalances, and of potential liquidity problems, but has several weaknesses, as follows:

- Because the groupings are discrete, the position can appear to change sharply from one day to the next. For example, a loan of 5 years plus one day would shift from one period to another a day later, given the schedule suggested above.
- For the same reason, if gap analysis shows a particular exposure which the bank wishes to cover, it is likely that the cover taken will create a new risk later: the cover might reduce the gap now, but re-create another one in due course.
- Most importantly, gap analysis does not take account of the time-value of money on the assets and liabilities, or the reinvestment risks. A 5-year zero-coupon asset appears to match a 5-year liability with semi-annual interest, whereas in fact the cashflow profiles are of course very different.

Other controls

There are other elements of control which should be in place, including the following:

- All deals should be input immediately to the bank's systems for both settlement processing and risk measurement.
- It is important that, for risk and accounting purposes, any trans-action intended to be a hedge is linked to the underlying deal it is intended to cover.
- There must be rigorous testing of computer valuation models before they are used.

CREDIT RISK

The risks

Credit risk is the risk that a counterparty might default on a trans-action by failing to pay amounts due or failing to deliver a security or failing in some other way (*counterparty risk*), or that the issuer of a security defaults on coupon or interest payments.

In the case of a loan made to a counterparty, the whole principal amount of the loan is potentially at risk. The same is true of a long position in a security if the issuer defaults.

In many cases, however, counterparty risk is rather smaller. For example, if the counterparty is bankrupted before a forward foreign exchange outright matures, our bank knows that it will not receive anything from the counterparty and therefore deliberately does not deliver its side of the deal either. In this case, how much will our bank lose? If the deal is showing a loss from our point of view, we will not lose anything. In practice, in this case the administrators of the bankrupt counterparty should insist on consummation of the deal anyway, so that there would be no effect on our bank.

Suppose, however, that the deal is showing a mark-to-market profit to our bank. That is, the deal would show a loss to the counterparty if it were closed out now. In this case, the deal will simply not be consummated. Our loss is therefore limited to the profit on the deal. This loss can be seen as how much it will cost our bank to replace the deal with a similar deal with another counterparty. The risk is therefore called *replacement risk.*

For a short period during the settlement cycle when a FX deal is delivered, the risk does involve the entire principal amount of the deal. After our bank has already committed itself to making payment on its part, but before it can be certain that its counterparty has done the same, the whole amount of the trade is at risk. This is known as *settlement risk* (also *Herstatt risk* in the case of foreign exchange after Bank Herstatt, which defaulted in 1974). This risk is removed when securities are delivered against payment through a clearing organization.

Example : On 15 August, the bank sells USD 10 million against CHF to a counterparty for value 17 September at 1.7324. By 22 August, the forward rate has moved to 1.7188. The bank has a potential profit of CHF 136,000 on 17 September, which it would lose if the counterparty goes bankrupt. The size of the replacement risk is therefore the present value of CHF 136,000.

$$10{,}000{,}000 \times (1.7324 - 1.7188) = 136{,}000$$

Settlement risk in foreign exchange should be rather short-term because payment instructions should be revocable (able to be cancel-led) until settlement date. In practice, however, the cut-off time for irrevocable instructions is sometimes earlier.

The clearing houses for futures exchanges are generally considered to be free of credit risk because of their arrangements for *margin.* This is a combination of collateral placed with the clearing house in case of default *(initial margin)* and the requirement to pay losses as they arise daily *(variation margin)* rather than on final settlement.

Exchanges do not all have the same rules, however, and, in extreme circumstances, could possibly still fail.

Credit risk can increase during the life of a deal for two reasons. Firstly, the credit rating of a counterparty, or of the issuer of a security in the bank's portfolio, might weaken after a deal has been transacted or a security purchased. Secondly, credit risk will change as the market moves. For example, the bank has no counterparty risk when a forward foreign exchange deal is first transacted. If the counterparty goes bankrupt immediately, there is no mark-to-market profit or loss, so that our bank can replace the deal with another counterparty at the same rate. If the market then moves so that our bank is in profit however, this creates a replacement risk. Credit risk and market risk are in this way interlinked. Credit risk includes both issuer default risk and counter-party risk. Counterparty risk is credit risk arising from default of a coun-terparty at any time.

Where a deal can be replaced, counterparty risk is called replacement risk and is limited to the cost of replacement – i.e. any mark-to-market profit.

After irrevocable payment instructions have been given, coun-terparty risk is called settlement risk and is potentially the entire amount of the deal.

Controls

The essential first step in reducing credit risk is rigorous credit assessment of counterparties and issuers. If there are no defaults, there is ~~no~~ credit risk. In practice, however, there will always be credit risk.

- As with market risk, there must be limits set on the size of outstanding transactions with any one counterparty together with the value of securities held which have been issued by that coun-terparty. Within the limit, the amount of business allowed will depend on the nature of the transaction. A USD 1 million loan to a counterparty is much riskier (because the whole principal amount is at risk) than a USD 1 million FRA transacted with the same counterparty.

- Limits are set not only on individual counterparties, but also, for example, on each sector of industry and each country.
- Monitoring of credit risk must take account of the fact that credit risk can depend on market movements, as described earlier.
- The value of any collateral taken from counterparties must be care-fully monitored and additional collateral called for when appro-priate.
- All settlements expected from counterparties must be reconciled promptly, as a warning system for potential default.
- Operations staff should be trained in what constitutes a default.
- The bank should negotiate the latest possible cut-off times for making payments.
- Wherever possible, the bank should set up legally enforceable documentation with each counterparty which incorporates *obliga-tion netting* and *close-out netting*. The bank should also use netting systems, and *DvP* and *PvP* systems where possible. These various areas are outlined in the next section.

Netting

Netting cash payments means transferring net amounts rather than gross amounts between parties. Transfers of a particular security can be netted in the same way.

Example : Bank A is due to make a payment of USD 5 million to Bank B on 15 June in settlement of one transaction and Bank B is due to make a payment of USD 4 million to Bank A on the same date in settlement of a different transaction. Instead of making both these payments gross, Banks A and B could agree that Bank A pays Bank B an amount of USD 1 million (=USD 5 million - USD 4 million) as full net settlement of the two transactions.

The purposes of netting are to reduce credit risk, improve liquidity and reduce operational risks and costs. In the above Example, if the two gross payments are made separately, Bank A must normally give irrevocable instructions to pay away USD 5 million before it knows whether it has received the USD 4 million from Bank B. If Bank B subsequently proves unable to pay the USD 4 million, Bank A might have a USD 4 million loss. Bank B is similarly exposed to the credit risk of Bank A. This risk reduction also enables an increase in the volume of business transactions between the two parties, because of the reduction in capital requirements allowed by supervisors where there is appropriate netting - see 'Capital adequacy requirements' later in this chapter. The bank's credit risk monitoring system should accurately reflect the effect of netting.

In the same Example, the net settlement improves liquidity. If Bank A only has to pay the net USD 1 million, its available funds are reduced by that amount. If, however, it must pay USD 5 million, its available funds are reduced by USD 5 million until it has finally received the USD 4 million from Bank B. The net settlement in the example should also reduce the operational cost and risk of error, as there is only one payment rather than two.

An arrangement to net should always be supported by a written master agreement between the parties to that effect. A master agree-ment is one which covers all deals of a particular type between the two parties, except those which are specifically agreed at the time of the deal to be treated separately. There are two netting aspects to a master agreement. The first is netting of settlements in the normal course of business as described in the example above; this is known as obligation netting. The second is close-out netting, which occurs when one of the parties is in default of the agreement for any reason; close-out netting allows the non-defaulting party to close-out all existing transactions – i.e., terminate them early. Agreement to close-out netting provides that, in these circumstances, a single net settlement is made for all outstanding transactions. This removes the possibility of *cherry-picking*, a term used to describe the way in which an administrator for a counterparty in liquidation might be able to insist on consummating profitable deals with a particular counterparty, while defaulting on unprofitable ones.

Netting in a master agreement is effective only if it will prove to be legally binding in the event of dispute. Whether this is so might depend on the various legal jurisdictions of the agreement itself, the parties and any correspondent banks or custodians involved in the settlements. It is therefore always important for legal opinions to be sought. Legal opinions in the UK and USA, for example, support the use of netting domestically, but there are still concerns over the enforceability of cross-border netting.

Netting in master agreements is often netting by novation. This involves legally substituting a new single contract between the two parties to combine and replace all existing similar contracts between them for a given settlement date. The major master agreements used internationally which cover the instruments described in this book are:

- IFEMA (International Foreign Exchange Master Agreement) for foreign exchange spot and forward deals.
- ISDA (International Swaps and Derivatives Association) master agreement for FRAs (also used for swaps, options and other transactions). FRABBA (The BBA's documentation for FRAs) is also used, but less frequently.
- GMRA (Global Master Repo Agreement) for repos and buy/sell-backs.
- SAFEBBA (The BBA's documentation for SAFEs)

Netting systems

The example above involves bilateral netting - netting between two parties. It is possible to organize such netting through a third-party bilateral netting system. FXNET is such an organization, which runs a bilateral netting system for banks involved in foreign exchange deals.

A multilateral netting system nets payments between more than two banks. Transactions between all the banks involved are netted so that, in each currency, each bank only receives one net amount or pays one net amount or does neither.

Example: Suppose the following gross amounts are due, all on the same date:

Bank A owes Bank B USD 5 million Bank B owes Bank A USD 4 million Bank A owes Bank C USD 3 million Bank C owes Bank A USD 5 million Bank B owes Bank C USD 10 million Bank C owes Bank B USD 8 million

The net result for Bank A is that it is owed USD 1 million (=— USD 5 million + USD 4 million — USD 3 million + USD 5 million). The net result for Bank B is that it owes USD 1 million (=—USD 5 million + USD 4 million + USD 10 million — USD 8 million).

The net result for Bank C is zero (= —USD 3 million + USD 5 million — USD 10 million + USD 8 million). In this case, multilateral settlement could be achieved by a simple payment of USD 1 million from Bank B to Bank A, instead of six gross bilateral payments.

PvP and DvP

Bilateral and multilateral netting systems operate by netting and settling the payments due on a particular date at certain times on that day - often at the end of the day. An alternative is a *payment versus payment (PvP)* system. In this, a payment from Bank A to Bank B is made only if, and at the same time as, the corresponding payment from Bank B to Bank A is made. The payments are made during the day on a real-time basis and, once made, are final. Such a system – *continuous real-time linked settlement (CLS)* – has been developed for FX settlements by CLS Bank, starting in 2002 with settlements for USD, CAD, EUR, GBP, CHF, AUD and JPY, and extending to SEK, NOK, DKK and SGD in 2003.

Settlement is avail-able during a 5-hour window from 07:00 to 12:00 Central European Time. Members of CLS need to maintain collateral in the system to cover the net risk they represent to other members. A danger of PvP is that there can be non-credit-related reasons for non-payment, such as systems failures, strikes, severe weather problems, human error etc. Non-settlement could cause the whole system to fail, causing a liquidity crisis. A systemic failure in one country, for example, could bring the system down.

Delivery versus payment (DvP) is the corresponding settlement mechanism, used widely both domestically and internationally, for settlement of securities transactions. In this, a payment from Bank A to Bank B is made only if, and at the same time as, the corresponding security is delivered from Bank B to Bank A.

Contracts for differences

A contract for differences is a transaction where only the net difference between two amounts is settled, and the principal amount involved is not transferred. This reduces credit risk very significantly. Generally the settlement is the difference between the rate or price dealt at the outset and a reference rate or price at maturity, calculated on a notional principal amount.

FRAs, Futures and SAFEs, covered earlier in this book, are contracts for differences.

Forward outrights are available as non-deliverable forwards (NDFs), also covered earlier. These contracts for differences are largely used in emerging currencies for exchange control reasons rather than risk control, but the concept can be extended to major currencies.

OPERATIONAL RISK

The risks

Operational risk is a wide term, covering the risk of losses due to failures in the bank's operations generally. This includes the activities of the operations department itself (deal input, confirmation, netting, payments and reconciliation) but also covers other areas such as the bank's computer systems (*system risk*), accounting, personnel problems and even third-party organizations such as custodians and correspondent banks. The problems might arise from staff mistakes, management weaknesses or system errors. Many of the risks can have knock-on effects on market risk or credit risk.

Example: Operational risk can arise in many ways. The following are just some examples:

A deal ticket for the purchase of USD 10 million from Bank A against CHF at 1.7324 is entered incorrectly in the bank's system as a sale of USD 10 million. A dealer covers the short USD expo-sure which the system is showing, by buying USD 10 million from Bank B. In fact this has doubled the size of the long posi-tion, rather than reducing the exposure to zero. The dollar now falls to 1.7188 and the bank makes a loss of CHF 272,000.

If in fact the dollar had risen instead, there would have been a profit on the original deal with bank A, giving rise to a credit risk from bank A. The system, however, would show no such credit risk because the deal would appear to show a loss.

The error could thus give rise to market risk or credit risk, by mis-stating the position in both.

A deal confirmation sent to a counterparty is incorrect, or an incorrect incoming confirmation is not checked properly. This could similarly give rise to market and/or credit risk, as well as harm the banks reputation (reputational risk). The payment in settlement of a deal is sent incorrectly, so that the counterparty, which does not receive the funds on time, makes a claim for interest.

A power cut causes the computer systems to crash and there is no adequate back-up power system.

The bank relies on a few key staff members for processing certain complex transactions and this whole team of staff leaves the bank to join a competitor. Errors are made as further deals of this type are processed, leading to market risk, credit risk and reputational risk.

A bomb or a natural disaster makes it impossible for the bank to carry on its business at its usual premises and there are no adequate back-up facilities. This could lead to the loss of a considerable volume of business, as well as creating market, credit and reputational risks.

Controls

The task of controlling operational risk is as broad as operational risk itself. It is paramount that staff are competent and well trained and that systems are thoroughly tested. An approach to reducing human error is the introduction of *straight-through processing (STP)*. This is a general term for the computerization of tasks in such a way that each process feeds automatically to the next. Other points include:

- No deal should be undertaken unless operations staff, risk managers, accounting staff and IT staff all understand the mechanics of the transaction. Existing systems might not be adequate, or input might be required to several incompatible systems for position recording, risk management, settlement etc.
- It is important that confirmations are sent, and incoming confir-mations checked, as quickly as possible. Speed is particularly important in areas where a loss could increase very quickly.
- It is important to have a team approach, as the individual proces-ses relating to a trade are completed by different people. Each person should know how his role fits into the whole process.

OTHER RISKS

Fraud

It is possible for the bank to try to address the risks mentioned so far – even though risk is rarely reduced to zero. The perpetrator of a fraud, however, is presumably circumventing exactly those controls which have been put in place to protect the bank. This could perhaps be seen as yet another type of operational risk. For example, it could be difficult to prevent fraud if there were sufficient collusion between dealers and operations staff in two counterparty banks.

Segregation of responsibilities

An important principle – particularly in seeking to avoid fraud but also to help control operational risks – is the segregation of responsi-bilities between the *front office* (the dealers) and the *back office* (the operational staff). It is essential that the two areas be totally separate in terms of both staff and management reporting. Ideally, they should be physically separate also, although this might not always be prac-ticable.

It is important also that computer access by dealing staff to the back-office systems is not possible. Operational errors or oddities are less likely to be noticed – or remedial action taken – if the same person is responsible for more than one of these areas. The internal audit function should also be totally separate.

Systemic risk

This is the risk of failure in the entire system of which the bank itself is only a part - for example, a failure of the entire payment clearing system or the entire banking system. This could, for example, be because of mechanical difficulties (a computer failure) or because a major payment default by another bank, which might be one with whom our bank has no dealings, has caused a chain reaction of defaults, seizing up the payment clearing.

Legal and regulatory risk

This is the risk that the banks business is affected by changes in laws and regulations, or by existing laws and regulations which it had not properly taken into account. Again, this may be seen as a type of operational risk, but some of the risks here arise from changes outside the bank's control and which it might not reasonably be likely to anticipate.

Example : The bank expects to receive an FRA settlement from a counter-party. Although financially healthy, the counterparty refuses to pay the settlement and the bank is unable to enforce settlement because the counterparty is in a legal jurisdiction which does not support the transaction. Alternatively, the counterparty did not have the authorization for the transaction, which is then considered legally void.

A corporate customer refuses to consummate a particular transaction, because it claims that it was misadvised by the bank in undertaking it, and the courts support the customer.

Some of the banks outstanding transactions are adversely affected by changes in taxation or changes in the requirements for capital adequacy (see later in this chapter).

The bank permits transactions, knowingly or unknowingly, which involve money laundering, and the bank is subsequently penalized by the authorities for doing so.

Business risk

The bank is at risk to general business conditions in the same way as any other business, although this can possibly be magnified. A severe recession, for example, as well as possibly reducing demand for the banks services, could result in a fall in creditworthiness of the bank's existing business across the board. The bank also faces other commercial risks, such as the commercial value of its buildings.

A fall in the bank's own credit rating for any reason will also result in higher funding costs compared with its competitors.

VALUE AT RISK (VAR)

A full treatment of VaR is mathematically complex and outside the scope of this book. This is therefore an overview only, aimed at giving the reader an understanding of the process. The details of the first section on basic statistics are not essential to understanding the VaR section which follows it, but they might be helpful if you are interested.

BASIC STATISTICS

Mean, variance and standard deviation

The arithmetic *mean* of a series of numbers is the average of the numbers as we normally understand it. The mean is useful, because it gives us an idea of the how big the numbers are - about 56. However, if we knew only this mean, 56, it would not give us any idea of how spread out all the numbers are around 56; perhaps they are all very close to 56, or perhaps they are very spread out.

The standard deviation of the same numbers is a measure of how spread out the numbers are around this mean. If all the numbers were exactly the same, the standard deviation would be zero. If the numbers were very spread out, the standard deviation would be very high. Effectively, the standard deviation gives an idea of the answer to the question: On average, how far away are the numbers from their mean?

The mean is the average of a set of numbers.

Standard deviation is a measure of how spread out the numbers are around the mean.

The standard deviation is defined as the square root of the *variance*. The variance in turn is defined as the average of the squared difference between each number and their average.

Consider the two sets of numbers in Figures 12.1 and 12.2. They also each have a mean of 56, but in Figure 12.1 the first set is closely packed together and the second set in Figure 12.2 is very spread out. In fact, the first set has a standard deviation of 1.4 and the second set has a standard deviation of 4.3. If the standard deviation or variance is lower, the histogram is compressed horizontally – it looks taller and thinner – and there is a lower probability that any particular number is a long way from the mean. If the standard deviation or variance is greater, the histogram is more stretched out horizontally – it looks lower and fatter – and more numbers are further from the mean.

Mean (μ) = sum of all the values divided by the number of values

Variance (σ^2) = mean of (difference from mean)^2

sum of all the (difference from the mean)^2 the number of values

This gives the variance of a set of numbers, given that all the numbers are known. Very often, however, a sample only of the numbers is used. For example, a representative sample of prices for a particular instrument might be the daily closing prices over a period of only one year, rather than over the entire history of that instrument since it began trading.

Correlation and covariance

Correlation and covariance are measures of the extent to which two things do, or do not, move together. The precise mathematical definitions are given below.

Consider, for example, the USD/DKK exchange rate and the USD/ EUR exchange rate. Generally, one rate will rise and fall in line with the other. The two rates are therefore very closely correlated. On the other hand, the USD/DKK exchange rate will fall as the EUR/USD exchange rate rises, so that there is a close negative correlation between these two rates. There is probably very little relationship at all between Mexican interest rates and the HUF/JPY exchange rate, so these 2 numbers have no correlation – the price of one moving up or down suggests no information about whether the other is moving up or down.

A correlation coefficient lies between +1 and -1. If two series of numbers are perfectly correlated – they move exactly in line – their correlation coefficient is +1. if they move exactly in line but in opposite directions, their correlation coefficient is -1. If there is no link at all between the two series, their correlation coefficient is 0.

A correlation coefficient lies between -1 and +1 and measures the extent to which two things do, or do not, move together.

Probability density

The *probability density* of a series of numbers is a description of how likely any one of them is to occur. Thus the probability density of the results of throwing a die is 1 for each possible result. The probability density of the heights of 100 adult men chosen at random will be relatively high for around 170 cm to 180 cm, and very low for less than 150 cm or more than 200 cm. The shape of the probability density therefore varies with the type of results being considered.

One particular probability density which is used as an approximate description of many circumstances in life is known as the *normal* probability function.

If the probabilities are as shown in Figure 12.4, for example, a number less than —3 or more than +3 is extremely unlikely, while a number between say — 1 and +1 is rather likely.

The normal probability function is not mathematically straightfor-ward – the equation for the graph is in fact:

This function is important here because it is widely used in VaR calculations.

Probability distribution

The *cumulative probability distribution* of a series of numbers is the probability that any one of them will be no greater than a particular number. Thus the probability distribution for throwing the die is:

probability $^{1}_{6}$ that the number thrown will be 1 probability $^{2}_{6}$ that the number thrown will be 1 or 2 probability $^{3}_{6}$ that the number thrown will be 1, 2 or 3 probability $^{4}_{6}$ that the number thrown will be 1, 2, 3 or 4 probability $^{5}_{6}$ that the number thrown will be 1, 2, 3, 4 or 5 probability $^{6}_{6}$ that the number thrown will be 1, 2, 3, 4, 5 or 6

The normal probability function shown in Figure 12.4 has the corresponding probability distribution shown in Figure 12.5. If the standard deviation were greater, so that the curve in Figure 12.4 was shorter and fatter, then the curve in Figure 12.5 would also be more stretched out horizontally. If the standard deviation were less, it would be compressed horizontally.

With this normal probability distribution, there is a probability of around 84.1% that the outcome will be less than or equal to 1 standard deviation higher than the mean; a probability of around 97.7% that the outcome will be less than or equal to 2 standard deviations higher than the mean; a probability of around 99.9% that the outcome will be less than or equal to 3 standard deviations higher than the mean, and so on.

In each of these examples, we are considering the probability of any number being in a range which goes down to minus infinity but goes up only to a certain defined level (1, 2, 3 and so on), leaving a *tail* excluded at the top. As the normal curve is symmetrical, we could equally well consider a range which goes up to plus infinity but goes down only to a certain defined level (—1, —2, —3 and so on), leaving a tail excluded at the bottom. This one-tailed measurement is what is generally used in risk calculations, because a risk manager is worried about how much loss the bank might make, rather than how much profit.

We have now reached the important point. If we assume that the probability distribution for a particular price is normal and can estimate the standard deviation, it is possible to calculate what is the probability of any particular number being less than — 1, or less than —2 etc. A similar calculation can also be made based on the assumption of a probability distribution other than a normal one. In financial risk management, this translates into being able to estimate the probability of a loss being worse than a particular level.

Overview of VaR

In order to control market risk, the bank needs to be in a position to measure it. In line with EU and BIS regulations, banks have therefore increasingly developed computer models to assess market risk, with a view to deriving an overall measurement of the bank's risk - value at risk (VaR) or *earnings at risk.*

VaR is the maximum potential loss which the bank might suffer on its positions over a given time period, estimated within a given confidence level. Suppose, for example, that the bank has a VaR of USD 10 million with a time horizon of 30 days and a confi-dence level of 95%. This means that if the bank's positions remain unchanged, there is a 95% probability that its total losses will not exceed USD 10 million over the next 30 days - or to put it another way, a 5% probability that the total losses will exceed this amount. The total expected loss would be smaller (greater) if the time horizon were less (more) than 30 days and smaller (greater) if the confidence level were lower (higher) than 95%.

VaR is: the maximum potential loss which the bank might suffer over a given time period estimated within a given confidence level.

In arriving at this summary number of USD 10 million, the bank must make certain assumptions. Firstly, there is an assumption about the probability distribution of price movements for each instru-ment in which the bank has a position – what is the pattern of price movement and are the price changes up and down expected to be large or small? Mathematically, this means: What is the probability distribution and what is its standard deviation? Typically, banks use an assumption that asset returns show a normal probability distri-bution as the basis for risk assessment, and the standard deviation used will be based on historic movements.

Secondly, the bank will take into account correlation between different instruments. Suppose, for example, that a particular dollar-based bank is long of 1 million euros and short of an equivalent amount of Swiss francs. Because there is some correlation between euros and Swiss francs, the bank is less vulnerable to market move-ments than if it were only long of 1 million euros without any offsetting position. In this particular case, the greater the correlation, the less risky the position. If the two positions were both long (rather than one long and one short), then the riskiness of the total position would instead increase with higher correlation, rather than decrease. In general, a portfolio of positions is less risky if it is more diversified.

VARIANCE/COVARIANCE, MONTE CARLO AND HISTORIC APPROACHES

There are 3 widely used approaches to calculating VaR, each with advantages and disadvantages.

Variance/covariance

The approach considered so far for estimating VaR is essentially the *variance/covariance* approach. This approach involves the following:

- Assume a probability distribution – generally taken to be the normal distribution.
- Assume a variance for each financial instrument and a covariance between each pair of different financial instruments – generally based on historic data.
- Because it is impractical (and gives rise to mathematical difficul-ties) to use variance and covariance data for each instrument in a portfolio, only a selection of standard instruments is used. Each instrument in the actual portfolio

is then expressed in terms of an equivalent number of these standard instruments. For example, a foreign exchange forward can be expressed in terms of a spot position and two loans or deposits; an interest rate-based security can be broken down to individual cashflows and expressed as an equivalent strip of zero-coupon instruments. This process is known as *mapping*, and vastly reduces the number of instruments to be considered.

CALCULATE THE VAR.

The variance/covariance approach has the advantage of being rela-tively straightforward. A matrix of variances and covariances for the standard instruments can be obtained from third parties, such as JP Morgan's *Riskmetrics*. The properties of the normal distribution are well known (a 95% confidence level, for example, implies a VaR of 1.65 standard deviations below the mean) and allow for relatively simple risk assessment. If the standard deviation is doubled, for example, the VaR is doubled as well; if the time horizon is doubled, the VaR is multiplied by the square root of 2.

A disadvantage is that the relationship between the VaR and the underlying risk variables is linear (i.e., they are directly propor-tional). For example, it assumes that if yields move by a certain amount, security prices will move in direct proportion. Similarly, it assumes that option values move in direct proportion to under-lying prices. In practice, this is not the case, so that for an option portfolio, the variance/covariance approach is generally unsatis-factory.

Monte Carlo simulation

An alternative is to use a *Monte Carlo* simulation. This involves generating a very large number of random prices, applying these to the current portfolio of instruments and measuring the net effect:

- For each instrument or set of instruments, choose a probability distribution and pricing model.
- Assume variances and covariances.
- Generate a random set of data (changes in prices, rates, option volatilities). Although this computer-generated series of prices is random, it must still fit an assumed

probability distribution; if the current price of an asset is 100, for example, a move to 50 is much less likely than a move to 99.

- Apply these data to the portfolio and calculate the resulting profit or loss.
- Repeat this process many times, to generate a large number of possible profit or loss outcomes.
- List these results in order. For a 95% confidence level, for example, exclude the worst 5% of results. The VaR will then be the worst result remaining.

A disadvantage of this technique is that it is more expensive in terms of computer time than the variance/covariance approach. It is also more complex to set up and to explain and still depends on the assumptions made about probability distributions and variances and covariances. It can, however, be much more reliable for option-related instruments.

Historic

Another possibility is to use historic price movements and apply these to the current portfolio of instruments, on the assumption that future price movements will mimic past ones, and look at the net effect, as with a Monte Carlo simulation. This approach is therefore as follows:

- Map the actual portfolio to a selection of standard instruments for which historic price data are available, either from a third party or from an in-house database.
- Estimate the change in value of the entire portfolio that would have arisen over a particular period in the past – for example, from 365 days ago until 335 days ago – by applying actual historic price changes. Then measure the change that would have arisen from 364 days ago until 334 days ago, then the change from 363 days ago until 333 days ago, and so on.
- List all these results and, for a 95% confidence level, exclude the worst 5% of results. The worst result remaining is the VaR for a 30-day time horizon.

This approach has the advantage of being a simpler technique mathematically than the variance/covariance and Monte Carlo appro-aches, and simple to explain in concept. No particular probability distribution (such as a normal one) needs to be assumed, as the prob-ability distribution is implicit in the historic data used. Similarly, the variances and covariances do not need to be measured or even known, because they are also implicit in the historic data. It also does not suffer from the same linear restrictions as the variance/covariance approach.

However, this method still suffers from the drawback that the size of price movements and the relationships between price movements of different instruments (i.e. their correlations or covariances) might not be the same in the future as in the past. It also depends on the choice of historic period. Too short a period might be unrepresentative (for example, it might have been a particularly volatile or quiet period). Too long a period might include a period so long ago that variances and/or covariances have changed significantly since then.

General problems with VaR calculations

One obvious difficulty with the variance/covariance calculation lies in the assumption of a normal probability distribution. In practice, the probability distribution relating to financial price movements tends to have fatter tails than suggested by the normal curve (the left-hand and right-hand ends of the graph are fatter than shown above). This suggests a greater probability of large profits or losses.

There is also a likelihood of *negative skewness* – a greater proba-bility of a large downward movement in prices than of a large upward movement. This is because a falling market can trigger panic stop-loss sales which accelerate prices downward.

Variances and correlations are also not constant. Those seen in the past are not necessarily a good guide to the future.

A further problem with correlation is that historic relationships sometimes break down under extreme circumstances. For example, in quiet markets, the US dollar and the Singapore dollar might be very closely correlated, so that a portfolio long of one and short of the other looks relatively safe. When the market panics, however, they might diverge significantly. The use of correlation in assessing risk must therefore be partly based on historic data and partly subjective.

In using VaR for risk management, the bank must also make

a decision on the holding period and confidence level (30 days and 95% in the examples above). These parameters are clearly arbitrary and depend on the bank's ability to accept risk and the speed with which it believes it can close out a loss-making position from a management point of view. They also depend on how liquid are the markets in which the bank is working, as this affects the speed and ease with which it is possible to close a position from a practical market point of view.

Stress-testing

An alternative approach to statistical analysis such as VaR is scenario analysis – assessing risk by assuming a particular scenario and seeing what happens:

- Choose a particular outcome for all the variables (FX rates, interest rates etc.).
- Calculate what would happen to the portfolio's value under these circumstances.
- Repeat the process for different assumptions.

A sensible check on a VaR model, for example, is stress testing by applying worst-case assumptions – not necessarily historical ones – to assess how different the result is for the portfolio compared with the VaR result. This might not necessarily be a basis for regulatory reporting, or for adjusting the portfolio, but is a useful additional view of both the portfolio and the VaR model.

For example, the bank can consider what is the greatest actual movement which has occurred in the past in each instrument or type of instrument. This gives rise to several problems. Firstly, history might not repeat itself because conditions do change. Secondly, the worst that has happened in the past might in fact not be as bad as the worst that could happen in the future. Thirdly, there is the problem of correlation: depending on the nature of the portfolio, it might be highly improbable that the worst will happen simultaneously in all the bank's positions.

The advantages of stress testing are that it is good for extreme events and shows up potential weaknesses in other models. As it can be based on any assumptions, it is good for 'what if' modeling. A disadvantage of course is that it is only as good as the assumptions made – garbage in, garbage out.

BIS recommendations on VaR

The BIS recommends that a supervisory authority should allow the bank to use its own internal VaR model for calculating its capital adequacy requirements (see the next section). The VaR is taken to be the greater of either the latest VaR measurement, or the average of the last 60 days' VaR measurements multiplied by a factor (which must be at least 3) determined by the supervisory authority.

This gives the capital charge for market risk. However, the recommendation is that an internal VaR model can only be used if the following conditions are met:

- There should be a qualitative check on the model's use: the bank should have a risk control unit which is independent of the dealers, and also the model's results should be integrated into the bank's day-to-day controls.
- There should be a quantitative check: a test portfolio should be run through the model to check its measurements.
- VaR using the model should be calculated at least daily.
- The holding period used should be 10 days and the confidence level should be 99% (i.e. there is only a 1% probability of the loss exceeding the VaR number over a 10-day period).
- The model should be tested against the previous year's historic data (*backtesting*) to check that the losses actually incurred by the bank did agree with the results estimated by the model. Four exceptions or less would be acceptable; between five and nine exceptions would require the multiplicative factor to be increased from 3; ten exceptions or more would require the model to be investigated before it could be used.
- VaR is measured for four separate areas of business or 'portfo-lios' – foreign exchange, interest rate instruments, equities and commodities – and the four figures added. The bank is allowed to take correlation (i.e. diversification) into account to reduce the measured VaR within each portfolio, but not across port-folios – i.e., it may not consider any correlation effects arising from positions in two different portfolios.

CAPITAL ADEQUACY REQUIREMENTS

In order to prevent banks from taking excessive risks (and hence to protect the banking system as a whole), the European Union (EU) and the *BIS* have established guideline limits to the risks which each bank may take. In turn, each country's regulator enforces these limits, or stronger ones if it prefers, on the banks under its control. The details of these guidelines are complex, and the following remarks are necessarily a simplification of them. The concept is that if some of the risks are realized, the bank should still have adequate capital to remain in business – hence the term *capital adequacy*. The various directives from the EU which together set out the risk measurement rules are known as the *Capital Adequacy Directives (CAD)*.

Risk asset ratio

Each loan or other transaction undertaken by the bank is measured in terms of risk according to certain rules, which currently combine measures of market risk and credit risk. The total of these risks is called its *risk-weighted assets*. These must be limited in relation to the bank's *own funds* – i.e. its available capital and reserves. The capital adequacy rules state that the bank's *risk asset ratio* – the ratio of own funds to risk-weighted assets – must always be equal to at least 8%. Each regulator may impose a higher requirement than 8% on any particular bank under its control if it so chooses.

The effect of the CAD is to limit the amount, and type, of business which the bank does. If the type of deals undertaken by a particular bank are measured as mostly having a low risk, it can do more of them than if they are measured as having a high risk.

Glossary

A

Acceptor: The person who accepts liability for a bill of exchange.

Accrued coupon: The proportion of the next coupon payment on a security earned so far, from the last coupon date until settlement date.

ACT/360: A day/year count convention taking the number of calendar days in a period and a 'year' of 360 days.

ACT/365: (Or ACT/365 fixed). A day/year count convention taking the number of calendar days in a period and a 'year' of 365 days.

Adjustable peg: Management of a currency at a fixed exchange rate against another currency or basket of currencies, with *ad hoc* adjustments to that fixed rate. *See* Crawling peg.

A/P: *See* Around par.

Appreciation: An increase in the market value of a currency in terms of other currencies. *See* Depreciation, Revaluation.

Arbitrage: The simultaneous operation in two different but related markets in order to take advantage of a discrepancy between them which will lock in a profit. The arbitrage operation itself usually tends to cause the different markets to converge. *See* Covered interest arbitrage.

Around par: (Or A/P). A foreign exchange swap price is around par if the left side is negative and the right side is positive.

Ask: *See* Offer.

B

BA: *See* Bankers' acceptance.

Back office: The operational department of the bank.

Backtesting: Testing a model, such as a VaR model, against historic data.

Balance sheet exposure: *See* Translation exposure.

Bankers' acceptance: Or BA. *See* Bill of exchange.

Banking book: For the purposes of capital adequacy, that part of a bank's busi-ness which broadly involves its lending department and long-term investments.

Base currency: Exchange rates are quoted in terms of the number of units of one currency (the variable or counter currency) which corresponds to one unit of the other currency (the base currency)

Basis: The difference between the futures price which would be implied by the current cash interest rate, and the actual futures price.

Basis points: In interest rate quotations, 0.01%.

Basis risk: The risk that the prices of two instruments will not move exactly in line – for example, the value of an FRA and the value of a futures contract being used to hedge the FRA.

Basket: A basket of currencies is a group of currencies, each weighted differ-ently, against which another currency is measured or managed.

Bear spread: A spread position taken with the expectation of a fall in value in the underlying.

Bearer security: A security where ownership for the purpose of paying coupons and principal is determined by whoever is physically in possession of the security. In order to maintain anonymity, there is no central record of ownership. *See* Registered security.

Bid: In general, the price at which the dealer quoting a price is prepared to buy or borrow. The bid price of a foreign exchange quotation is the rate at which the dealer will buy the base currency and sell the variable currency. The bid rate in a deposit quotation is the interest rate at which the dealer will borrow the currency involved. The bid rate in a repo is the interest rate at which the dealer will borrow the collateral and lend the cash. *See* Offer.

Big figure: In a foreign exchange quotation, the exchange rate omitting the last two decimal places. For example, when USD/CHF is 1.7510/20, the big figure is 1.75. *See* Points.

Bilateral netting: Obligation netting between two parties.

Bill of exchange: A short-term zero-coupon debt issued by a company to finance commercial trading. If it is guaranteed by a bank, it becomes a banker's acceptance.

BIS: Bank for International Settlements, the central banks' forum in Basle.

Bond basis: An interest rate is quoted on a bond basis if it is on an ACT/365, 30/360 or ACT/ACT basis. *See* Money-market basis.

Broken date: (Or odd date). A maturity date other than the standard ones normally quoted.

Bull spread: A spread position taken with the expectation of a rise in value in the underlying.

Buy/sell-back: Opposite of sell/buy-back.

C

Cable: The exchange rate for sterling against the US dollar.

CAD: *See* Capital adequacy directives.

Calendar spread: The simultaneous purchase (or sale) of an FRA or futures contract for one date and the sale (or purchase) of an FRA or futures contract for a different date. *See* Spread.

Capital adequacy: The concept that if some of a bank's risks are realized, the bank should still have adequate capital to remain in business.

Capital adequacy directives: (Or CAD). The various directives from the EU which together set out the capital adequacy rules.

Capital market: Long-term market (generally longer than one year) for financial instru-ments. *See* Money market.

Cash: *See* Cash market.

Cash market: The market for trading an underlying financial instrument, where the whole value of the instrument will potentially be settled on the normal delivery date – as opposed to contracts for differences, futures etc. (where the cash amount to be settled is not intended to be the full value of the underlying) or forwards (where delivery is for a later date than normal). *See* Derivative.

CD: *See* Certificate of deposit.

Certificate of deposit: (Or CD). A security, generally coupon-bearing, issued by a bank to borrow money.

Charting: *See* Technical analysis.

Cherry picking: Insistence by a defaulting organization on consummating profitable deals with a particular counterparty, while defaulting on unprofitable ones.

Chicago Mercantile Exchange: (Or CME). A futures exchange in Chicago.

Choice: A choice price is one with a zero spread – i.e. the bid and offer are the same.

Classic repo: (Or repo or US-style repo). Repo is short for 'sale and repurchase agreement' – a simultaneous spot sale and forward purchase of something, equivalent to borrowing money against a loan of collat-eral. A reverse repo is the opposite. The terminology is usually applied from the perspective of the repo dealer. For example, when a central bank does repos, it is lending cash (the repo dealer is borrowing cash from the central bank).

Clean deposit: Same as fixed deposit.

Clean price: The price of a security excluding accrued coupon.

Close-out netting: *See* Netting.

CLS: *See* Continuous linked settlement.

CME: *See* Chicago Mercantile Exchange.

Collateral: (Or security). Something of value, often of good creditworthiness such as a government bond, given temporarily to a counterparty to enhance a party's creditworthiness. In a repo, the collateral is actually sold temporarily by one party to the other rather than merely lodged with it.

Commercial paper: A short-term security issued by a company or bank, generally with a zero coupon.

Competitive exposure: Economic exposure which arises specifically because of a competitor.

Compound interest: When some interest on an investment is paid before maturity and the investor can reinvest it to earn interest on interest, the interest is said to be compounded. Compounding often assumes that the reinvestment rate is the same as the original rate. *See* Simple interest.

Continuous linked settlement: (Or CLS). A real-time PvP clearing system for settlement of FX trans-actions, where a payment from Bank A to Bank B is made only if, and at the same time as, the corresponding payment from Bank B to Bank A is made.

Contract date: The date on which a transaction is negotiated. *See* Value date.

Contract for differences: A transaction such as an FRA, NDF or SAFE where only the net difference between two amounts is settled, and the principal amount involved is not transferred.

Convertible currency: A currency that may be freely exchanged for other currencies.

Correlation coefficient: A measure of the extent to which two things do, or do not, move together.

Counter currency: *See* Variable currency

Counterparty risk: The risk that a counterparty might default on a contract by failing to pay amounts due or failing to fulfill the delivery conditions of the contract.

Coupon: The interest payment(s) made by the issuer of a security to the holders, based on the coupon rate and face value.

Covariance: A measure of the extent to which two things do, or do not, move together.

Cover: To cover an exposure is to deal in such a way as to remove the risk – either reversing the position, or hedging it by dealing in an instrument with a similar but opposite risk profile.

Covered interest arbitrage: Creating a loan/deposit in one currency by combining a loan/deposit in another currency with a forward foreign exchange swap.

CP: *See* Commercial paper.

Crawling peg: Management of a currency at a fixed exchange rate against another currency or basket of currencies, with a regular pre-determined adjustment to that fixed rate. *See* Adjustable peg.

Credit risk: The risk that a counterparty defaults on a transaction or that the issuer of a security defaults on coupon or interest payments.

Cross: *See* Cross-rate.

Cross-rate: Generally an exchange rate between two currencies, neither of which is the US dollar.

Cumulative probability distribution: The probability that any one of a series of numbers will be no greater than a particular number.

D

Daylight limit: The maximum size of a position which a dealer is allowed to take during the day.

Delivery versus payment: (Or DvP). A method for the settlement of a securities transaction, whereby a payment from Bank A to Bank B is made only if, and at the same time as, the corresponding security is delivered from Bank B to Bank A.

Deposit: An investment of cash in return for interest.

Depreciation: A decrease in the market value of a currency in terms of other currencies. *See* Appreciation, Devaluation.

Derivative: Strictly, any financial instrument whose value is derived from another, such as a forward foreign exchange outright, a futures contract, an FRA etc. Forward deals to be settled in full are not always called derivatives, however.

Devaluation: An official one-off decrease in the value of a currency in terms of other currencies. *See* Revaluation, Depreciation.

Direct: An exchange rate quotation against the US dollar in which the dollar is the variable currency and the other currency is the base currency.

Dirty floating: A floating-rate regime with some government intervention.

Dirty price: The price of a security including accrued coupon.

Discount: The amount by which a currency is cheaper, in terms of another currency, for future delivery than for spot, is the forward discount (in general, a reflection of interest rate differentials between two curren-cies). If an exchange rate is 'at a discount' (without specifying to which of the two currencies this refers), this means in London (but generally not elsewhere) that the variable currency is at a discount. *See* Premium.

Discount instrument: An instrument which pays no coupon and is therefore always worth less than its face value unless interest rates are negative.

Discount rate: The method of market quotation for certain securities (US and UK treasury bills, for example), expressing the return on the security as a proportion of the face value of the security received at maturity – as opposed to a yield which expresses the return as a proportion of the original investment. *See also* Discount.

Drawee: The person to whom a bill of exchange is addressed, and who owes the money.

Drawer: The originator of a bill of exchange.

Dual rate: A system of two or more exchange rates for a currency, each used for a different type of transaction.

DvP: *See* Delivery versus payment.

E

Economic exposure: A company's exposure to currency movements other than transac-tion exposure and translation exposure.

ECU: *See* European currency unit.

Effective date: The start date of the forward period to which an FRA relates.

Effective exchange rate: An index of a currency's value against a basket of other currencies, weighted by trade importance to the country.

Effective rate: (Or annual equivalent rate). An effective interest rate is the rate which, earned as simple interest over 1 year, gives the same return as interest paid more frequently than once per year and then compounded. *See* Nominal rate.

Eligible bill: A bankers' acceptance which the Bank of England is willing to purchase because it has been accepted by an eligible bank.

EMS: *See* European monetary system.

EMU: *See* European monetary union.

End-end: A foreign exchange swap or money-market deal commencing on the last working day of a month and lasting for a whole number of months, maturing on the last working day of the corresponding month.

Equivalent rate: The rate of interest which would be equivalent to the nominal rate quoted, after compounding at a different frequency of interest payment.

ERA: *See* Exchange rate agreement.

ERM: *See* Exchange rate mechanism.

EU: European Union.

Euro: The name for the single currency of the European monetary union.

Eurocurrency: A currency owned by a non-resident of the country in which the currency is legal tender.

Euromarket: The international market in which Eurocurrencies are traded.

European currency unit: (Or ECU). The former basket of EU currencies which was replaced by the euro.

European monetary system: A former grouping of EU currencies.

European monetary union: The formation of a single currency, the euro, for a group of EU countries.

Exchange controls: Regulations restricting the free convertibility of a currency into other currencies.

Exchange rate agreement: (Or ERA). A contract for differences based on the movement in a forward-forward foreign exchange swap price. It does not take account of the effect of spot rate changes as an FXA does. *See* SAFE.

Exchange rate mechanism: That part of the European monetary system which controlled the exchange rates of its member currencies.

Exchange-traded: Instruments such as futures which are traded on a recognized exchange, as opposed to forward deals which are OTC.

Exposure: Risk.

F

Face value: (Or nominal value). The principal amount of a security, generally repaid ('redeemed') all at maturity, but sometimes repaid in stages, on which the coupon amounts are calculated.

FEER: *See* Fundamental equilibrium exchange rate.

Figure: When the last two digits in a foreign exchange price are zero. For example, a price of 1.7895/00 would be "One seventy-eight ninety-five, figure".

Fixed deposit: (Or time deposit or term deposit or clean deposit). A non-negotiable deposit for a specific term.

Fixed-rate regime: Management of a currency at a fixed exchange rate against another currency or basket of currencies.

Flat yield curve: A yield curve where rates are similar for all maturities.

Floating rate CD: (Or FRCD). CD on which the rate of interest payable is refixed in line with market conditions at regular intervals (usually 6 months).

Floating rate: In interest rates, an instrument paying a floating rate is one where the rate of interest is refixed in line with market conditions at regular intervals such as every 3 or 6 months. *See also* Floating-rate regime.

Floating-rate note: A security where the coupon is refixed at regular intervals according to an index such as LIBOR.

Floating-rate regime: Allowing a currency to find its own free-market level against other currencies, with no government intervention.

Forward: In general, a deal for value later than the normal value date for that particular commodity or instrument. In the foreign exchange market, a forward price is the price quoted for the purchase or sale of one currency against another where the value date is at least one month after the spot date. *See* Short date.

Forward exchange agreement: (Or FXA). A contract for differences designed to create exactly the same economic result as a foreign exchange cash forward-forward deal. *See* ERA, SAFE.

Forward-forward: An FX swap, loan or other interest-rate agreement starting on one forward date and ending on another.

Forward rate agreement: (Or FRA). A contract for differences based on a forward-forward interest rate.

FRA: *See* Forward rate agreement.

FRCD: *See* Floating rate CD.

FRN: *See* Floating rate note.

Front office: The trading department of the bank.

Fundamental Equilibrium Exchange Rate: (Or FEER). The exchange rate necessary to achieve a sustainable balance in the country's external current account. *See* Purchasing power parity.

Fundamental analysis: (Or judgemental analysis). An approach to forecasting based on external factors such as economics, government policy and political events. *See* Technical analysis.

Funds: The USD/CAD exchange rate for value on the next business day (standard practice for USD/CAD, in preference to spot).

Fungible: Able to be combined indistinguishably with an existing position in the same instrument.

Future value: The amount of money achieved in the future, including interest, by investing a given amount of money now. *See* Time value of money, Present value.

Futures contract: A deal to buy or sell some financial instrument or commodity for value on a future date. Unlike a forward deal, futures contracts are traded only on an exchange (rather than OTC), have standardized contract sizes and value dates, and are often only contracts for differences rather than deliverable.

FX: Foreign exchange.

FXA: *See* Forward exchange agreement.

G

Gap analysis: Analysis of the difference in exposures to interest rates in different periods.

General risk: In measuring position risk for capital adequacy purposes, the risk arising from the market position held by the bank. *See* Specific risk.

GMRA: Global Master Repo Agreement, a master agreement for repos and buy/sell-backs.

H

Hedge: Protect against the risks arising from potential market movements in exchange rates, interest rates or other variables. *See* Cover, Arbi-trage, Speculation.

Herstatt risk: Same as settlement risk in FX.

Historic rate rollover: A forward swap in FX where the settlement exchange rate for the near date is based on a historic off-market rate rather than the current market rate. This is prohibited by many regulators.

Historic VaR: A method of calculating VaR by applying historic price movements to the current portfolio of instruments. *See* Monte Carlo simulation, Variance/covariance.

I

IFEMA: International Foreign Exchange Master Agreement, a master agree-ment for foreign exchange spot and forward deals.

IMM: *See* International Monetary Market.

Indirect: An exchange rate quotation against the US dollar in which the dollar is the base currency and the other currency is the variable currency.

Initial margin: *See* Margin.

Interbank: An interbank transaction is one between two banks, as opposed to one between a bank and an end-user.

International Monetary Market: The financial sector of the Chicago Mercantile Exchange.

Interpolation: The process of estimating a price or rate for value on a particular date by comparing the prices actually quoted for value dates either side.

Intervention: Purchases or sales of currencies in the market by central banks in an attempt to reduce exchange rate fluctuations or to maintain the value of a currency within a particular band, or at a particular level. Similarly, central bank operations in the money markets to maintain interest rates at a certain level.

Inverted yield curve: *See* Negative yield curve.

ISDA master agreement: International Swaps and Derivatives Association master agreement for FRAs, swaps, options and other transactions.

J

Judgemental analysis: *See* Fundamental analysis.

L

Large exposure risk: The requirement to allocate more capital for capital adequacy purposes if the total exposure to any one counterparty is a particularly large proportion of the bank's total.

Legacy currency: (Or national currency unit). One of the former national currencies which became a unit of the euro.

Legal risk: The risk that the bank's business is affected by changes in laws and regulations, or by existing laws and regulations which it had not properly taken into account.

LIBID: *See* LIBOR.

LIBOR: London inter-bank offered rate, the rate at which banks are willing to lend to other banks of top creditworthiness. The term is used both generally to mean the interest rate at any time, and specifically to mean the reference rate at 11:00 a.m., published by the British Bankers' Association, for the purpose of providing a benchmark to fix an interest payment such as on an FRA settlement. LIBID is similarly London inter-bank bid rate. LIMEAN is the average between LIBID and LIBOR.

LIFFE: London International Financial Futures and Options Exchange.

Lift: To lift an offer is to deal on the offered price quoted by someone.

LIMEAN: *See* LIBOR.

Liquid: A liquid market is one where it is easy to find buyers and sellers at good prices. A liquid investment is one which can easily be turned into cash because there is a liquid market in that instrument.

Liquidity: *See* Liquid.

Liquidity risk: The risk of being unable to find a liquid market for a particular instrument.

Locals: Private traders on a futures exchange dealing for their own account.

Long: A long position is a surplus of purchases over sales of a given currency or asset, or a situation which naturally gives rise to an organization benefiting from a strengthening of that currency or asset. To a money market dealer, however, a long position is a surplus of borrowings taken in over money lent out, (which gives rise to a benefit if that currency weakens rather than strengthens). *See* Short.

M

Managed floating: Same as dirty floating.

Mapping: In the variance/covariance approach to VaR, the process of repre-senting a position in terms of other standardized instruments.

Margin call: A call by one party in a transaction for variation margin to be transferred by the other.

Margin transfer: The transfer of a margin call.

Margin: Initial margin is collateral placed by one party with a counterparty at the time of a deal, against the possibility that the market price will move against the first party, thereby leaving the counterparty with a credit risk. Variation margin is a payment made, or extra collateral transferred, subsequently from one party to the other because the market price has moved. Variation margin payment is either in effect a settlement of profit/loss (for example, in the case of a futures contract) or the reduction of credit exposure (for example, in the case of a repo). In a loan, margin is the extra interest above a benchmark (e.g. a margin of 0.5% over LIBOR) required by a lender to compensate for the credit risk of that particular borrower.

Market risk: The risk that the value of a position falls due to changes in market rates or prices.

Mark-to-market: The process of revaluing a position at current market rates.

Mean: Average.

Mine: "I buy the base currency." For example, if someone who has asked for and received a price says "5 mine!" he means "I buy 5 million units of the base currency". *See* Yours.

Model risk: The risk that the computer model used to price and value an instru-ment is wrong.

Modified duration: A factor measuring the sensitivity of a position to changes in interest rates.

Modified following: The convention that if a value date in the future falls on a non-business day, the value date will be moved to the next following business day, unless this moves the value date to the next month, in which case the value date is moved back to the last previous business day.

Money market: Short-term market (generally up to 1 year) for financial instruments. *See* Capital market.

Money-market basis: An interest rate quoted on an ACT/360 basis is said to be on a money-market basis. *See* Bond basis.

Monte Carlo simulation: A method of calculating VaR by generating a very large number of random prices, applying these to the current portfolio of instru-ments and measuring the net effect. *See* Historic VaR, Variance/co-variance.

Multilateral netting: Obligation netting between more than two parties.

My risk: If someone who has asked for a price says "my risk", he is acknowl-edging that the price may change before he has accepted it.

N

National currency unit: *See* Legacy currency.

Negative skewness: A greater probability of a large downward movement than of a large upward movement.

Negative yield curve: (Or inverted yield curve). A downward-sloping yield curve. *See* Posi-tive yield curve.

Negotiable: A security which can be bought and sold in a secondary market is negotiable.

Net present value: (Or NPV). The net present value of a series of cashflows is the sum of the present values of each cashflow (some or all of which may be negative).

Netting: Obligation netting is the payment, in the normal course of business, of one net amount from one party to another instead of a gross payment in each direction. Close-out netting allows, in the event of a default, the non-defaulting party to terminate all outstanding transactions and settle them with a single net payment or receipt.

Nominal amount: Same as face value of a security.

Nominal rate: A rate of interest as quoted, rather than the effective rate to which it is equivalent.

Non-deliverable forward: A forward outright where the two parties settle only the change in value between the forward rate dealt and the spot rate 2 working days before maturity, based on a notional principal amount.

Normal probability function: A particular probability density, with the formula.

Normal yield curve: (Or positive yield curve). An upward-sloping yield curve. *See* Nega-tive yield curve.

Notional: Contracts for differences require a notional principal amount on which settlement can be calculated.

NPV: *See* Net present value.

O

O/N: *See* Overnight.

Obligation netting: *See* Netting.

Odd date: *See* Broken date.

Off: If a market maker says "Off!" he means "The price that I last quoted is no longer valid".

Off-balance sheet: An instrument where the principal amount is either not transferred, or is transferred simultaneously in both directions.

Offer: (Or ask). In general, the price at which the dealer quoting a price is prepared to sell or lend. The offered price of a foreign exchange quotation is the rate at which the dealer will sell the base currency and buy the variable currency. The offered rate in a deposit quotation is the interest rate at which the dealer will lend the currency involved. The offered rate in a repo is the interest rate at which the dealer will lend the collateral and borrow the cash. *See* Bid.

Off-market: A rate which is not the current market rate.

Open outcry: Trading face-to-face on a physical exchange.

Operational risk: The risk of losses due to failures in the bank's operations generally.

Option forward: *See* Time option.

OTC: *See* Over the counter.

Outright: An outright is the sale or purchase of one foreign currency against another for value on any date other than spot. *See* Spot, Swap, Forward, Short date.

Over the counter: (Or OTC). An OTC transaction is one dealt privately between any two parties, with all details agreed between them, as opposed to one dealt on an exchange – for example, a forward deal as opposed to a futures contract. *See* Exchange-traded.

Overborrowed: A position in which a dealer's liabilities (borrowings taken in) are of longer maturity than the assets (loans out). *See* Overlent.

Overlent: A position in which a dealer's assets (loans out) are of longer maturity than the liabilities (borrowings taken in). *See* Overborrowed.

Overnight: (Or O/N or today/tomorrow). A deal from today until the next working day ('tomorrow').

Overnight limit: The maximum size of a position which a dealer is allowed to take overnight.

Own funds: A bank's available capital and reserves for the purposes of capital adequacy rules.

P

Par: In foreign exchange, when the outright and spot exchange rates are equal, the forward swap is zero or par. When the price of a security is equal to the face value, usually expressed as 100, it is said to be trading at par.

Par value: *See* Parity.

Parity: The exchange rate for a currency against another currency or basket of currencies, considered by the government as its official fixed rate, central rate or target rate.

Payee: The person to whom something is payable (for example, a bill of exchange).

Payment versus payment: (Or PvP). Method for the settlement of a FX transaction, whereby a payment from Bank A to Bank B is made only if, and at the same time as, the corresponding payment is made from Bank B to Bank A.

Pips: *See* Points.

Points: (Or pips). The last two decimal places in an exchange rate. For example, when USD/CHF is 1.7510/1.7520, the points are 10/20. *See* Big figure.

Position risk: Same as market risk, used particularly in capital adequacy calcula-tions.

Positive yield curve: *See* Normal yield curve.

PPP: *See* Purchasing power parity.

Premium: The amount by which a currency is more expensive, in terms of another currency, for future delivery than for spot, is the forward premium (in general, a reflection of interest rate differentials between two currencies). If an exchange rate is 'at a premium' (without spec-ifying to which of the two currencies this refers), this means in London (but generally not elsewhere) that the variable currency is at a premium. *See* Discount.

Present value: The amount of money which needs to be invested now to achieve a given amount in the future when interest is added. Hence, the value of future cashflow. *See* Time value of money, Future value.

Primary market: The primary market for a security refers to its original issue. *See* Secondary market.

Probability density: A description of how likely any one of a series of numbers is to occur.

Probability distribution: *See* Cumulative probability distribution.

Produce: To produce dollars (for example, via covered interest arbitrage) gener-ally means effectively to borrow dollars.

Promissory note: A written promise to pay.

Public order member: A member of a futures exchange able to enter into transactions on behalf of customers.

Purchasing power parity: The idea that a currency's exchange rate must move, in the long term, to adjust for inflation differentials against other countries. *See* Fundamental equilibrium exchange rate.

PvP: *See* Payment versus payment.

R

Real effective exchange rate: An effective exchange rate adjusted for inflation differentials bet-ween countries.

Reciprocal rate: An exchange rate quoted in such a way that the base currency and variable currency are reversed.

Redeem: A security is said to be redeemed when the principal is repaid.

Registered security: A security where ownership for the purpose of paying coupons and principal is determined by whoever is recorded centrally as the owner. There might or might not also be a physical piece of paper evidencing ownership. *See* Bearer security.

Replacement risk: The risk of losing an unrealized profit because the counterparty defaults.

Repo: (Or RP). Usually refers in particular to classic repo. Also used as a general term to include classic repos, buy/sell-backs and securities lending.

Repurchase agreement: *See* Repo.

Reputational risk: The risk of damage to a bank's reputation.

Revaluation: An official one-off increase in the value of a currency in terms of other currencies. *See* Devaluation.

Reverse repo: (Or reverse). The opposite of a repo.

Reverse: *See* Reverse repo.

Risk asset ratio: The ratio of a bank's own funds to its risk-weighted assets.

Riskmetrics: A variance/covariance model for VaR, made available by JP Morgan.

Risk-weighted assets: The money which a bank has put at risk for the purposes of capital adequacy rules.

Rollover: *See* Tom-next. Also refers to renewal of a loan.

RP: *See* Repo.

S

S/N: *See* Spot-next.

S/W: *See* spot-a-week.

SAFE: *See* Synthetic agreement for forward exchange.

SDR: *See* Special drawing right.

Secondary market: The market for buying and selling a security after it has been issued. *See* Primary market.

Secured: Collateralized.

Security: A financial asset sold initially for cash by a borrowing organization (the issuer). The security is often negotiable and usually has a maturity date when it is redeemed.

Same as collateral.: Sell/buy-back Simultaneous spot sale and forward purchase of something, with the forward price calculated to achieve an effect equivalent to a classic repo.

Serial months: Additional futures delivery months added to the regular cycle, so that the three nearest possible months are always available.

Settlement risk: The risk that the counterparty does not deliver its side of the deal after we have irrevocably paid or delivered our side.

Short date: A deal for value on a date other than spot but less than one month after spot.

Short: A short position is a surplus of sales over purchases of a given currency or asset, or a situation which naturally gives rise to an organization benefiting from a weakening of that currency or asset. To a money market dealer, however, a short position is a surplus of money lent out over borrowings taken in (which gives rise to a benefit if that currency strengthens rather than weakens). *See* Long.

Simple interest: When interest on an investment is paid all at maturity or not rein-vested to earn interest-on-interest, the interest is said to be simple. *See* Compound interest.

Special drawing right: (Or SDR). The artificial basket currency of the IMF.

Specific risk: In measuring position risk for capital adequacy purposes, the risk arising from the issuer of a particular security held by the bank. *See* General risk.

Speculation: A deal undertaken because the dealer expects prices to move in his favor, as opposed to a hedge or arbitrage.

Spot: A deal to be settled on the customary value date for that particular market. In the foreign exchange market, this is for value in 2 working days' time.

Spot-a-week: (Or S/W). A transaction from spot until a week later.

Spot-next: (Or S/N). A transaction from spot until the next working day.

Spread: The difference between the bid and offer prices in a quotation. A strategy in which a particular instrument is purchased and a similar instrument is sold, such as a futures spread, in which one futures contract is purchased and another is sold.

Square: A position in which sales exactly match purchases, or in which assets exactly match liabilities. *See* Long, Short.

Standard deviation: A measure of how spread out a series of numbers is around its mean.

STIR futures: Short-term interest rate futures contract.

Stop-loss: A price or rate which, if touched in the market, will trigger the closing of a position in order to avoid any further loss. *See* take profit.

STP: *See* Straight-through processing.

Straight-through processing: (Or STP). The computerization of operational tasks in such a way that each process feeds automatically to the next.

Strip: A strip of FRAs is a series of FRAs covering consecutive periods, which together create the effect of a longer-term instrument (for example, 4 consecutive 3-month FRAs have an effect similar to a 1 year FRA). A strip of futures is similar.

Swap: A foreign exchange swap is the purchase of one currency against another for delivery on one date, with a simultaneous sale to reverse the transaction on another value date.

SWIFT: Society for Worldwide Interbank Financial Transfers, the system for international payments between banks.

Synthetic agreement for forward exchange: (or SAFE). A generic term for ERAs and FXAs.

System risk: The risk of losses due to failures in the bank's computer systems.

Systemic risk: The risk of failure in the entire payment clearing system or banking system of which the bank is a part.

T

T/N: *See* Tom-next.

Tail: The exposure to interest rates over a forward-forward period arising from a mismatched position (such as a 2-month borrowing against a 3-month loan). A forward foreign exchange dealer's exposure to spot movements. The extreme left- and right-hand ends of a probability distribution.

Take-profit: A price or rate which, if touched in the market, will trigger the closing of a position in order to ensure that an existing profit is captured. *See* Stop-loss.

Technical analysis: (Or charting). An approach to forecasting which considers only past price movements. *See* Fundamental forecasting.

Tenor: The tenor of a security is the length of time until its maturity.

Term: The time between the beginning and end of a deal or investment.

Term deposit: Same as fixed deposit.

Tick: The minimum allowed price movement on a futures contract.

Tick value: The value of a one tick price change on one futures contract.

Time deposit: Same as fixed deposit.

Time option: (Or option forward). A forward currency deal in which the value date is set to be within a period rather than on a particular day. The customer sets the exact date 2 working days before settlement.

Time value of money: The concept that a future cashflow can be valued as the amount of money which it is necessary to invest now in order to achieve that cashflow in the future. *See* Present value, Future value.

Today–tomorrow: *See* Overnight.

Tom-next: (Or T/N or rollover). A transaction from the next working day ('tomorrow') until the working day after ('next' day – i.e. spot in the foreign exchange market.)

Trading book: For the purposes of capital adequacy, that part of a bank's business which broadly involves its trading department.

Transaction exposure: The risk to currency movements arising from a definite, or closely forecast, transaction.

Translation exposure: (Or balance sheet exposure). The risk to currency movements arising from an asset or liability on the balance sheet which is denominated in a foreign currency.

Treasury bill: A short-term security issued by a government, generally with a zero coupon.

True yield: The yield which is equivalent to the quoted discount rate (for a US or UK treasury bill, for example).

U

Under reference: If a market-maker or his broker says that a price he has quoted is "under reference", he means that the price must be reconfirmed before a counterparty can deal on it.

Underlying: The underlying of a futures contract is the commodity or financial instrument on which the contract depends.

US-style repo: Same as classic repo.

V

Value at risk: (Or VaR). The maximum potential loss which an organization might suffer on its positions over a given time period, estimated within a given confidence level.

Value basis: The theoretical futures price, less the actual futures price.

Value date: (Or settlement date or maturity date). The date on which a deal is to be consummated.

VaR: *See* Value-at-risk.

Variable currency: (Or counter currency). Exchange rates are quoted in terms of the number of units of one currency (the variable or counter currency) which corresponds to 1 unit of the other currency (the base currency).

Variance: The square of the standard deviation of a series of numbers.

Variance/covariance: A method of calculating VaR which applies assumed variances and covariances to a probability distribution which is generally taken as normal. *See* Historic VaR, Monte Carlo simulation.

Variation margin: *See* Margin.

Y

Yard: One American billion – i.e. 1,000,000,000.

Yield: The interest rate which can be earned on an investment, currently quoted by the market or implied by the current market price for the investment – as opposed to the coupon paid by an issuer on a security, which is based on the coupon rate and the face value.

Yield curve: A graph showing the current interest rate for each maturity.

Yours: "I sell the base currency". For example, if someone who has asked for and received a price says "5 yours!", he means "I sell 5 million units of the base currency". *See* Mine.

Z

Zero-coupon: A zero-coupon security is one that does not pay a coupon. Its price is correspondingly less to compensate for this.

Bibliography

Aliber, R. Z.: *The International Market for Foreign Exchange,* New York, Praeger, 1969.

Baldassarri, M.: *Global Disequilibrium,* London: MacMillan. 1992.

Dalrymple A : *Observations on the Copper Coinage wanted in Circars,* Oxford, London, 1794.

Hauft, Ottomar: *Distribution of Stock of Money,* Effingham, London, 1892.

Jones, J. F. : *Trade, Balance of Payments and Growth,* Amsterdam, North-Holland Publishing Company, 1971.

Laughlin J. L. : *History of Bimetallism,* Oxford, New York, 1886.

Muller, John : *Indian Tables,* Calcutta, 1836.

Polak, J.J. : *The New International Monetary System,* New York, Columbia University Press, 1978.

Summner, Prof. : *History of American Currency,* MacMillan, New York, 1874.

Swoboda, A. : *Monetary Problems of the International Economy,* Chicago, University of Chicago Press, 1969.

Swoboda, A.: *International Monetary Problems,* Chicago. University of Chicago Press, 1967.

Taylor, M.: *The Fiscal System of Peru,* Washington, DC: The Pan American Union, 1969.

Tremblay, R.: *Africa and Monetary Integration,* Montreal, Les Editions HRW, 1972.

Whitakar, A. C. : *Foreign Exchange. Appleton,* New York, 1920.

Wolfe, J.N.: *Value, Capital and Growth,* Chicago, Edinburgh University Press. 1968.

Index

A

Applications, 135.
Approach, 9, 119, 126, 136, 155, 174, 200, 204, 205, 213, 231, 239, 240, 241, 242, 243, 254.

B

Bank Risk Management, 204.
Bearing Instruments, 116.

C

Conservation, 42, 43, 49, 51, 76.
Coupon Period, 118, 119, 121.
Currency Relationships, 193.

D

Developments, 201, 203.
Discount Instruments, 113, 121.

E

European Monetary Union, 6, 196, 197.
Exchange Rate Regimes, 194.

F

Foreign Exchange Management, 10.
Foreign Trade, 89, 90, 98, 99, 100, 107, 108.
Forward Exchange, 158, 179, 240, 241, 249, 251.
Forward Interest Rates, 124, 168.
Forward Outrights, 156, 158, 160, 173, 217.
Forward Rate Agreement, 126, 240.

G

Governments, 195, 196, 197, 199.

L

Laws, 75, 79, 87, 219, 243.

M

Market Environment, 155.
Money Market Instruments, 109.

O

Operational Risk, 205, 207, 217, 218, 219, 220, 246.
Organization, 5, 111, 112, 190, 205, 211, 215, 235, 252, 254.

P

Production, 32, 54, 74, 86, 87, 91, 95, 102, 114, 124, 134.
Protection, 52, 88, 96, 106, 132.

R

Reciprocal Rates, 152.
Risk Measurement, 207, 210, 231.

S

Smuggling Activities Act, 42, 76.
Spot Foreign Exchange, 145, 147, 149.
Spot Rates, 147.

T

Treasury Bills, 6, 113, 122, 123, 238.